JOSSEY-BASS TEACHER

Jossey-Bass Teacher provides educators with practical knowledge and tools to create a positive and lifelong impact on student learning. We offer classroom-tested and research-based teaching resources for a variety of grade levels and subject areas. Whether you are an aspiring, new, or veteran teacher, we want to help you make every teaching day your best.

From ready-to-use classroom activities to the latest teaching framework, our value-packed books provide insightful, practical, and comprehensive materials on the topics that matter most to K–12 teachers. We hope to become your trusted source for the best ideas from the most experienced and respected experts in the field.

Algebra Teacher's Activities Kit, Grades 6-12

Algebra Teacher's Activities Kit, Grades 6-12

150 Activities that Support Algebra in the Common Core Math Standards

Second Edition

Judith A. Muschla

Gary Robert Muschla

Erin Muschla-Berry

JB JOSSEY-BASS™

A Wiley Brand

Published by Jossey-Bass
A Wiley Brand
One Montgomery Street, Suite 1000, San Francisco, CA 94104-4594-www.josseybass.com

Jossey-Bass books and products are available through most bookstores. To contact Jossey-Bass directly call our Customer Care Department within the U.S. at 800-956-7739, outside the U.S. at 317-572-3986, or fax 317-572-4002.

Wiley publishes in a variety of print and electronic formats and by print-on-demand. Some material included with standard print versions of this book may not be included in e-books or in print-on-demand. If this book refers to media such as a CD or DVD that is not included in the version you purchased, you may download this material at http://booksupport.wiley.com. For more information about Wiley products, visit www.wiley.com.

Library of Congress Cataloging-in-Publication Data
Muschla, Judith A.
   Algebra teacher's activities kit : 150 activities that support algebra in the common core math standards, grades 6-12 / Judith A. Muschla, Gary Robert Muschla, and Erin Muschla-Berry. – Second edition.
       pages cm.
     ISBN 978-1-119-04574-8 (paperback), 978-1-119-04560-1 (ePDF) and 978-1-119-04559-5 (epub)
   1. Algebra–Study and teaching (Secondary)–Activity programs. I. Muschla, Gary Robert. II. Muschla-Berry, Erin. III. Title.
     QA159.M87 2016
     512.9071′2073–dc23
                               2015026767

Cover image: Wiley
Cover design: ©Linda Bucklin/iStockphoto

Printed in the United States of America

SECOND EDITION
HB Printing   10 9 8 7 6 5 4 3 2 1
PB Printing   V10009411_041219

ABOUT THE AUTHORS

Judith A. Muschla received her B.A. in mathematics from Douglass College at Rutgers University and is certified to teach K–12. She taught mathematics in South River, New Jersey, for over 25 years at various levels at both South River High School and South River Middle School. She wrote several math curriculums and conducted mathematics workshops for teachers and parents.

Together, Judith and Gary Muschla have coauthored several math books published by Jossey-Bass: *Hands-On Math Projects with Real-Life Applications, Grades 3–5* (2009); *The Math Teacher's Problem-a-Day, Grades 4–8* (2008); *Hands-On Math Projects with Real-Life Applications, Grades 6–12* (1996; second edition, 2006); *The Math Teacher's Book of Lists* (1995; second edition, 2005); *Math Games: 180 Reproducible Activities to Motivate, Excite, and Challenge Students, Grades 6–12* (2004); *Algebra Teacher's Activities Kit* (2003); *Math Smart! Over 220 Ready-to-Use Activities to Motivate and Challenge Students, Grades 6–12* (2002); *Geometry Teacher's Activities Kit* (2000); and *Math Starters! 5- to 10-Minute Activities to Make Kids Think, Grades 6–12* (1999).

Gary Robert Muschla received his B.A. and M.A.T. from Trenton State College and taught sixth grade in Spotswood, New Jersey, for more than 25 years. In addition to math resources, he has written several resources for English and writing teachers, among them *Writing Workshop Survival Kit* (1993; second edition, 2005); *The Writing Teacher's Book of Lists* (1991; second edition, 2004); *Ready-to-Use Reading Proficiency Lessons and Activities, 10th Grade Level* (2003); *Ready-to-Use Reading Proficiency Lessons and Activities, 8th Grade Level* (2002); *Ready-to-Use Reading Proficiency Lessons and Activities, 4th Grade Level* (2002); *Reading Workshop Survival Kit* (1997); and *English Teacher's Great Books Activities Kit* (1994), all published by Jossey-Bass.

Erin Muschla-Berry received her B.S. and M.Ed. from The College of New Jersey. She is certified to teach grades K–8 with Mathematics Specialization in Grades 5–8. She currently teaches math at Monroe Township Middle School in Monroe, New Jersey, and has presented workshops for math teachers for the Association of Mathematics Teachers of New Jersey. She has coauthored eight books with Judith and Gary Muschla for Jossey-Bass: *Teaching the Common Core Math Standards with Hands-On Activities, Grades 9–12* (2015); *Teaching the Common Core Math Standards with Hands-On Activities, Grades K–2* (2014); *Teaching the Common Core Math Standards with Hands-On Activities, Grades 3–5* (2014); *Math Starters, Second Edition: 5- to 10- Minute Activities Aligned with the Common Core Standards, Grades 6–12* (2013); *Teaching the Common Core Math Standards with Hands-On Activities, Grades 6–8* (2012); *The Algebra Teacher's Guide to Reteaching Essential Concepts and Skills* (2011); *The Elementary Teacher's Book of Lists* (2010); and *Math Teacher's Survival Guide, Grades 5–12* (2010).

ACKNOWLEDGMENTS

We thank Chari Chanley, Ed.S., principal of Monroe Township Middle School, James Higgins, vice-principal of Monroe Township Middle School, and Scott Sidler, vice-principal of Monroe Township Middle School, for their support.

We also thank Kate Bradford, our editor at Jossey-Bass, for her support and suggestions as we developed this book.

We appreciate the support of our many colleagues who have encouraged us in our work over the years.

And we wish to acknowledge the many students we have had the satisfaction of teaching.

CONTENTS

SECTION 6: STATISTICS AND PROBABILITY   221

PREFACE

Algebra is the foundation for learning higher mathematics. Mastery of algebra prepares a student for subjects such as geometry, trigonometry, and calculus; hones a student's problem-solving skills; and fosters a student's ability to understand and express mathematical relationships.

The *Algebra Teacher's Activities Kit, Grades 6–12, Second Edition: 150 Activities that Support Algebra in the Common Core Math Standards* follows the same general structure as the first edition but with thoroughly updated activities. The original activities that have been retained have been revised, many activities have been retired, and many new activities have been added.

The new edition is divided into six sections:

Section 1: "Ratios and Proportional Relationships," covering Standards from grade 6 through grade 7.

Section 2: "The Number System and Number and Quantity," covering Standards from grade 6 through high school.

Section 3: "Basic Expressions, Equations, and Inequalities," covering Standards from grade 6 through grade 8.

Section 4: "Polynomial, Rational, Exponential, and Radical Expressions, Equations, and Inequalities," covering Standards for high school algebra.

Section 5: "Functions," covering Standards from grade 8 through high school.

Section 6: "Statistics and Probability," covering Standards from grade 6 through high school.

Each section is divided into two parts. The first part contains teaching notes for each activity that include a brief summary of what students are to do, suggestions for implementation, and an answer key. The second part contains the reproducibles of the section.

Every activity stands alone, is numbered according to its section, and is labeled with the Standard it supports. Reproducibles are numbered according to their activity. For example, Activity 3–23: (8.EE.8) "Solving Systems of Linear Equations Algebraically" is the 23rd activity in Section 3. Its reproducible is numbered 3–23 and shares the same title.

The activities in each section follow the general sequence of the Standards and progress from basic to advanced. The activities are suitable for supplementing your math program, for reinforcement, and for challenges. To provide students with quick feedback, as well as reduce your workload, many of the activities are self-correcting. Correct answers enable students to complete a statement or answer a question about math, which will verify that their answers are right. We suggest that you utilize the activities in a manner that best supports your program and meets the needs of your students.

The algebra skills covered in this book were drawn from the Common Core Math Standards for grades 6, 7, and 8; the algebra Standards for high school; and the Standards included in algebra I and algebra II courses in the traditional pathway, as noted in the Common Core State Standards for Mathematics, Appendix A, "Designing High School Mathematics Courses Based on the Common Core Standards." Consequently, many Standards from number and quantity, functions, and statistics and probability that address algebraic concepts and skills are included in this book. Standards designated with a plus, which go beyond the typical curriculum, are not included. Because some of the Standards address skills and concepts that require multiple class periods of instruction, activities supporting these Standards usually focus on an aspect of the Standard.

We hope this book proves to be a useful addition to your math program and we wish you a successful and rewarding year of teaching.

Judith A. Muschla
Gary Robert Muschla
Erin Muschla-Berry

Algebra Teacher's Activities Kit, Grades 6-12

SECTION 1

Ratios and Proportional Relationships

Teaching Notes for the Activities of Section 1

1-1: (6.RP.1) UNDERSTANDING RATIOS

For this activity, your students will read statements that describe ratios. They will be given choices of ratios and must select the ratio that matches each statement. Answering a question at the end of the worksheet will enable students to check their answers.

Explain that a ratio compares two numbers or quantities. For example, if you have 5 markers and 2 are green and 3 are red, you can write a ratio comparing green markers to red markers as 2 to 3. You may instead write a ratio comparing the red markers to green markers as 3 to 2. Ratios can also be written with a colon, 2:3, or as a fraction, $\frac{2}{3}$.

Discuss the directions on the worksheet, emphasizing that students are to choose the ratio that matches each statement. Remind students to answer the question at the end.

ANSWERS

(1) O, 5:7   (2) A, 32:8   (3) H, 12 to 5   (4) T, 6 to 10   (5) E, $\frac{6}{4}$ (6) O, $\frac{13}{14}$

(7) T, 5 to 6   (8) P, $\frac{10}{12}$ (9) W, 8 to 2   (10) L, 3:2   (11) R, 2:25

The answer to the question is "whole to part."

1-2: (6.RP.2) UNIT RATES AND RATIOS

For this activity, your students are to determine if statements that describe unit rates associated with ratios are true or false. Answering a question at the end of the worksheet will enable them to check their answers.

Explain that a ratio that has a denominator of 1 is a unit rate. Examples of unit rates include: 4:1, $\frac{7}{1}$, or 3 to 1. Unit rates may also be expressed as a quantity of 1, for example: 30 miles per gallon of gasoline or $3 per pound. Ratios such as 6:3, $\frac{4}{5}$, and 2 to 9 do not represent unit rates. However, any ratio that compares two different quantities can be converted to a unit rate by writing the ratio as a fraction and dividing both numerator and denominator by the denominator. For example, $\frac{6}{3} = \frac{6 \div 3}{3 \div 3} = \frac{2}{1}$ or 2:1.

Discuss the directions on the worksheet with your students. After deciding whether a statement is true or false, they are to use the letters of correct answers to answer the question at the end.

1-3: (6.RP.3) EQUIVALENT RATIOS AND THE COORDINATE PLANE

For this activity, your students will complete tables of equivalent ratios and then plot the pairs of values in the coordinate plane. They will need rulers and graph paper.

Discuss the example on the worksheet. Explain that equivalent ratios can be found by writing the ratio as a fraction, and then multiplying or dividing the numerator and denominator by the same nonzero number. Note that the process is the same as finding equivalent fractions.

Explain that ratios can be expressed as ordered pairs in the coordinate plane. If necessary, review the coordinate plane, ordered pairs, and how students can plot points. Instruct them to place the origin of their coordinate plane near the center of their graph paper to ensure that they will have enough space to plot all of the points.

Go over the directions with your students. Emphasize that after completing the tables they must use the first value of each ratio as the x-coordinate and the second value as the y-coordinate. They are then to plot the ordered pairs and use their rulers to connect the points.

ANSWERS

Table 1: 1:2, 2:4, 3:6, 4:8, 5:10   Table 2: 2:3, 4:6, 8:12   Table 3: 12:8, 6:4, 3:2

1-4: (6.RP.3) FINDING THE PERCENT OF A NUMBER AND FINDING THE WHOLE

For this activity, your students will have two tasks: Find the percent of a number and find a whole, given the percent and a part.

If necessary, review that to find the percent of a number students should change the percent to a decimal or fraction and multiply. For example, 75% of 92 = 0.75 × 92 = 69, or $\frac{3}{4} \times \frac{92}{1} = \frac{3}{1} \times \frac{92^{23}}{1} = \frac{69}{1} = 69$.

Also review the process for finding the whole, given the percent and a part. Offer the following example: 35% of _____ = 14. In this case, students should say to themselves, "35% of what number is 14." To find this number using a decimal, students should change the percent to a decimal and divide, 14 ÷ 0.35 = 40. To find the number using a fraction, they should first change the percent to a fraction and simplify, $\frac{35}{100} = \frac{7}{20}$ and then divide, $\frac{14}{1} \div \frac{7}{20} = \frac{14^2}{1} \times \frac{20}{7_1} = \frac{40}{1} = 40$. You may want to note that solving these kinds of problems is usually easier when converting the percents to decimals.

Discuss the directions on the worksheet. Suggest that students follow the instructions at the end to see if their answers are most likely to be correct. (The term most likely is necessary for the rare case that students may make mistakes but still find the correct sum when adding their answers.)

ANSWERS

(1) 16   (2) 27   (3) 6   (4) 3   (5) 24   (6) 12   (7) 35   (8) 15   (9) 80   (10) 32
The sum of the answers is 250. 40% of 250 = 100.

1-5: (7.RP.1) FINDING UNIT RATES

For this activity, your students will be given various problems for which they must find unit rates. Answering a question at the end of the worksheet will enable them to check their answers.

Explain that a unit rate is a ratio written as a fraction with a denominator of 1. Ratios such as feet per second, dollars per hour, and pounds per square inch are unit rates.

Offer this example: During his morning office hours, a doctor saw 15 patients in 3 hours. The unit rate can be found by writing a ratio of the number of patients to the number of hours as a fraction and simplifying: $\frac{15}{3} = \frac{15 \div 3}{3 \div 3} = \frac{5}{1}$, which is a rate of 5 patients per hour. Note that some problems on the worksheet can be expressed as complex fractions. If necessary, review simplifying complex fractions.

Discuss the directions on the worksheet with your students. Remind them to answer the question at the end.

ANSWERS

(1) M, 52   (2) E, $0.01   (3) R, $1.85   (4) S, 61   (5) U, $8.50   (6) R, $1.85   (7) K, 1
(8) P, $0.11   (9) S, 61   (10) E, $0.01   (11) A, 5   (12) T, $1.29   The stores are "supermarkets."

1-6: (7.RP.2) GRAPHING PROPORTIONAL RELATIONSHIPS

For this activity, your students are to determine equivalent ratios by graphing. They will need rulers and graph paper.

Explain that a proportion is a statement that two ratios are equal. One way to determine if two or more quantities are in a proportional relationship is to graph the quantities in the coordinate plane. Quantities that result in a graph that is a line through the origin are equivalent ratios.

To complete this activity, students will need to be familiar with graphing points in the coordinate plane in all quadrants. If necessary, review these skills.

Discuss the directions on the worksheet with your students. After plotting all of the points, students should find three groups of equivalent ratios by identifying points that lie on lines through the origin. Not all of the plotted points can be expressed as equivalent ratios. Caution your students that they will need to examine the points carefully and use their rulers to draw the lines. For the final part of the activity, students are to express the groups of equivalent ratios as $\frac{y}{x}$.

ANSWERS

Following are the three groups of ratios. $\frac{-9}{-3}$, $\frac{3}{1}$, $\frac{6}{2}$, $\frac{12}{4}$; $\frac{3}{-3}$, $\frac{-3}{3}$, $\frac{-6}{6}$; $\frac{-6}{-3}$, $\frac{2}{1}$, $\frac{4}{2}$, $\frac{8}{4}$, $\frac{-4}{2}$

1–7: (7.RP.2) REPRESENTING PROPORTIONAL RELATIONSHIPS

For this activity, your students will write equations to represent proportional relationships. Answering a question at the end of the worksheet will enable them to check their answers.

Explain that a proportion is an equation that states two ratios are equal. Proportions can be written to represent relationships. For example, suppose that 4 bean seeds germinate for every 5 seeds that are planted. This relationship can be shown by the ratio of $\frac{4}{5}$. The number of seeds expected to grow if 100 seeds were planted can be shown by the proportion of $\frac{4}{5} = \frac{x}{100}$. ($x = 80$)

Discuss the directions on the worksheet with your students. They are to write a proportion to show the relationship in each problem and express the proportions to match the proportions in the Answer Bank. Note that students are not to solve the proportions (as this is not a focus of this Standard). To check if their work is correct, students should answer the question at the end.

ANSWERS

(1) I, $\frac{3}{5} = \frac{x}{10}$ (2) N, $\frac{2}{1} = \frac{54}{x}$ (3) S, $\frac{20}{\$1.00} = \frac{x}{\$5.00}$ (4) R, $\frac{2}{\$1.89} = \frac{5}{x}$ (5) E, $\frac{3}{5} = \frac{6}{x}$

(6) T, $\frac{3}{10} = \frac{x}{120}$ (7) W, $\frac{2}{1} = \frac{x}{52}$ (8) H, $\frac{5}{\$2.00} = \frac{30}{x}$ (9) F, $\frac{1}{20} = \frac{x}{120}$

(10) O, $\frac{10}{25} = \frac{x}{100}$ (11) A, $\frac{\$2.00}{\$5.00} = \frac{x}{\$100.00}$ "Proportio" means "for its own share."

1–8: (7.RP.3) SOLVING WORD PROBLEMS INVOLVING PERCENTS

This activity requires your students to solve a variety of word problems on topics such as commissions, tax, discounts, and percent increase and percent decrease. Students are to determine if given answers are correct, explain why incorrect answers are wrong, and correct wrong answers.

Start the activity by reviewing percents and basic types of percent problems. Explain that whenever attempting to solve a problem, it is essential to formulate a strategy and follow the proper procedure. Understanding the problem and identifying what one wishes to find is vital to finding the solution.

Discuss the directions on the worksheet with your students. Emphasize that some of the provided answers are incorrect. The errors are not computational. If an answer is incorrect, your students must identify the error and solve the problem. Point out that 40% of the problems are correct.

ANSWERS

(1) Incorrect—The weekly salary was not added; correct answer is $685.80. (2) Correct
(3) Incorrect—The student found 6% of $368,000 (which he rounded to the nearest hundred). The correct equation is 94% of $n = \$368,000$, where n represents the selling price of the home, which should be $391,489.36 or about $391,500. (4) Correct
(5) Incorrect—The student found $0.21 \times \$350,000$ instead of $0.021 \times \$350,000$. The correct answer is $7,350. (6) Incorrect—The student found 20% of 15 and subtracted the answer from 15. The correct equation is $0.8n = 15$, where n represents the original price which is $18.75. (7) Incorrect—The student found 6% of $14.31 and rounded to the nearest penny. The correct equation is $1.06n \times \$14.31$ where n is the cost of the bill without the tax. The cost is $13.50. (8) Correct (9) Correct (10) Incorrect—The student found the difference in price. To find the percent decrease he needed to find the difference in price (which he did) and then write a ratio of that difference to the original price. The percent decrease was 30%.

Reproducibles for Section 1 follow.

1–1: UNDERSTANDING RATIOS

A ratio is a comparison of two numbers. Ratios may be written in different ways, for example: 3:5, 3 to 5, or $\frac{3}{5}$.

Directions: Read each statement and find the ratio. Choose your answers from the ratios after each statement. Answer the question at the end by writing the letter of each answer in the space above its problem number. You will need to reverse the letters and divide them into words.

1. Five out of 7 days were rainy last week. What was the ratio of rainy days to the total number of days last week? (U. 7:5   O. 5:7)

2. A punch recipe called for 32 ounces of juice and 8 ounces of soda. What was the ratio of juice to soda? (A. 32:8   R. 8 to 32)

3. Twelve ducks and 5 swans were on a pond. What was the ratio of ducks to swans? (U. 5:12   H. 12 to 5)

4. Callie's teacher handed out 10 red counters and 6 blue counters to each student. What was the ratio of blue counters to red counters? (E. $\frac{10}{6}$ T. 6 to 10)

5. In the election for class president, Reynaldo received 6 votes for every 10 votes that were cast. What was the ratio of Reynaldo's votes to his opponent's votes? (E. $\frac{6}{4}$ I. 6 to 10)

6. Tasha's math class had 14 girls and 13 boys. What was the ratio of boys to girls? (D. 14:13   O. $\frac{13}{14}$)

7. For every 6 dogs waiting in the veterinarian's office 5 cats were also waiting. What was the ratio of cats to dogs? (U. 6 to 5   T. 5 to 6)

8. A green ribbon was 10 inches long. A red ribbon was 12 inches long. What was the ratio of the length of the green ribbon to the length of the red ribbon? (P. $\frac{10}{12}$ H. 12:10)

9. The Lions won 8 of their 10 basketball games. What was the ratio of the number of games they won to the number of games they lost? (R. $\frac{8}{10}$ W. 8 to 2)

10. Randy bought 3 jelly donuts, 1 chocolate donut, and 2 cream-filled donuts. What was the ratio of jelly donuts to cream-filled donuts? (S. 3:1   M. 2:3   L. 3:2)

(Continued)

11. Melinda got 23 out of 25 math problems correct. What was the ratio of incorrect problems to the total number of problems? (E. 25:23   R. 2:25   L. 25:2)

Ratios can be used to compare numbers in three ways. Two of these ways are "part to whole" and "part to part." What is the third way?

$$\overline{7} \qquad \overline{11} \qquad \overline{2} \qquad \overline{8} \qquad \overline{1} \qquad \overline{4} \qquad \overline{5} \qquad \overline{10} \qquad \overline{6} \qquad \overline{3} \qquad \overline{9}$$

1–2: UNIT RATES AND RATIOS

A unit rate is a rate expressed as a quantity of 1. Examples of unit rates include 40 miles per gallon of gasoline, $12 per hour, or 3 pounds per bag. These unit rates can be written as ratios: 40:1, $12:1, or 3:1.

Directions: Read each statement. Decide whether the statement is *true* or *false* and circle your answer. Then answer the question at the end by writing the letter of each correct answer in the space above its problem number.

1. During a one-day sale, Sara's mom bought 20 bags of frozen vegetables for $10. This was a unit rate of $\frac{2}{\$1}$. (R. True   M. False)

2. Paying $24 for 3 movie tickets is a unit rate of $8 per ticket. (O. True   E. False)

3. A bakery sold 20 blueberry muffins and 25 bran muffins. The unit rate of blueberry muffins sold to bran muffins sold was $\frac{25}{20}$ or $\frac{5}{4}$. (E. True   O. False)

4. A local pizzeria offered a special to their customers: Join the pizza-a-week club for 10 weeks and buy 10 pies for a total of $120. This unit rate can be expressed as $\frac{10}{\$120}$. (R. True   I. False)

5. A ratio of 6 quarts of juice to 2 quarts of water is a unit rate of 3 quarts of juice to 1 quart of water. (O. True   U. False)

6. In 22 minutes Emmie walked 2 miles. This is a unit rate of 11 miles per minute. (S. True   N. False)

7. A cookie recipe calls for 2 cups of brown sugar to 4 cups of flour. This is a unit rate of $\frac{2}{4}$. (I. True   R. False)

8. Chad drove 147 miles in 3 hours. This is a unit rate of 49 miles per hour. (T. True   H. False)

9. Ethan bought 24 bottles of spring water for $4, which is a unit rate of 24:4. (A. True   P. False)

10. The Harris family spent $20 for 5 ice-cream cones. This is a unit rate of $4 per cone. (P. True   S. False)

What kind of equation shows that two ratios are equal?

$\overline{9}$ $\overline{7}$ $\overline{2}$ $\overline{10}$ $\overline{5}$ $\overline{1}$ $\overline{8}$ $\overline{4}$ $\overline{3}$ $\overline{6}$

1–3: EQUIVALENT RATIOS AND THE COORDINATE PLANE

You can find equivalent ratios by doing the following:

1. Write the ratio as a fraction.

2. Multiply or divide the numerator and denominator by the same nonzero number.

For example, the ratio 3:4 is equivalent to 6:8 because $\frac{3}{4} \times \frac{2}{2} = \frac{6}{8}$.

Directions: Write equivalent ratios to complete each table below. Express each ratio as an ordered pair. Use the first value of each ratio as the x-coordinate and the second value as the y-coordinate. Then graph the ratios listed in table 1 and connect the points. Follow the same procedure for tables 2 and 3.

1. 1:2

1	2
	4
3	
4	
	10

2. 2:3

2	3
	6
8	

3. 12:8

12	8
6	
	2

After connecting the points of the ratios in each table, you should see three line segments.

Copyright © 2016 by Judith A. Muschla, Gary Robert Muschla, and Erin Muschla-Berry.

Name _____ Date _____ Period _____

1–4: FINDING THE PERCENT OF A NUMBER AND FINDING THE WHOLE

The word percent means "per hundred." Percents are ratios that when written in fraction form have a denominator of 100. For example, $25\% = \frac{25}{100}$. Because the denominator is 100, percents can easily be written in decimal form, $25\% = \frac{25}{100} = 0.25$.

Directions: For numbers 1 to 6, find the percent of a number. For numbers 7 to 10, find the whole, given the percent and a part. Then follow the instructions at the bottom of the worksheet.

1. What is 25% of 64? _____

2. What is 36% of 75? _____

3. What is 12% of 50? _____

4. What is 5% of 60? _____

5. What is 10% of 240? _____

6. What is 50% of 24? _____

7. 20% of _____ = 7.

8. 60% of _____ = 9.

9. 35% of _____ = 28.

10. 75% of _____ = 24.

To check that your answers are most likely correct, add your answers. Find 40% of the sum. This final answer should equal 100!

Name _____ Date _____ Period _____

1–5: FINDING UNIT RATES

A unit rate is a ratio written as a fraction with a denominator of 1. Terms such as $3.50 per gallon, 60 miles per hour, and $2.00 per pound are unit rates.

Directions: Find the unit rates. If necessary, round your answers to the nearest cent or whole number. Match each answer with an answer in the Answer Bank. Some answers will be used more than once, and one answer will not be used. Then answer the question at the end by writing the letter of each answer in the space above its problem number.

1. On a recent class trip, 208 students were divided equally to travel on 4 buses. What was the number of students per bus? _____

2. A store sold 400 sheets of notebook paper for $3.99. What was the cost of 1 sheet of paper? _____

3. Giorgio bought 12 flowers for $22.19. All of the flowers were the same price. What was the cost per flower? _____

4. Leeann typed 305 words in 5 minutes. How many words did she type per minute? _____

5. Sami earned $85 working 10 hours last week at her part-time job. How much did she earn per hour? _____

6. A case containing 36 boxes of nails cost $66.59. What was the cost per box? _____

7. A car traveled 60 miles in one hour. What was the speed in miles per minute? _____

8. 36 bottles of spring water were on sale for $3.99. What was the cost per bottle? _____

9. A salesperson drove 260 miles in 4 hours, 15 minutes. What was the rate in miles per hour? _____

10. During a store special, 5 bags each containing 50 peppermint candies were on sale for a total of $2.50. What was the cost of 1 candy? _____

11. Janelle jogged $3\frac{4}{5}$ miles in $\frac{3}{4}$ of an hour. What was the rate in miles per hour? _____

12. James paid $4.50 for $3\frac{1}{2}$ pounds of apples. What was the cost per pound? _____

(Continued)

Answer Bank

E. $0.01	A. 5	K. 1	R. $1.85	O. 5.2
S. 61	P. $0.11	T. $1.29	M. 52	U. $8.50

Many stores display the unit price of items. What is a popular type of store that displays unit prices?

$\overline{9}$ $\overline{5}$ $\overline{8}$ $\overline{2}$ $\overline{6}$ $\overline{1}$ $\overline{11}$ $\overline{3}$ $\overline{7}$ $\overline{10}$ $\overline{12}$ $\overline{4}$

Name ______________________ Date ____________ Period ____________

1-6: GRAPHING PROPORTIONAL RELATIONSHIPS

A proportion is a statement that two ratios are equal. When equivalent ratios are graphed, they result in a line through the origin.

Directions: Plot the following points in the coordinate plane. Decide which points can be written as equivalent ratios.

(4, 12)	(7, 3)	(2, 4)	(−2, −4)	(3, −3)
(1, 2)	(−6, −3)	(−3, −6)	(4, 7)	(−5, 2)
(2, −3)	(−3, −9)	(4, −2)	(−5, 1)	(−4, −5)
(6, −4)	(−2, 4)	(2, 6)	(4, 8)	(6, −6)
(1, 3)	(−3, 3)	(−6, −4)	(−4, 11)	(2, −10)

Write the equivalent ratios as $\frac{y}{x}$.

____

____

____

Name _____ Date _____ Period _____

1–7: REPRESENTING PROPORTIONAL RELATIONSHIPS

A proportion is an equation that contains two equivalent ratios. For example, $\frac{1}{2} = \frac{8}{16}$ is a proportion.

Directions: Write a proportion for each problem. (You do not have to solve the proportions.) Choose your answers from the Answer Bank. Some answers will not be used. Then answer the question at the end by writing the letter of each answer in the space above its problem number. You will need to divide the letters into words.

1. Annie made 3 of 5 free throws. Write a proportion showing how many free throws Annie could expect to make if she took 10 free throws.

2. Yesterday the Sunny Side Bakery sold twice as many blueberry muffins as bran muffins. Write a proportion showing how many bran muffins they sold if they sold 54 blueberry muffins.

3. If 20 mints cost $1.00, write a proportion showing the number of mints you could buy for $5.00.

4. Bradley bought 2 pounds of pears at $1.89 per pound. Write a proportion showing how much Bradley would pay for 5 pounds of pears.

5. Last season, Richard scored 3 goals for every 5 games of hockey he played. Assuming he scored goals at the same rate this year, write a proportion showing how many games he played if he scored 6 goals.

6. A bag contained marbles of different colors. 3 out of 10 marbles were red. Write a proportion showing how many red marbles you would expect to find if the bag contained 120 marbles.

7. In Crystal's town, on average it rains 2 days every week. Given this average, write a proportion showing how many days she should expect it to rain in a year.

8. Mrs. Rogers purchased 5 protractors for $2.00 for her classroom. Write a proportion showing how much 30 protractors would cost.

9. Jacob has a lawn-mowing service in the summer. He can mow an average-sized lawn in about 20 minutes. Write a proportion showing how many average-sized lawns he can mow in 2 hours.

10. Kayleigh is an excellent baseball player. In her last 25 at-bats, she got 10 hits. Write a proportion showing how many hits she can expect to have in 100 at-bats.

(Continued)

11. DeShawn manages to save $2.00 for every $5.00 he earns at his part-time job. Write a proportion showing how much he can expect to save if he earns $100.00.

Answer Bank

G. $\frac{2}{1} = \frac{x}{365}$ F. $\frac{1}{20} = \frac{x}{120}$ R. $\frac{2}{\$1.89} = \frac{5}{x}$

V. $\frac{5}{\$2.00} = \frac{x}{\$100.00}$ E. $\frac{3}{5} = \frac{6}{x}$ S. $\frac{20}{\$1.00} = \frac{x}{\$5.00}$

I. $\frac{3}{5} = \frac{x}{10}$ N. $\frac{2}{1} = \frac{54}{x}$ M. $\frac{\$2.00}{30} = \frac{x}{5}$

U. $\frac{\$1.89}{21} = \frac{x}{5}$ A. $\frac{\$2.00}{\$5.00} = \frac{x}{\$100.00}$ T. $\frac{3}{10} = \frac{x}{120}$

O. $\frac{10}{25} = \frac{x}{100}$ W. $\frac{2}{1} = \frac{x}{52}$ H. $\frac{5}{\$2.00} = \frac{30}{x}$

The word "proportion" is taken from a Latin word, "proportio." What does "proportio" mean?

$\overline{9}$ $\overline{10}$ $\overline{4}$ $\overline{1}$ $\overline{6}$ $\overline{3}$ $\overline{10}$ $\overline{7}$ $\overline{2}$ $\overline{3}$ $\overline{8}$ $\overline{11}$ $\overline{4}$ $\overline{5}$

Name _____ Date _____ Period _____

1–8: SOLVING WORD PROBLEMS INVOLVING PERCENTS

Percents are used in countless everyday situations. Understanding percents and being able to solve problems are important skills in mathematics.

   Directions: Solve each problem and compare your answer to the one provided. If the answer is correct, write "correct" on the line. If the answer is wrong, write "incorrect," explain why the original answer is wrong and write the correct answer. Hint: 40% of the problems are correct.

1. Juan works in a sporting goods store for a salary of $450 per week, plus a 6% commission on his sales. One week his sales were $3,930. What was his income that week?
   $235.80 _____

   _____

2. How much money is saved by purchasing a bicycle priced $320 at a 20% discount rather than one marked $320 with discounts of 10% and 10%?
   $3.20 _____

   _____

3. The Smiths wish to sell their home. They agreed to pay the real estate agent 6% of the selling price. After they pay the commission, they need to have $368,000 left to be able to buy their new home. What must the selling price of their current home be? (Round your answer to the nearest hundred.)
   $22,100 _____

   _____

4. Kara recently lost interest in tennis. She sold her $58 tennis racket to a friend at a 20% loss from the amount she originally paid for the racket. How much did Kara charge her friend for the tennis racket?
   $46.40 _____

   _____

5. School taxes are 2.1% of the assessed value of property in the town of Centerville. Find the school tax on a home whose value is assessed at $350,000.
   $73,500 _____

   _____

6. John purchased a CD for $15 after receiving a discount of 20%. Find the original price of the CD.
   $12.00 _____

   _____

(Continued)

7. A state's sales tax is 6%. If the bill, including the tax, on a meal at a fast food restaurant is $14.31, what is the cost of the meal without the tax?

$0.86 _____

_____

8. Ten years ago, the population of Pleasant Lake was 35,680. Now it is 51,736. What is the percent of increase?

45% _____

_____

9. In a recent city election, 27,720 people out of 70,000 registered voters voted. What percent of the voters cast a ballot?

39.6% _____

_____

10. A pair of sneakers originally cost $90.00. A year later, the price of the sneakers was reduced to $63.00. What was the percent of decrease?

27% _____

_____

The Number System and Number and Quantity

Teaching Notes for the Activities of Section 2

2-1: (6.NS.5) REPRESENTING POSITIVE AND NEGATIVE NUMBERS

This activity requires your students to apply the concepts of positive and negative numbers to everyday situations. Answering a question at the end of the worksheet will enable students to check their work.

Begin the activity by reviewing that positive numbers are greater than zero and negative numbers are less than zero. Note how these numbers are essential to describing real-world situations by referring to the information on the worksheet. Ask your students to volunteer other examples of how positive and negative numbers can be used to describe everyday occurrences.

Discuss the directions on the worksheet. Remind your students to answer the question at the end.

ANSWERS

(1) N, opposite   (2) S, before   (3) A, sign   (4) O, negative   (5) T, positive   (6) E, below
(7) I, gain   (8) P, loss   (9) O, negative   (10) P, loss   Every number except zero has "an opposite."

2-2: (6.NS.6) GRAPHING RATIONAL NUMBERS ON A NUMBER LINE

For this activity, your students will graph rational numbers on a number line. Completing a statement at the end of the worksheet will enable them to check their answers.

Start this activity by explaining that a rational number is a number that can be expressed as a fraction. Offer examples such as $\frac{2}{9}$, $-\frac{3}{4}$, 7, which can be expressed as $\frac{7}{1}$, -6, which can be expressed as $-\frac{6}{1}$, and $-5\frac{1}{3}$, which can be expressed as $-\frac{16}{3}$.

Explain that the number line on the worksheet ranges from -3 to 3. Although the intervals between the integers are the same length, the intervals are broken down into various units. For example, the interval between -3 and -2 is divided into thirds, the interval between -2 and -1 is divided into fourths, the interval between 0 and 1 is divided into halves, and so on.

Explain that to graph a positive number such as $1\frac{3}{4}$ on the number line, students should start at zero, move $1\frac{3}{4}$ units to right, and mark a point on the number line at that position. This corresponds to point S on the number line. To graph a negative number such as $-2\frac{1}{3}$, students should start at zero, move $2\frac{1}{3}$ units to the left, and mark a point on the number line at that position. This corresponds to point L on the number line.

Go over the directions on the worksheet with your students. After graphing the points on the number line, students should complete the statement at the end.

-2, G; $2\frac{1}{5}$, R; $\frac{1}{2}$, A; $-1\frac{1}{4}$, P; 3, H; -3, E; $-\frac{2}{3}$, D; $1\frac{1}{4}$, O; $-2\frac{2}{3}$, N   Every rational number can be "graphed on" a number line.

2-3: (6.NS.6) GRAPHING POINTS IN THE COORDINATE PLANE

For this activity, students will graph points in the coordinate plane. Graphing and connecting the points correctly will result in an optical illusion. Students will need rulers and two sheets of graph paper.

Provide an example of the coordinate plane, and explain that the origin (0, 0) is the point at which the x- and y-axes intersect. Instruct your students to draw a coordinate plane on a sheet of graph paper. To graph a point, students should start at the origin and then move according to the coordinates. The coordinates are the numbers in an ordered pair, for example (3, 4). 3 is the x-coordinate, and 4 is the y-coordinate. Instruct your students to graph the following points for practice: $(-3, 4)$, $(5, -6)$, and $\left(2\frac{1}{2}, 3\frac{1}{2}\right)$. Note that students will have to estimate to graph $\left(2\frac{1}{2}, 3\frac{1}{2}\right)$. Point out that $2\frac{1}{2}$ is halfway between 2 and 3 on the x-axis and $3\frac{1}{2}$ is halfway between 3 and 4 on the y-axis.

Discuss the directions on the worksheet. Students should use their second sheet of graph paper to graph the points on the worksheet. If your students graph and connect the points correctly, they will draw an optical illusion. Note that an optical illusion is a deceiving image. If necessary, remind students that congruent line segments have the same length.

A sketch of the graph is pictured below. Although the two vertical line segments appear to be different lengths, they are congruent. Students may confirm that the vertical line segments are congruent by measuring them. You may wish to discuss that the direction of the segments at the endpoints of the vertical segments gives the impression that the vertical segment on the right is longer than the one on the left.

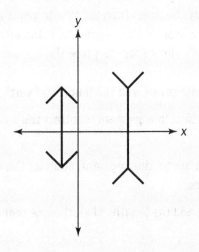

2-4: (6.NS.7) THE ABSOLUTE VALUE AND ORDER OF RATIONAL NUMBERS

This activity requires your students to decide whether statements about absolute value and the order of rational numbers are true or false. They can check their answers by completing a sentence at the end of the worksheet.

Start by reviewing that a rational number is a number that can be expressed as a fraction. Examples include $\frac{4}{5}$, $\frac{17}{4}$, $2\frac{1}{2}$, which equals $\frac{5}{2}$, 3, which equals $\frac{3}{1}$, and 0.7, which equals $\frac{7}{10}$.

Explain the concepts of absolute value and order that are provided on the worksheet. Model absolute value on a number line by showing that -5 is five units from 0. Note that the absolute value of a number is always positive because it represents the distance from 0 and distance is always positive. Therefore, $|-5| = 5$. Next show that 3 is three units from 0 and that $|3| = 3$.

Go over the directions on the worksheet. Suggest that students sketch a number line to help them determine the correct answers to the statements. Writing the letter of the each answer in the space above its statement number at the end will reveal a sentence.

ANSWERS

(1) R, false   (2) R, true   (3) E, true   (4) T, false   (5) U, true   (6) C, true   (7) A, true
(8) C, true   (9) O, false   (10) R, true   (11) Y, false   (12) O, false   (13) E, false   The sentence is "You are correct."

2-5: (6.NS.8) USING THE COORDINATE PLANE TO SOLVE PROBLEMS

For this activity, your students will plot a trail in the coordinate plane that leads to a treasure. They will need rulers and graph paper.

Read the introduction and discuss the directions on the worksheet with your students. They are to draw a coordinate plane on their graph paper, graph the given points, and use a ruler to connect the points in alphabetical order.

Explain that after connecting the points, they are to find the total distance in paces (units) Timmy would walk along the line segments from point A to point I. They may do this in either of two ways. They may simply count the units from point A to point I, or they may find the sum of the lengths of the vertical and horizontal line segments. Using either method should provide them with the total distance, which will allow them to place the treasure at a correct point 40 paces from point A.

If necessary, explain how students can find the lengths of vertical and horizontal line segments:

- To find the length of a vertical line segment, subtract the y-coordinates and find the absolute value of the difference.

- To find the length of a horizontal line segment, subtract the x-coordinates and find the absolute value of the difference.

- To find the total distance, add the lengths of all the line segments.

Remind your students that once they find the total distance, they must decide where Serena could place the treasure. Three places are possible.

ANSWERS

$\overline{AB} = 6$, $\overline{BC} = 5$, $\overline{CD} = 8$, $\overline{DE} = 2$, $\overline{EF} = 2$, $\overline{FG} = 10$, $\overline{GH} = 3$, $\overline{HI} = 3$ The total distance from A to I along the indicated path is 39 units. A sketch of the graph is pictured below.

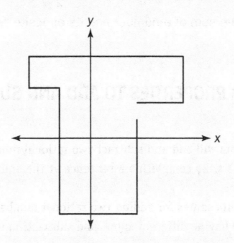

Serena could place the treasure at A (3, 1) or point (2, 2) or point (3, 3), each of which would require 40 paces from point A.

2-6: (7.NS.1) USING THE NUMBER LINE TO ADD AND SUBTRACT RATIONAL NUMBERS

For this activity, your students will use a number line to reinforce the meaning of addition and subtraction. They will also add and subtract rational numbers. By completing a sentence at the end of the worksheet, they can check their answers.

Explain that students can use a number line to show addition and subtraction of rational numbers. To add two rational numbers, students should start at zero on the number line. They should then move the number of units represented by the first number in the problem. If the number is positive, they must move to the right. If the number is negative, they must move to the left. From that point, they must move the number of units represented by the second number. If the second number is positive, they must move to the right. If the second number is negative, they must move to the left.

Explain that subtraction can be thought of as adding the opposite of the number being subtracted. To subtract rational numbers, students should rewrite each subtraction problem as an addition problem and follow the procedure for adding rational numbers. To find the distance between any two points, students should subtract and find the absolute value of the difference.

Discuss the directions on the worksheet. Students are to read each statement and fill in the blanks, referring to the number line, if necessary. Remind them that after completing the statements they are to complete the sentence at the end.

ANSWERS

(1) E, 2   (2) Q, $-\dfrac{1}{2}$ (3) A, −2   (4) R, $\dfrac{1}{4}$ (5) Z, $-1\dfrac{1}{2}$ (6) E, 2   (7) O, $2\dfrac{1}{2}$ (8) S, $-\dfrac{3}{4}$

(9) L, −1   (10) U, $1\dfrac{1}{4}$ The sum of a number and its opposite "equals zero."

2-7: (7.NS.1) USING PROPERTIES TO ADD AND SUBTRACT RATIONAL NUMBERS

For this activity, your students will add and subtract two rational numbers. They will also add three or more rational numbers. By completing a sentence at the end of the worksheet, they can check their answers.

If necessary, review the procedures for adding two rational numbers having the same sign, adding two rational numbers having different signs, and subtracting rational numbers. Refer to the information on the worksheet.

Explain that understanding and applying properties of addition can make adding or subtracting three or more rational numbers easier.

- Commutative Property: $a + b = b + a$, where a and b are rational numbers. The order of adding two rational numbers does not change the sum.

- Associative Property: $(a + b) + c = a + (b + c)$, where a, b, and c are rational numbers. The way numbers are grouped does not affect the sum.

- Identity Property: $a + 0 = a$, which states that the sum of a number and 0 is the number.

- Property of Zero: $a + (-a) = 0$, which states that the sum of a number and its opposite is 0.

Offer the following example:

$$
\begin{aligned}
-1.9 + 2.7 - (-1.9) \quad &= -1.9 + 2.7 + 1.9 && \text{Subtract } -1.9 \\
&= -1.9 + 1.9 + 2.7 && \text{Commutative Property} \\
&= (-1.9 + 1.9) + 2.7 && \text{Associative Property} \\
&= 0 + 2.7 && \text{Property of Zero} \\
&= 2.7 && \text{Identity Property}
\end{aligned}
$$

Your students may, of course, simply rewrite subtraction as addition and then add from left to right. Or they may use a combination of properties, even if they are computing mentally. Understanding and applying the properties can help ensure accurate work.

Discuss the directions on the worksheet. After completing the problems, students should find the answers in the Answer Bank and complete the sentence at the bottom of the page.

(1) A, 5.8 (2) D, –6 (3) S, 0.8 (4) E, 0 (5) O, $-12\frac{4}{5}$ (6) L, –1.7 (7) I, $6\frac{4}{5}$

(8) T, 1 (9) R, $-1\frac{1}{2}$ The mathematical meaning of rational "is related to ratio."

2-8: (7.NS.2) MULTIPLYING AND DIVIDING RATIONAL NUMBERS

This activity requires your students to multiply and divide rational numbers. By answering a question at the end of the worksheet, students can check their answers.

Discuss the procedures for multiplying two rational numbers having the same sign, multiplying two rational numbers having different signs, and dividing two rational numbers, as noted on the worksheet. Remind your students that when dividing fractions, they must change the divisor to its reciprocal and then multiply.

Your students might find it helpful if you also discuss the following properties of multiplication, the understanding of which can make both multiplying and dividing rational numbers easier.

- Commutative Property: $a \times b = b \times a$, where a and b are rational numbers. The order of multiplying two rational numbers does not change the product.

- Associative Property: $(a \times b) \times c = a \times (b \times c)$, where a, b, and c are rational numbers. The way numbers are grouped does not change the product.

- Distributive Property: $a(b + c) = ab + ac$ or $(b + c)a = ba + ca$, where a, b, and c are rational numbers. The product of a rational number and the sum of two rational numbers is the same as the sum of the products.

- Identity Property: $a \times 1 = a$, which states that the product of a number and 1 is the number.

- Inverse Property of Multiplication: $a \times \left(\frac{1}{a}\right) = 1$, where $a \neq 0$. The product of any nonzero number and its reciprocal is 1.

- Property of Zero: $a \times 0 = 0$, which states that the product of a number and 0 is 0.

- Property of Opposites: $(-1) \times a = -a$, which states that the product of a number and –1 is the opposite of the number.

Explain that understanding these properties can make multiplying or dividing three rational numbers easier. Present the following example:

$$-\frac{3}{8} \times \frac{1}{5} \div \left(-\frac{3}{8}\right) = -\frac{3}{8} \times \frac{1}{5} \times \left(-\frac{8}{3}\right) \qquad \text{Change the divisor to its reciprocal and multiply}$$

$$= -\frac{3}{8} \times \left(-\frac{8}{3}\right) \times \frac{1}{5} \qquad \text{Commutative Property}$$

$$= \left[-\frac{3}{8} \times \left(-\frac{8}{3}\right)\right] \times \frac{1}{5} \qquad \text{Associative Property}$$

$$= 1 \times \frac{1}{5} \qquad \text{Inverse Property of Multiplication}$$

$$= \frac{1}{5} \qquad \text{Identity Property}$$

Go over the directions on the worksheet. Note that the problems contain positive and negative whole numbers, fractions, and decimals. If necessary, review the skills needed for multiplying or dividing decimals and fractions. Remind students to answer the question at the end.

ANSWERS

(1) I, −2   (2) L, −2.44   (3) A, $13\frac{1}{2}$ (4) N, $\frac{3}{8}$ (5) R, −7.125   (6) C, $-1\frac{3}{4}$

(7) S, −2.5   (8) E, $-9\frac{3}{5}$ (9) V, −14   (10) M, 1   (11) U, $10\frac{1}{2}$ (12) T, −11

(13) P, 15.96   Another name for the reciprocal is "multiplicative inverse."

2-9: (7.NS.2) CONVERTING RATIONAL NUMBERS TO DECIMALS

This activity requires your students to express rational numbers as terminating or repeating decimals. By answering a question at the end of the worksheet students can check their answers.

Explain that the decimal expansion of a terminating decimal ends, while the decimal expansion of a repeating decimal does not end. For example, 0.65 is a terminating decimal; it ends with 5 hundredths. But $0.6\overline{5}$ is a repeating decimal. The bar over the 5 indicates that the 5 repeats forever. Thus, $0.6\overline{5}$ is actually 0.655555....

Review the process for expressing rational numbers as decimals.

- If the number is positive, divide the numerator by the denominator. Add a decimal point and a zero after the numerator. Add more zeroes if necessary. Keep dividing until the remainder is zero or until a number or group of numbers repeats in the quotient. A remainder of zero results in a terminating decimal. If a number or group of numbers repeats, the decimal is nonterminating and is a repeating decimal. (Note: You may want to mention that some decimals will neither terminate nor repeat. These are irrational numbers and not included in this activity.)

- If the number is negative, divide the numerator by the denominator. Follow the procedure above. Keep the negative sign.

Discuss the directions on the worksheet. Note that after completing the problems, students are to complete the sentence at the end.

ANSWERS

(1) U, 0.1875   (2) G, $-0.58\overline{3}$ (3) E, $0.\overline{285714}$ (4) N, $-0.\overline{5}$ (5) R, 0.875
(6) M, $-0.8\overline{3}$ (7) A, 0.45   (8) C, $-0.\overline{6}$ (9) D, −0.25   (10) I, 0.18   (11) L, $0.2\overline{142857}$
A repeating decimal is also known as a "recurring decimal."

2-10: (7.NS.3) SOLVING WORD PROBLEMS INVOLVING RATIONAL NUMBERS

This activity requires your students to solve a variety of word problems with rational numbers by identifying correct problems and correcting incorrect problems. By arranging the letters of the correct problems to form a word, your students can verify that they did in fact identify all of the correct problems.

Discuss the directions on the worksheet with your students. Emphasize that some of the provided answers are incorrect. If an answer is incorrect, your students must identify the error and solve the problem. After completing the problems, students are to write the letters of the problems that provided the correct answers and rearrange these letters to form a word that describes their work.

ANSWERS

(S) Incorrect—The mistake was adding $-\frac{5}{8}$ to 10 instead of subtracting $-\frac{5}{8}$ from 10. The correct answer is $\$10\frac{5}{8}$.   (M) Incorrect—The mistake was dividing the total ticket sales, $\$1,041.50$, by $\$3.50$. The student ticket sales, $\$268$, needed to be subtracted from the total sales first, resulting in $\$773.50$, which must then be divided by $\$3.50$. The correct answer is 221 adult tickets were sold.   (R) Correct   (U) Incorrect—The mistake was subtracting 282 from 20,237 instead of subtracting -282 from 20,237. The correct answer is 20,519 feet.   (T) Correct   (P) Incorrect—The reduced price from Monday to Tuesday was found. The correct answer for the total reduction in price is $\$15$.   (E) Correct   (A) Correct   (B) Incorrect—The interest earned was not included. The correct answer is $\$162.71$ (G) Correct   Your work is "great."

2-11: (8.NS.1) EXPRESSING FRACTIONS AS REPEATING DECIMALS AND REPEATING DECIMALS AS FRACTIONS

For this activity, your students will express rational numbers in fraction form and as repeating decimals. By completing a sentence at the end of the worksheet, they can check their answers.

Review that students can convert a fraction such as $\frac{1}{8}$ to a decimal by dividing the numerator by the denominator and finding that $\frac{1}{8} = 0.125$. Note that the same procedure is used if a decimal repeats. Also note that negative fractions must be expressed as negative decimals and negative decimals must be expressed as negative fractions.

Discuss the examples on the worksheet that detail expressing a fraction as a repeating decimal. Note that the bar is placed over the digit or digits that repeat.

Next, discuss the example that details the procedure for changing a repeating decimal to a fraction. Emphasize that because two digits repeat in $0.\overline{86}$, students must multiply $0.\overline{86}$ by 100 to find $86.\overline{86}$. Explain the reasoning that $0.868686\ldots \times 100 = 86.\overline{86}$ because the decimal still repeats. After multiplying, students must subtract the original number from the product and then solve to find the fraction.

Go over the instructions on the worksheet. After students have completed the problems, they are to complete the sentence at the end.

2–12: (8.NS.2) USING RATIONAL APPROXIMATIONS OF IRRATIONAL NUMBERS

For this activity, your students will determine whether statements about irrational numbers are true or false. Answering a question at the end of the worksheet will enable them to check their work. They will need calculators and rulers for this activity.

Explain to your students that although rational numbers are terminal or have a decimal expansion in which a digit or group of digits repeats, irrational numbers do not. Show your students how to use their calculators to approximate the square roots of irrational numbers. Provide an example of $\sqrt{3}$ that shows one, two, and three decimal places. Note that the more decimal places that are considered, the more accurate the approximation.

- $\sqrt{3} \approx 1.7$
- $\sqrt{3} \approx 1.73$
- $\sqrt{3} \approx 1.732$

Explain that rational approximations of irrational numbers can be graphed on a number line. You may wish to show where the rational approximation of $\sqrt{3}$ is placed on the number line by first locating 1.7 and 1.8. $\sqrt{3}$ is about a third of the distance from 1.7 to 1.8.

Discuss the directions on the worksheet. In order to determine whether some statements are true or false, students will need to use their calculators to find the approximation of irrational numbers. Suggest that drawing a number line can be helpful to locating the approximation of an irrational number in relation to other numbers on the number line. After they are done identifying the statements correctly, students should write the letters of their answers in order to reveal a word.

2-13: (N-RN.1) USING THE PROPERTIES OF EXPONENTS

For this activity, your students will use the properties of exponents to find values of n that make equations true. By completing the statement at the end of the worksheet, they can check their answers.

Start the activity by reviewing the following properties of exponents with your students. Note that the exponents are integers, which is unlike the properties of exponents shown on the worksheet that include rational exponents.

- Product of Powers Property: $x^m \cdot x^n = x^{m+n}$, where m and n are integers.

- Power of a Power Property: $(x^m)^n = x^{mn}$, where m and n are integers.

- Negative Exponent Property: $x^{-m} = \frac{1}{x^m}$, where x is a nonzero number and m is an integer.

Explain how to extend the Product of Powers Property to rational exponents by providing this example:

Find the value of n that would make this equation true: $3^n \cdot 3^n = 3^1$ or 3. By the Product of Powers Property, $3^n \cdot 3^n = 3^{2n}$. Because $3^1 = 3^{2n}$, $2n = 1$. Therefore, $n = \frac{1}{2}$, which means that $3^{\frac{1}{2}} = \sqrt{3}$. This can be checked by substituting $\sqrt{3}$ for 3^n into the first equation: $\sqrt{3} \cdot \sqrt{3} = 3$. If necessary, use a similar process to demonstrate how the other properties can be extended to include rational exponents.

Discuss the properties of exponents on the worksheet. Note that these have been extended to include rational numbers; provide more examples, if needed.

Go over the directions with your students. Remind them to complete the statement at the end of the worksheet.

ANSWERS

(1) O, 2   (2) U, $\frac{3}{2}$ (3) E, $\frac{1}{3}$ (4) A, $\frac{1}{2}$ (5) N, $-\frac{1}{2}$ (6) L, 1   (7) S, 4   (8) R, $-\frac{2}{3}$

(9) M, $\frac{1}{4}$ James Hume suggested using "Roman Numerals."

2-14: (N-RN.2) REWRITING EXPRESSIONS INVOLVING RADICALS AND RATIONAL EXPONENTS

For this activity, your students will rewrite expressions using the properties of exponents. By completing a statement at the end of the worksheet, they can check their work.

Review that $x^{\frac{1}{n}}$ is the nth root of x and can be written as $\sqrt[n]{x}$. Discuss the properties of the exponents that are shown on the worksheet and explain that they can be used to rewrite expressions. Provide the following examples:

- Rewrite $\left(\sqrt[3]{125}\right)^2$ so that it does not contain a radical. Using the Rational Exponent Property and the Power of a Power Property, $\left(\sqrt[3]{125}\right)^2 = 125^{\frac{2}{3}} = \left(125^{\frac{1}{3}}\right)^2 = 5^2 = 25$.

- Rewrite $9^{\frac{-1}{2}}$ so that it does not contain an exponent. Using the Negative Exponent Property and the Rational Exponent Property, $9^{\frac{-1}{2}} = \frac{1}{9^{\frac{1}{2}}} = \frac{1}{\sqrt{9}} = \frac{1}{3}$.

Discuss the directions on the worksheet with your students. Emphasize that if an expression contains a radical, it should be matched with an expression that does not contain a radical. If an expression contains an exponent, it should be matched with an expression that does not contain an exponent. Remind your students to complete the statement at the end.

ANSWERS

(1) E, 3   (2) O, 32   (3) H, $15\frac{1}{2}$ (4) I, 343   (5) S, 125   (6) D, 64   (7) A, 27   (8) U, 4
(9) T, 10^{-1} (10) Y, 6   (11) L, $\frac{1}{25}$ Christoff Rudolff first used the radical sign "that is still used today."

2–15: (N-RN.3) SUMS AND PRODUCTS OF RATIONAL AND IRRATIONAL NUMBERS

This activity requires your students to determine if a sum or product is rational or irrational. By finding a word related to a definition of rational, students can check their answers.

Discuss the definitions of rational and irrational numbers. Note the examples on the worksheet and be sure that students realize that some square roots may be simplified as rational numbers.

Provide the following examples of addition and multiplication:

- Ask your students to find the sum of two rational numbers, $2.8 + (-3.5)$. The sum is -0.7, which is a rational number.

- Ask your students to find the sum of a rational number and an irrational number, $\sqrt{11} + 2.5$. The sum is $\sqrt{11} + 2.5$, which is an irrational number. The sum of a terminating decimal and a nonrepeating, nonterminating decimal results in a nonrepeating, nonterminating decimal.

- Ask your students to find the product of two rational numbers, $2.8 \times (-3.5)$. The product is -9.8, a rational number.

- Ask your students to find the product of a rational number and an irrational number, $\sqrt{11} \times 2.5$. The product is $2.5\sqrt{11}$, which is an irrational number. The product of a terminating decimal and a nonrepeating, nonterminating decimal results in a nonrepeating, nonterminating decimal.

You may provide an example of the sum of a repeating decimal and a nonrepeating, nonterminating decimal, such as $0.\overline{9} + \sqrt{7}$. The sum is $0.\overline{9} + \sqrt{7}$, which is an irrational number. You may also provide an example of the product of a repeating decimal and a nonrepeating, nonterminating decimal, such as $1.\overline{6} \times \sqrt{3}$. The product is $1.\overline{6}\sqrt{3}$, which is an irrational number.

Go over the directions on the worksheet. Note that students are to use only the letters of the sums or products of rational numbers in the unscrambling of the word.

(1) I, rational   (2) C, rational   (3) B, irrational   (4) Z, irrational   (5) O, rational
(6) L, rational   (7) K, irrational   (8) R, irrational   (9) N, irrational   (10) L, rational
(11) A, rational   (12) G, rational   The scrambled word is "icollag," which can be
unscrambled as "logical."

2-16: (N-Q.1) INTERPRETING AND USING UNITS

For this activity, your students will create a graph that shows the expenses of a fictional election campaign in a small town. In creating the graph, students will need to choose and interpret units, as well as select the type of graph and scale. Your students will need rulers and graph paper.

Read and discuss the scenario presented on the worksheet. In any election, a candidate does not want to run out of campaign funds. The costs of the campaign must be balanced against the amount of money that is available.

Go over the directions with your students and discuss the possible graphs they might consider. Also discuss the scale and units they might use. Because it is impractical to try to graph amounts of money to the nearest cent, students should round the weekly expenses. You might suggest that they round to hundreds. They could then use a scale starting at $3,500 and increase each unit by a hundred: $3,500, $3,600, $3,700, and so on up to $5,000, spanning 16 units on the grid. Students should plot the expenses by weeks.

Remind your students that after creating their graphs, they are to answer the questions at the end. They should support their answers.

Graphs and answers will vary. One practical graph is to plot the expenses, rounded to the nearest hundred by weeks. This graph would show an increase in expenses from $3,500 to $4,600, which is accelerating as the campaign goes on. If this trend in spending continues, Clarice's campaign funds will not last to election day.

2-17: (N-Q.2) DEFINING APPROPRIATE QUANTITIES

This activity requires your students to choose appropriate measures and units to solve problems. Given problems with incorrect answers because of the selection of inappropriate quantities, students must identify the mistake in the problem, select the appropriate quantity, and find the correct solution.

Explain that selecting the appropriate quantities is critical to problem solving. To ensure that they choose the right measures and units, students should identify the measures and units presented in a problem, and then ask themselves which measures and units are necessary to solve the problem. They should also be aware that sometimes they may need to convert a measure to an equivalent form. For example, 15 minutes can be expressed both as 0.25 hour or $\frac{1}{4}$ hour.

Go over the directions on the worksheet with your students. Emphasize that they are to identify and explain the mistake that was made in the answer that was provided, and then use the appropriate measures and units to find the correct solution.

ANSWERS

(1) The answer provided was found by dividing 536 miles by 32 miles per gallon. However, because the question asks for the time spent driving on the highway, the total miles must be divided by 61 miles per hour. The correct answer is about 9 hours.   (2) The answer provided was found by dividing 25,000 gallons by 14 hours. But the question required the answer to find the rate of water draining per minute. The given answer of about 1,786 must be divided by 60 minutes, resulting in a correct answer of about 30 gallons per minute.   (3) The answer provided was found by multiplying 120 pounds × 30 minutes × 4.2 calories burned per pound per hour. But because the calories burned are calculated per hour, the time must also be calculated in hours. Instead of the time being 30 minutes, it should be 0.5 hours, resulting in an answer of 252 calories.   (4) The answer provided was found by dividing the price of the tablet by $8.50 per hour. However, the question asked how long (in weeks) Evan must work. This answer would be found by dividing the cost of the tablet, $483.75, by $85 (Evan's earnings per week), resulting in 5.69 or 6 full weeks.

2–18: (N-Q.3) CHOOSING APPROPRIATE LEVELS OF ACCURACY FOR MEASUREMENT

For this activity, your students are to decide whether levels of accuracy for various measurements are appropriate. Understanding rounding and significant digits will be helpful to students in completing this activity.

Explain that measurements are seldom exact because measuring instruments are not perfect. In many cases, measurements are rounded off to practical numbers. For example, in measuring a car's fuel efficiency in miles per gallon, rounding measurements to whole numbers is practical. 30 miles per gallon, as opposed to 30.15 miles per gallon under ideal test conditions, is a sensible and appropriate level of accuracy.

If necessary, review that significant digits indicate how exactly a number is known. Offer the following guidelines:

- All nonzero digits are significant.

- All zeroes between two nonzero digits are significant.

- For a decimal, all zeroes after the last nonzero digit are significant.

- For a whole number, unless zeroes after the last nonzero number are known to be significant, they should be assumed to be not significant.

- For addition and subtraction, the answer should have the same number of decimal places as the least number of decimal places in any of the numbers being added or subtracted.

If necessary, round the answer to this place. Examples: The sum of $6.7 + 3.421$ is rounded to 10.1, and the difference of $40.22 - 2.6790$ is rounded to 37.54.

- For multiplication and division, the answer should have the same number of significant digits as the least number of significant digits in any one of the numbers being multiplied or divided. If necessary, round the answer accordingly. Examples: The product of 3.401×2.3 is rounded to 7.8, and the quotient of $28.6 \div 3.8$ is rounded to 7.5.

Go over the directions on the worksheet. Students are to answer the questions on the worksheet regarding the appropriate levels of accuracy and justify their answers. You might want to suggest that students consider significant digits in their answers.

ANSWERS

Answers may vary; possible answers follow.   (1) Miles, because feet is an impractical measure for distance between towns.   (2) No, because a sum is accurate only to the smallest number of decimal places being added, which in this case is 112.6 meters. (You may want to mention that in real life when ordering items such as fencing, it is wise to order a little more than the exact length you need.)   (3) Yes, because rounding 3 hundredths to tenths is meaningless, and attempting to measure the speed beyond hundredths is impractical.   (4) Yes, because this is an average. While measuring to tenths provides more accuracy than whole number degrees, measuring to hundredths or beyond would not be practical.   (5) No, because a product is accurate only to the least number of significant digits in any one of the numbers being multiplied. The area of the floor should be calculated as 26.9 square meters.   (6) Yes, because the difference should have the same number of decimal places as the least number of decimal places in either of the numbers being subtracted.   (7) No, because a quotient should have the same number of significant digits as the smaller number of significant digits in the divisor or dividend. The answer should be 1.6 feet.   (8) 2.5 ounces is the more appropriate level of accuracy as 0.15625 pound is essentially meaningless.

2-19: (N-CN.1) WRITING COMPLEX NUMBERS

This activity requires your students to write complex numbers in the form of $a + bi$ where a and b are real numbers. Answering a question at the end of the worksheet will enable students to check their answers.

Explain to your students that the set of real numbers and the set of imaginary numbers are subsets of the complex numbers. Every real number and every imaginary number can be written as a complex number expressed as $a + bi$, where a and b are real numbers. Numbers such as $-3 + i$ are expressed in the form $a + bi$, where $a = -3$ and $b = 1$.

Provide an example of a real number such as -7 and show that it can be written as a complex number, $-7 + 0i$. In this example, $a = -7$ and $b = 0$. Also provide an example of an imaginary number such as $0.75i$ and show that it can be written as a complex number, $0 + 0.75i$. In this example, $a = 0$ and $b = 0.75$.

Go over the directions on the worksheet with your students. Remind them to answer the question at the end.

2-20: (N-CN.2) ADDING, SUBTRACTING, AND MULTIPLYING COMPLEX NUMBERS

For this activity, your students must add, subtract, and multiply complex numbers. To complete this activity successfully, they will need to use the Commutative, Associative, and Distributive Properties to simplify expressions. By completing a statement at the end of the worksheet, students can check their answers.

Explain that complex numbers include both real and imaginary numbers. If necessary, review examples of imaginary numbers such as $\sqrt{-10} = i\sqrt{10}$, $2i$, $3 + 2i$, and $-i\sqrt{2}$. Also, review simplifying expressions such as $(3i)(4i) = 12i^2$ or -12.

Discuss the directions and examples on the worksheet, emphasizing that it is necessary to simplify radicals before adding, subtracting, and multiplying. If necessary, remind your students that FOIL is a procedure for multiplying two binomials: First, Outer, Inner, Last. Students are to complete the statement at the end of the worksheet.

2-21: (N-CN.7) SOLVING QUADRATIC EQUATIONS THAT HAVE COMPLEX SOLUTIONS

For this activity, your students will solve quadratic equations with real coefficients that have complex solutions. They are to identify solutions that are right and correct solutions that are wrong. Unscrambling the letters of the correct solutions will reveal a word that will confirm that students did in fact identify the correct solutions.

Discuss the quadratic formula, $x = \frac{-b \pm \sqrt{b^2 - 4ac}}{2a}$, with your students and provide this example: Solve $3x^2 + x + 4 = 0$. $a = 3$, $b = 1$, $c = 4$

Explain that students should substitute these values into the formula and then solve,

$$x = \frac{-1 \pm \sqrt{1^2 - 4(3)(4)}}{2(3)} = \frac{-1 \pm \sqrt{-47}}{6} = \frac{-1 \pm i\sqrt{47}}{6}.$$

Review the directions on the worksheet with your students. Note that they may have to rewrite some equations into the form $ax^2 + bx + c = 0$. Remind them to unscramble the letters of the problems that were correct to form a word.

ANSWERS

Correct answers are followed by their letter; incorrect answers are followed by the correct solution. (1) Correct, U (2) Incorrect, $x = -1 \pm i\sqrt{3}$ (3) Correct, R (4) Correct, E (5) Incorrect, $x = \frac{-1 \pm i\sqrt{7}}{-2}$ (6) Correct, S (7) Incorrect, $x = -1 \pm \frac{i\sqrt{3}}{3}$ (8) Incorrect, $x = 1 \pm i$ (9) Incorrect, $x = \frac{-1 \pm i}{2}$ (10) Correct, P The unscrambled letters spell "super."

Reproducibles for Section 2 follow.

Name _____ Date _____ Period _____

2-1: REPRESENTING POSITIVE AND NEGATIVE NUMBERS

Positive and negative numbers are used to represent common occurrences. We experience gains and losses every day. Stocks go up and down, a football team gains or loses yards, and temperatures increase or decrease. All of these situations can be described with positive and negative numbers.

Directions: The sentences below relate to positive and negative numbers. Complete each sentence using the words in the Answer Bank. Some answers will be used more than once. Some answers will not be used. Then answer the question by writing the letter of each answer in the space above its sentence number. You will need to divide the letter into words.

1. −4 can be read as negative four or the _____ of four.

2. When launching a spacecraft, "T minus one" refers to one second _____ liftoff.

3. Positive numbers can be written without any _____.

4. All _____ numbers are less than zero.

5. All _____ numbers are greater than 0.

6. −300 feet means three hundred feet _____ sea level.

7. Winning $10 is a _____ of $10.

8. +8 mean a gain of 8; therefore −7 means a _____ of 7.

9. On a number line, moving to the left is moving in a _____ direction.

10. In banking, a _____ of $350 can be written as −$350.

Answer Bank

U. left	N. opposite	P. loss	A. sign
W. zero	M. less	E. below	O. negative
S. before	L. right	I. gain	T. positive

Every number except zero has this. What is it?

$\overline{3}$ $\quad$ $\overline{1}$ $\quad$ $\overline{4}$ $\quad$ $\overline{8}$ $\quad$ $\overline{10}$ $\quad$ $\overline{9}$ $\quad$ $\overline{2}$ $\quad$ $\overline{7}$ $\quad$ $\overline{5}$ $\quad$ $\overline{6}$

Name_____ Date_____ Period_____   37

2-2: GRAPHING RATIONAL NUMBERS ON A NUMBER LINE

A rational number is a number that can be expressed as a fraction. For example, $\frac{2}{3}$, $-\frac{3}{4}$, and 5, which can be expressed as $\frac{5}{1}$, are rational numbers. Each point on the number line below represents a rational number.

Directions: Graph -2, $2\frac{1}{5}$, $\frac{1}{2}$, $-1\frac{1}{4}$, 3, -3, $-\frac{2}{3}$, $1\frac{1}{4}$, and $-2\frac{2}{3}$ on the number line. Complete the statement by writing the letter of each point you graphed in the space above the point. You will need to divide the letters into words.

Every rational number can be _____ a number line.

$\overline{-2}$ $\overline{2\frac{1}{5}}$ $\overline{\frac{1}{2}}$ $\overline{-1\frac{1}{4}}$ $\overline{3}$ $\overline{-3}$ $\overline{-\frac{2}{3}}$ $\overline{1\frac{1}{4}}$ $\overline{-2\frac{2}{3}}$

Name_____ Date_____ Period_____

2–3: GRAPHING POINTS IN THE COORDINATE PLANE

The coordinate plane is a plane that is formed by two intersecting perpendicular lines called the *x*-axis and the *y*-axis. These lines intersect at point (0, 0), which is called the origin.

Directions: Follow the steps below to draw an optical illusion.

1. Draw a coordinate plane on graph paper and graph each point. Label each point with the given letter.

$$A. \left(-4\tfrac{1}{2},\ 5\tfrac{1}{2}\right) \qquad B. \left(-2\tfrac{1}{2},\ 7\right) \qquad C. \left(0,\ 5\tfrac{1}{2}\right)$$

$$D. \left(-4\tfrac{1}{2},\ -3\tfrac{1}{2}\right) \qquad E. \left(-2\tfrac{1}{2},\ -5\right) \qquad F. \left(0,\ -3\tfrac{1}{2}\right)$$

$$G.\ (5, 9) \qquad\qquad H.\ (7, 7) \qquad\qquad I.\ (9, 9)$$

$$J.\ (5, -7) \qquad\qquad K.\ (7, -5) \qquad\qquad L.\ (9, -7)$$

2. Connect the points in the following order. *A* to *B*. *B* to *C*. *D* to *E*. *E* to *F*. *B* to *E*. *G* to *H*. *H* to *I*. *J* to *K*. *K* to *L*. *H* to *K*.

3. If you have graphed and connected the points correctly, you have drawn two congruent vertical line segments. How can you prove that the segments are congruent?

Copyright © 2016 by Judith A. Muschla, Gary Robert Muschla, and Erin Muschla-Berry.

Name _____ Date _____ Period _____

2–4: THE ABSOLUTE VALUE AND ORDER OF RATIONAL NUMBERS

The absolute value of a number is its distance from zero on the number line. For example, $|10| = 10$ and $|−10| = 10$. Both numbers are 10 units from zero. The direction does not matter.

But direction does matter with the order of numbers. A number is always smaller than the numbers to its right on the number line. Conversely, a number is always larger than the numbers to its left on the number line.

Directions: Determine if each statement is *true* or *false*. If a statement is true, circle the letter for true. If a statement is false, circle the letter for false. Then write the letter of each correct answer in the space above its statement number. Divide the letters into words to reveal a sentence that describes your work.

1. $−2 > −1$ because $−2$ is to the left of $−1$ on the number line.   (Z. True   R. False)

2. 3 ounces $<$ 4 ounces because $3 < 4$.   (R. True   N. False)

3. $|6| = |−6|$ because 6 and $−6$ are the same distance from 0 on the number line. (E. True   F. False)

4. $\left|1\frac{1}{2}\right| = \left|2\frac{1}{2}\right|$ because $1\frac{1}{2}$ and $2\frac{1}{2}$ are the same distance from 2 on the number line. (I. True   T. False)

5. Moving 7 units right on a number line is less than moving 10 units left because $|7| < |−10|$. (U. True   H. False)

6. $−6$ shows a loss of 6 points and $|−6|$ shows the number of points that were lost. (C. True   P. False)

7. A point 3 feet above sea level is higher than a point 3 feet below sea level because $3 > −3$. (A. True   D. False)

8. Because all positive numbers are to the right of 0 on the number line, all positive numbers are greater than negative numbers. (C. True   K. False)

9. Since $|−2.5°C|$ is equal to $|2.5°C|$, $−2.5°C$ is equal to $2.5°C$. (J. True   O. False)

10. $−3$ and 3 have opposite signs, but their absolute values are the same. (R. True   M. False)

11. $|−5|$ is $−5$ units from 0 on a number line. (D. True   Y. False)

(Continued)

39

12. Since $-4\frac{1}{4}$ is closer to 0 than -5, $\left|-4\frac{1}{4}\right| > |-5|$. (W. True   O. False)

13. Two numbers that are the same distance from 0 on a number line may not have the same absolute value. (U. True   E. False)

$\overline{11}$ $\overline{9}$ $\overline{5}$ $\overline{7}$ $\overline{1}$ $\overline{13}$ $\overline{6}$ $\overline{12}$ $\overline{2}$ $\overline{10}$ $\overline{3}$ $\overline{8}$ $\overline{4}$

Name _____ Date _____ Period _____

2–5: USING THE COORDINATE PLANE TO SOLVE PROBLEMS

Serena's younger brother Timmy loves pirates. One day, Serena decided to make a treasure map and hide a small box full of play coins in the backyard. To plan the map and decide where to place the coins, she graphed points in the coordinate plane. She started at a large bush in the backyard and marked the bush at point A (3, 1) on the graph. Each unit of the graph equaled the length of Timmy's foot. This allowed him to pace out the steps in the yard. Serena placed markers in the yard corresponding to points A, B, C, D, E, F, G, H, and I. Using the map, she wrote a set of steps that Timmy could follow to find the treasure. You have to decide where to place the treasure so that Timmy passes each point and the treasure is 40 paces from A.

Directions: Follow the steps below.

1. Draw a coordinate plane on graph paper.

2. Graph and label each point.

A (3, 1)	B (3, −5)	C (−2, −5)	D (−2, 3)	E (−4, 3)
F (−4, 5)	G (6, 5)	H (6, 2)	I (3, 2)	

3. Connect the points in alphabetical order: A to B, B to C, C to D, and so on finally connecting H to I.

4. Find the length of each line segment.

5. Find the total distance along the line segments from A to I.

6. Decide where Serena should place the treasure so that Timmy can follow the map and walk along the trail to find the treasure. Remember, the treasure must be 40 paces from point A.

2–6: USING THE NUMBER LINE TO ADD AND SUBTRACT RATIONAL NUMBERS

A number line can help you to add and subtract rational numbers.

Directions: Complete each sentence or equation with a rational number. Choose your answers from the answers in the Answer Bank. One answer will be used more than once. Some answers will not be used. Then complete the sentence at the end by writing the letter of each answer in the space above its problem number. You will need to divide the letters into words.

1. $1\frac{1}{2}$ feet of ribbon was cut from a strip that was _____ feet long. $\frac{1}{2}$ foot of the original strip of ribbon was left.

2. $\frac{1}{2} +$ _____ $= 0$

3. A temperature of _____°C increased 2°C. The temperature is now 0°C.

4. $1\frac{1}{4} + \left(-\frac{1}{4}\right)$ is the same as $1\frac{1}{4} -$ _____.

5. $2\frac{1}{2}$ and _____ are the same distance from $\frac{1}{2}$.

6. $-\frac{1}{4} - (-2) = -\frac{1}{4} +$ _____

7. Traveling east 2 miles and then traveling west _____ miles places you $\frac{1}{2}$ mile west of the starting point.

8. _____ and $\frac{1}{4}$ are the same distance from $-\frac{1}{4}$.

9. $|-2 - (-1)| =$ the absolute value of _____.

10. The distance between $-\frac{1}{2}$ and $\frac{3}{4}$ is $\left|-\frac{1}{2} - \frac{3}{4}\right| =$ _____.

Answer Bank

P. $-1\frac{3}{4}$	A. -2	S. $-\frac{3}{4}$	Q. $-\frac{1}{2}$	N. $2\frac{3}{4}$	L. -1
R. $\frac{1}{4}$	E. 2	O. $2\frac{1}{2}$	U. $1\frac{1}{4}$	T. $-\frac{1}{4}$	Z. $-1\frac{1}{2}$

The sum of a number and its opposite _____.

$\overline{6}$ ___ $\overline{2}$ ___ $\overline{10}$ ___ $\overline{3}$ ___ $\overline{9}$ ___ $\overline{8}$ ___ $\overline{5}$ ___ $\overline{1}$ ___ $\overline{4}$ ___ $\overline{7}$

Name _____   Date _____   Period _____

2–7: USING PROPERTIES TO ADD AND SUBTRACT RATIONAL NUMBERS

Following are guidelines for adding and subtracting rational numbers:

- To add two rational numbers that have the same sign, add and keep the sign.

- To add two rational numbers that have different signs, subtract the smaller absolute value from the larger absolute value. Use the sign of the number with the larger absolute value.

- To subtract two rational numbers, write a related addition problem and add the opposite of the second number. Then follow the rules for adding rational numbers.

Directions: Find each sum or difference and match each answer with an answer in the Answer Bank. One answer will not be used. Complete the sentence at the end by writing the letter of each answer in the space above its problem number. You will need to divide the letters into words.

1. $8.2 + (-2.4)$

2. $-4\frac{1}{3} + \left(-1\frac{2}{3}\right)$

3. $5.4 - 4.6$

4. $-4.2 + (-7.8) + 12$

5. $-6\frac{4}{5} - 6\frac{3}{5} + \frac{3}{5}$

6. $4.8 + 5.5 - 12$

7. $2\frac{4}{5} - \left(-1\frac{3}{5}\right) + 2\frac{2}{5}$

8. $4\frac{1}{4} - 3\frac{1}{2} + \frac{1}{4}$

9. $-2\frac{1}{3} + 1\frac{1}{2} - \frac{2}{3}$

Answer Bank

S. 0.8	E. 0	I. $6\frac{4}{5}$	P. 6	T. 1
L. −1.7	D. −6	A. 5.8	R. $-1\frac{1}{2}$	O. $-12\frac{4}{5}$

The mathematical meaning of rational _____.

$\overline{7}$ $\overline{3}$ $\overline{9}$ $\overline{4}$ $\overline{6}$ $\overline{1}$ $\overline{8}$ $\overline{4}$ $\overline{2}$ $\overline{8}$ $\overline{5}$ $\overline{9}$ $\overline{1}$ $\overline{8}$ $\overline{7}$ $\overline{5}$

Name _____ Date _____ Period _____

2–8: MULTIPLYING AND DIVIDING RATIONAL NUMBERS

To multiply two rational numbers, multiply the absolute values. Then determine the sign of the product.

- If two rational numbers have the same sign, the product is positive.

- If two rational numbers have different signs, the product is negative.

To divide a rational number by a nonzero number, divide the absolute values. Then determine the sign of the quotient using the guidelines above.

Directions: Find each product or quotient and match each answer with an answer in the Answer Bank. One answer will not be used. Then answer the question at the end by writing the letter of each answer in the space above its problem number.

1. -8×0.25

2. $-12.2 \div 5$

3. $-3 \times \left(-4\frac{1}{2}\right)$

4. $2\frac{1}{2} \times \left(-\frac{3}{4}\right) \times \left(-\frac{1}{5}\right)$

5. $-28.5 \div 4$

6. $-\frac{7}{8} \times \frac{1}{2} \div \frac{1}{4}$

7. $12.5 \div (-5)$

8. $\frac{3}{5} \div \frac{1}{2} \div \left(-\frac{1}{8}\right)$

9. $7 \div \left(-\frac{1}{2}\right)$

10. $\frac{5}{9} \times \frac{1}{5} \times 9$

11. $-12 \times \left(-\frac{7}{8}\right)$

12. $-121 \div 11$

13. $-4.2 \times (-3.8)$

Answer Bank

C. $-1\frac{3}{4}$	H. 14	S. -2.5	R. -7.125	U. $10\frac{1}{2}$	T. -11	M. 1
P. 15.96	L. -2.44	I. -2	A. $13\frac{1}{2}$	N. $\frac{3}{8}$	E. $-9\frac{3}{5}$	V. -14

What is another name for the reciprocal?

$\overline{10}$ $\overline{11}$ $\overline{2}$ $\overline{12}$ $\overline{1}$ $\overline{13}$ $\overline{2}$ $\overline{1}$ $\overline{6}$ $\overline{3}$ $\overline{12}$ $\overline{1}$ $\overline{9}$ $\overline{8}$

$\overline{1}$ $\overline{4}$ $\overline{9}$ $\overline{8}$ $\overline{5}$ $\overline{7}$ $\overline{8}$

2-9: CONVERTING RATIONAL NUMBERS TO DECIMALS

Every rational number can be expressed as a terminating or repeating decimal. For example, 0.34 is a terminating decimal while $0.3\overline{4}$ is a repeating decimal. The bar over the 4 shows that the 4 repeats. $0.3\overline{4}$ means $0.344444444\ldots$.

Directions: Express each rational number as a decimal and match each answer with an answer in the Answer Bank. One answer will not be used. Then answer the question at the end by writing the letter of each answer in the space above its problem number. You will need to divide the letters into words.

1. $\frac{3}{16}$ 2. $-\frac{7}{12}$ 3. $\frac{2}{7}$ 4. $-\frac{5}{9}$ 5. $\frac{7}{8}$ 6. $-\frac{5}{6}$

7. $\frac{9}{20}$ 8. $-\frac{2}{3}$ 9. $-\frac{1}{4}$ 10. $\frac{9}{50}$ 11. $\frac{3}{14}$

Answer Bank

N. $-0.\overline{5}$	I. 0.18	R. 0.875	C. $-0.\overline{6}$
G. $-0.58\overline{3}$	L. $0.\overline{214285}7$	D. -0.25	M. $-0.8\overline{3}$
B. 0.55	A. 0.45	E. $0.\overline{285714}$	U. 0.1875

What is another name for a decimal that repeats?

$\overline{5}$ $\overline{3}$ $\overline{8}$ $\overline{1}$ $\overline{5}$ $\overline{5}$ $\overline{10}$ $\overline{4}$ $\overline{2}$ $\overline{9}$ $\overline{3}$ $\overline{8}$ $\overline{10}$ $\overline{6}$ $\overline{7}$ $\overline{11}$

2–10: SOLVING WORD PROBLEMS INVOLVING RATIONAL NUMBERS

Rational numbers are used in countless real-world situations. The following problems represent only a few of the many applications.

Directions: Solve each problem and compare your answer to the one provided. If the answer is correct, write *correct* on the line. If the answer is wrong, write *incorrect*, explain why it is wrong, and write the correct answer. Write the letter of each problem that contains a correct answer and rearrange these letters to form a word that describes your work.

S. On Tuesday a particular stock sold at $10 per share. This was a change of $-\frac{5}{8}$ from the previous day. What was the closing price of the stock on Monday?

$9\frac{3}{8}$ _____

_____

M. Ticket sales for the spring play at Jefferson Middle School totaled $1,041.50. Tickets for adults cost $3.50 each, and tickets for students cost $2.00 each. 134 students purchased tickets. How many adults purchased tickets?

298 _____

_____

R. Last night, Jana spent 20 minutes doing her math homework, $\frac{3}{4}$ of an hour on history, and a half hour on science. How much time did Jana spend doing her homework?

$1\frac{7}{12}$ hours or 95 minutes _____

_____

U. The highest point in the United States is Mt. McKinley in Alaska with an elevation of 20,237 feet. The lowest point in the United States is the Badwater Basin in Death Valley in California. It is 282 feet below sea level. Find the difference in the elevations.

19,955 feet _____

_____

T. Margie spent $12.50 on five school lunches this week. Using this amount, what would she expect to spend on school lunches for the year if she bought lunch for 175 days?

$437.50_____

_____

(Continued)

Copyright © 2016 by Judith A. Muschla, Gary Robert Muschla, and Erin Muschla-Berry.

P. For a Monday sale, the price of a sweater that originally cost $49.95 was reduced to $39.95. On Tuesday, the price was further reduced to $34.95. What was the total amount the sweater was reduced in price?

$5.00 _____

_____

E. Ricky's little brother Bobby is $\frac{2}{3}$ as tall as Ricky, who is 5 feet, 3 inches tall. How tall is Bobby?

42 inches or 3 feet, 6 inches _____

_____

A. The number of beach badges sold this year was 1,214, which was 92 fewer than the number of badges sold last year. How many badges were sold last year?

1,306 _____

_____

B. Last year, Megan started a savings account with $150 that she received for her birthday. During the next six months, she deposited $50, $25, and $15 into the account. She also earned $1.96 in interest. She then withdrew $79.25 to purchase a new printer. How much money was in the savings account after her withdrawal?

$160.75_____

_____

G. To pay off the loan on her new car, Maria pays $487.54 each month. The period of the loan is for five years. After the five-year period, how much money will Maria have paid?

$29,252.40_____

_____

Your work is _____.

2–11: EXPRESSING FRACTIONS AS REPEATING DECIMALS AND REPEATING DECIMALS AS FRACTIONS

Although only some fractions can be expressed as repeating decimals, every repeating decimal can be expressed as a fraction.

To express a fraction as a repeating decimal, divide the numerator by the denominator. Add a decimal point and zeroes, and keep dividing until a digit or digits repeat. Here are two examples:

- $\frac{3}{11} = 3 \div 11 = 0.\overline{27}$

- $-\frac{7}{15} = -7 \div 15 = -0.4\overline{6}$

To express a repeating decimal as a fraction, do the following:

Let n = the number.

1. If one digit repeats, multiply by 10. If two digits repeat, multiply by 100. If three digits repeat, multiply by 1,000, and so on.

2. Subtract the original number from the product you found in step 1.

3. Solve for n.

Here is an example:

$$
\begin{aligned}
n &= 0.\overline{86} && \text{Start with the number.} \\
100n &= 86.\overline{86} && \text{Multiply by 100.} \\
-n &= -0.\overline{86} && \text{Subtract original number.} \\
99n &= 86 && \text{Find the difference.} \\
n &= \frac{86}{99} && \text{Divide both sides by 99.}
\end{aligned}
$$

Directions: Match each number with its equivalent form in the Answer Bank. Answer the question at the end by writing the letter of each answer in the space above its problem number. You will need to divide the letters into words.

1. $\frac{2}{9}$ 2. $-0.\overline{6}$ 3. $0.\overline{14}$ 4. $\frac{2}{13}$ 5. $-\frac{1}{6}$ 6. $\frac{6}{7}$

7. $-0.\overline{09}$ 8. $0.\overline{4}$ 9. $-0.\overline{72}$ 10. $-\frac{5}{6}$ 11. $-\frac{2}{7}$ 12. $0.\overline{8}$

(Continued)

Copyright © 2016 by Judith A. Muschla, Gary Robert Muschla, and Erin Muschla-Berry.

Answer Bank

U. $-\frac{8}{11}$	O. $\frac{8}{9}$	M. $-\frac{1}{11}$	L. $0.\overline{153846}$
D. $-0.\overline{285714}$	S. $-0.1\overline{6}$	E. $\frac{14}{99}$	H. $\frac{4}{9}$
Y. $-0.8\overline{3}$	B. $-\frac{2}{3}$	I. $0.\overline{2}$	T. $0.\overline{857142}$

What is the name of the slanted line that separates the numerator from the denominator in a fraction?

$\overline{6}$ $\overline{8}$ $\overline{3}$ $\overline{5}$ $\overline{12}$ $\overline{4}$ $\overline{1}$ $\overline{11}$ $\overline{9}$ $\overline{5}$ $\overline{5}$ $\overline{10}$ $\overline{7}$ $\overline{2}$ $\overline{12}$ $\overline{4}$

2–12: USING RATIONAL APPROXIMATIONS OF IRRATIONAL NUMBERS

Although rational numbers can be expressed as fractions and decimals, irrational numbers cannot. Using a calculator, you can find an approximate value of an irrational number. The more decimal places you consider, the more accurate the approximation is. All irrational numbers can be graphed on a number line by considering their decimal approximations.

Directions: Determine if each statement is *true* or *false*. If a statement is true, circle the letter for true after the statement. If a statement is false, circle the letter for false. Answer the question at the end by writing the letters you have circled in order.

1. Irrational numbers do not terminate nor repeat in a specific pattern.
   (M. True   R. False)

2. All irrational numbers can be approximated and graphed on a number line.
   (U. True   N. False)

3. $\sqrt{2}$ is between 1.3 and 1.4 on the number line. (E. True   L. False)

4. $\sqrt{2}$ and $\sqrt{3}$ are located between 1 and 2 on the number line. (T. True   I. False)

5. $\sqrt{10}$ is about 2 times $\sqrt{5}$. (U. True   I. False)

6. $\sqrt{1}$, $\sqrt{2}$, and $\sqrt{4}$ are irrational numbers. (C. True   T. False)

7. $\sqrt{6}$, $\sqrt{7}$, and $\sqrt{8}$ are between 2.4 and 2.8 on the number line.
   (A. True   U. False)

8. $-\sqrt{2}$ is to the left of $-\sqrt{1}$ on the number line. (D. True   K. False)

9. $(\sqrt{3})^2 = 3$. (I. True   O. False)

10. $3\sqrt{3} = 9$. (R. True   N. False)

11. 9.1 is a very close approximation of π^2. (D. True   O. False)

12. $\sqrt{16}$ is the only integer between $\sqrt{9}$ and $\sqrt{25}$. (U. True   O. False)

13. $\sqrt{5}$, $\sqrt{6}$, $\sqrt{7}$, and $\sqrt{8}$ are between 2 and 3 on the number line.
    (S. True   E. False)

This adjective means "very numerous or existing in great numbers." What is it?

_____

Name_____ Date_____ Period_____

2–13: USING THE PROPERTIES OF EXPONENTS

Some properties of exponents that include rational exponents follow:

- Product of Powers Property: $x^m \cdot x^n = x^{m+n}$, where m and n are rational numbers.

- Power of a Power Property: $(x^m)^n = x^{mn}$, where m and n are rational numbers.

- Negative Exponent Property: $x^{-m} = \frac{1}{x^m}$, where x is a nonzero number and m is a rational number.

- Rational Exponent Property: Let $x^{\frac{1}{n}}$ be an nth root of x. $x^{\frac{m}{n}} = \left(x^{\frac{1}{n}}\right)^m = \left(\sqrt[n]{x}\right)^m$, where m is a positive integer.

Directions: Use the properties of exponents to find the values of n that will make each equation true. Find your answers in the Answer Bank and then complete the statement at the end by writing the letter of each answer in the space above its problem number. One answer will not be used. You will need to divide the letters into words.

1. $8^{\frac{2}{3}} = \left(8^{\frac{1}{3}}\right)^n = 4$

2. $4^{\frac{1}{2}} \times 4^{\frac{1}{2}} \times 4^{\frac{1}{2}} = 4^n = 8$

3. $27^{\frac{1}{3}} \times 27^{\frac{1}{3}} \times 27^n = 27^1 = 27$

4. $10^{\frac{1}{2}} \times 10^n = 10^1 = 10$

5. $25^n = \frac{1}{25^{\frac{1}{2}}} = \frac{1}{\sqrt{25}} = \frac{1}{5}$

6. $\left(3^{\frac{1}{2}}\right)^2 = 3^n = 3$

7. $\left(8^{-\frac{1}{2}}\right)^n = 8^{-2} = \frac{1}{64}$

8. $\left(1{,}000^{\frac{1}{3}}\right)^{-2} = 1{,}000^n = \frac{1}{100}$

9. $(16^n)^2 = 16^{\frac{1}{2}} = 4$

Answer Bank

E. $\frac{1}{3}$	U. $\frac{3}{2}$	S. 4	R. $-\frac{2}{3}$	A. $\frac{1}{2}$
O. 2	L. 1	N. $-\frac{1}{2}$	H. -3	M. $\frac{1}{4}$

In 1636, Scottish mathematician James Hume suggested using raised _____ to represent exponents.

$\overline{8}$ $\overline{1}$ $\overline{9}$ $\overline{4}$ $\overline{5}$ $\overline{5}$ $\overline{2}$ $\overline{9}$ $\overline{3}$ $\overline{8}$ $\overline{4}$ $\overline{6}$ $\overline{7}$

Name _____ Date _____ Period _____

2–14: REWRITING EXPRESSIONS INVOLVING RADICALS AND RATIONAL EXPONENTS

Some properties of exponents that include rational exponents are shown below. These properties can be used to rewrite expressions in different forms.

- Product of Powers Property: $x^m \cdot x^n = x^{m+n}$, where m and n are rational numbers.

- Power of a Power Property: $(x^m)^n = x^{mn}$, where m and n are rational numbers.

- Negative Exponent Property: $x^{-m} = \frac{1}{x^m}$, where x is a nonzero number and m is a rational number.

- Rational Exponent Property: Let $x^{\frac{1}{n}}$ be an nth root of x. $x^{\frac{m}{n}} = \left(x^{\frac{1}{n}}\right)^m = \left(\sqrt[n]{x}\right)^m$, where m is a positive integer.

Directions: Following are radical expressions and expressions with rational exponents. Match each radical expression with an expression in the Answer Bank that does not contain a radical. Match each expression that has a rational exponent with an expression in the Answer Bank that does not have an exponent. Complete the statement at the end by writing the letter of each answer in the space above its problem number. One answer will not be used. You will need to divide the letters into words.

1. $\sqrt[3]{27}$ 2. $4^{\frac{5}{2}}$ 3. $\sqrt{15}$ 4. $49^{\frac{3}{2}}$ 5. $\left(\sqrt{25}\right)^3$ 6. $16^{\frac{3}{2}}$

7. $81^{\frac{3}{4}}$ 8. $\left(\sqrt[3]{8}\right)^2$ 9. $\frac{1}{\sqrt{100}}$ 10. $\left(\sqrt{6}\right)^2$ 11. 5^{-2}

Answer Bank

L. $\frac{1}{25}$	T. 10^{-1}	I. 343	Y. 6	H. $15^{\frac{1}{2}}$	A. 27
O. 32	D. 64	N. $\frac{1}{3}$	U. 4	S. 125	E. 3

In the 1500s, Christoff Rudolff first used the radical sign _____.

$\overline{9}$ $\overline{3}$ $\overline{7}$ $\overline{9}$ $\overline{4}$ $\overline{5}$ $\overline{5}$ $\overline{9}$ $\overline{4}$ $\overline{11}$ $\overline{11}$

$\overline{8}$ $\overline{5}$ $\overline{1}$ $\overline{6}$ $\overline{9}$ $\overline{2}$ $\overline{6}$ $\overline{7}$ $\overline{10}$

Name_____ Date_____ Period_____

2-15: SUMS AND PRODUCTS OF RATIONAL AND IRRATIONAL NUMBERS

Rational numbers can be expressed as a fraction, but irrational numbers cannot. Examples of irrational numbers are $\sqrt{2}$, $-\sqrt{3}$, and π. Although most square roots are irrational numbers, some, for example $\sqrt{25}$, which equals 5, and $\sqrt{49}$, which equals 7, are rational numbers.

Directions: Determine if the sum or product in each problem is rational or irrational. Circle the letter of each answer and write the letters of the sums or products that are rational numbers. Rearrange the letters to spell a word related to the definition of "rational."

1. $0.1\overline{6} + 0.\overline{3}$ (I. Rational   R. Irrational)

2. $0.1\overline{6} \times 0.\overline{3}$ (C. Rational   N. Irrational)

3. $1\frac{1}{2} + \sqrt{2}$ (E. Rational   B. Irrational)

4. $\sqrt{3} + 3$ (U. Rational   Z. Irrational)

5. $\sqrt{1} \times \sqrt{4}$ (O. Rational   T. Irrational)

6. $\sqrt{1} + (-1)$ (L. Rational   U. Irrational)

7. $\sqrt{1} + \sqrt{5}$ (D. Rational   K. Irrational)

8. $3 \times \pi$ (F. Rational   R. Irrational)

9. $3 \times \sqrt{3}$ (R. Rational   N. Irrational)

10. $7.5 + 8\frac{1}{3}$ (L. Rational   M. Irrational)

11. $5 \times \sqrt{25}$ (A. Rational   W. Irrational)

12. $7.5 \times 8\frac{1}{3}$ (G. Rational   E. Irrational)

The letters _____ can be unscrambled to spell _____.

Copyright © 2016 by Judith A. Muschla, Gary Robert Muschla, and Erin Muschla-Berry.

Name_____ Date_____ Period_____

2-16: INTERPRETING AND USING UNITS

Clarice is an independent candidate for mayor of Taylorville, a small town. Being an independent candidate, she does not receive any support from any political party, and she has built her campaign fund from the donations of a few friends and her own savings.

Clarice tries to manage her campaign costs efficiently in order to avoid running out of money before election day, which is November 2. To help keep track of her spending, she has decided to create a graph that shows how much money she has spent so far. She hopes to be able to use the graph to identify any trends in her spending and then estimate if she will have enough money to finish the campaign.

Directions: Given the data below, create a graph showing the money Clarice has spent on her campaign. Consider the following in designing your graph:

- Choose a type of graph that you feel will best show the data, for example, a line or bar graph. (You can, of course, choose another type of graph.)

- Select a practical scale.

- Select the units for displaying the data.

As of September 1, the beginning of her campaign, Clarice's campaign fund contained $34,180.00. She does not expect any more contributions. Following are her weekly expenses so far.

Week Of	Expenses
9/3	$3,502.75
9/10	$3,584.69
9/17	$3,672.45
9/24	$3,910.59
10/1	$4,205.29
10/8	$4,593.95

After creating your graph, answer the following questions.

1. Describe the trend of spending.

2. Based on the graph, do you think Clarice will have enough money in her campaign fund to pay for expenses up to election day, November 2? Support your answer.

Name_____ Date_____ Period_____

2–17: DEFINING APPROPRIATE QUANTITIES

Choosing appropriate measures and units is necessary for problem solving. If you choose an inappropriate measurement or unit, you may compute an answer correctly, but it will not be the answer to the problem you attempted to solve.

Directions: Read each problem. In each case, an answer is calculated correctly, but the answer is not the solution to the problem. Explain why the answer is wrong and find the correct solution.

1. Latonya is a salesperson who drove 536 miles on the highway last week. Her car averages 32 miles per gallon of gas while driving at highway speeds. Her average speed for highway driving last week was 61 miles per hour. About how long did Latonya spend driving on the highway last week? Answer: about 17 hours.

2. Jayson drained his swimming pool. The pool contained 25,000 gallons of water and required about 14 hours to drain. About how much water was draining from the pool per minute? Answer: about 1,786 gallons.

3. Emma likes to jog. She read in a book that jogging can burn about 4.2 calories per hour per pound of a person's weight. Emma can find out how many calories, C, she burns while jogging by using the formula Weight × Time × Calories per Hour per Pound = C. If Emma weighs 120 pounds and she jogged for a half-hour, about how many calories did she burn? Answer: about 15,120 calories.

4. Evan works part-time after school. He is saving to buy a new tablet that costs $483.75, which includes the tax. He earns $8.50 per hour and works 10 hours per week. If he saves all of his earnings, how many full weeks must he work in order to save enough money to buy the tablet? Answer: 57 weeks.

2-18: CHOOSING APPROPRIATE LEVELS OF ACCURACY FOR MEASUREMENT

Accuracy is important in measurement. But measurements are seldom perfect. For example, when measuring length with a ruler, the measurements are not exact because rulers are not perfectly straight. This results in inaccuracy and is why choosing an appropriate level of accuracy is important.

Directions: Read each problem and answer the question. Explain your answers.

1. The distance from Potterstown to Riverville is 23 miles or 121,440 feet. Which is the more appropriate level of accuracy in measuring the distance between these two towns?

2. Roger wanted to install a fence around his yard. When he measured its perimeter, he found the sides to be 30.4 meters, 30.43 meters, 25.9 meters, and 25.91 meters. He then found the total length of the fence he needed, which was 112.64 meters. Was this an appropriate level of accuracy?

3. A snail moves at a speed of about 0.03 miles per hour. Is this an appropriate level of accuracy when describing a snail's speed?

4. The normal temperature of the human body is 98.6°F. Is this measurement an appropriate level of accuracy?

5. The area of a floor of a small room is 4.8 meters by 5.6 meters. Is 26.88 square meters an appropriate level of accuracy when calculating the area of the floor?

6. For the month of April, Allenville had 5.75 inches of rain. For May, Allenville had 3.5 inches of rain. Is 2.3 inches of rain an appropriate level of accuracy when determining the difference in rainfall for these two months?

7. Kayleigh wants to hang a set of 14 decorative lights along her porch rail. The rail is $22\frac{3}{4}$ (or 22.75) feet long. In order to space the lights evenly, Kayleigh divided the length of the rail by 14 and found that the lights should be placed every 1.625 feet. Is this an appropriate level of accuracy for measuring the distance between the lights?

8. Stegosaurus was a dinosaur that lived during the late Jurassic period, about 156–140 million years ago. It was about 30 feet long and weighed about 6,800 pounds. Despite its size, Stegosaurus had the smallest brain of any dinosaur. Which is the more appropriate level of accuracy in describing the size of a Stegosaurus's brain—2.5 ounces or 0.15625 pound?

Copyright © 2016 by Judith A. Muschla, Gary Robert Muschla, and Erin Muschla-Berry.

Name_____ Date_____ Period_____

2-19: WRITING COMPLEX NUMBERS

The set of real numbers and the set of imaginary numbers form the set of complex numbers. Every complex number can be written as $a + bi$, where a and b are real numbers. a is the real part and b is the imaginary part.

Directions: Rewrite each complex number in the form $a + bi$. Find the values of a and b and match your answers with the answers in the Answer Bank. Some answers will be used more than once, and one answer will not be used. Record the letters of your answers, and then answer the question at the end by writing the letters of the values for a and b in order, 1a, 1b, 2a, 2b, and so on. You will need to divide the letters into words.

1. $-6 - 7i =$ $a = $ _____ $b = $ _____

2. $-8 =$ $a = $ _____ $b = $ _____

3. $\frac{2}{3}i - 6 =$ $a = $ _____ $b = $ _____

4. $-8 - 0.6i =$ $a = $ _____ $b = $ _____

5. $8 + \frac{2}{3}i =$ $a = $ _____ $b = $ _____

6. $5 - 7i =$ $a = $ _____ $b = $ _____

7. $2 - 3i =$ $a = $ _____ $b = $ _____

8. $-0.6 + 3i =$ $a = $ _____ $b = $ _____

Answer Bank

A. -8	B. 2	E. -3	G. 0	I. -6	M. -7
N. $\frac{2}{3}$	R. -0.6	U. 5	C. -2	S. 3	Y. 8

René Descartes introduced this expression in the seventeenth century. What is the expression?

_____

Name_____ Date_____ Period_____

2-20: ADDING, SUBTRACTING, AND MULTIPLYING COMPLEX NUMBERS

The real numbers and imaginary numbers form the set of complex numbers. A complex number can written as $a + bi$ where a and b are real numbers: a is the real part of the complex number and b is the imaginary part.

To add and subtract complex numbers, combine the real parts and the imaginary parts. For example:

$$(3 + 2i) + (6 - 4i) = 3 + 2i + 6 - 4i = 3 + 6 + (2 - 4)i = 9 - 2i$$

$$(3 + 2i) - (6 - 4i) = 3 + 2i - 6 + 4i = 3 - 6 + (2 + 4)i = -3 + 6i$$

To multiply two complex numbers, use FOIL and then substitute -1 for i^2. For example:

$$(3 + 2i)(6 - 4i) = 18 - 12i + 12i - 8i^2 = 18 - 8(-1) = 26$$

Directions: Simplify each expression. Find your answers in the Answer Bank and complete the statement at the end by writing the letter of each answer in the space above its problem number. You will need to divide the letters into words.

1. $(4 + 3i) + (3 - 7i) =$

2. $(6 - 8i) + (5 - 2i) =$

3. $(5 + 4i) - (2 - 6i) =$

4. $(2 - 3i) - (4 + 7i) =$

5. $(4 + 3i) - 2(7 + i) =$

6. $2i(3 + 6i) =$

7. $(1 + i)(1 - i) =$

8. $(5 + 3i)(5 - 3i) =$

9. $(5 + i)(4 - 3i) =$

10. $(3 - 4i)^2 =$

11. $(1 + i\sqrt{6})^2 =$

12. $(2 - 5i)(3 + 5i) =$

13. $-2i(i - 4) =$

14. $(4 + 2i)(3 + i) =$

15. $(4 + 2i) - (3 + i) =$

Answer Bank

E. $2 + 8i$	P. $-5 + 2i\sqrt{6}$	L. 34	S. $-12 + 6i$	X. $10 + 10i$
A. $7 - 4i$	R. 2	N. $11 - 10i$	Y. $-2 - 10i$	C. $1 + i$
O. $3 + 10i$	W. $-7 - 24i$	B. $-10 + i$	M. $23 - 11i$	U. $31 - 5i$

The sum, difference, product, and quotient of two complex numbers is

_____.

$\overline{1}$ $\overline{8}$ $\overline{10}$ $\overline{1}$ $\overline{4}$ $\overline{6}$ $\overline{1}$

$\overline{15}$ $\overline{3}$ $\overline{9}$ $\overline{11}$ $\overline{8}$ $\overline{13}$ $\overline{14}$ $\overline{2}$ $\overline{12}$ $\overline{9}$ $\overline{5}$ $\overline{13}$ $\overline{7}$

Name_____ Date_____ Period_____

2-21: SOLVING QUADRATIC EQUATIONS THAT HAVE COMPLEX SOLUTIONS

The quadratic formula, $x = \frac{-b \pm \sqrt{b^2 - 4ac}}{2a}$, may always be used to solve second-degree equations of the form $ax^2 + bx + c = 0$, $a \neq 0$. If an equation is not written in this form, rewrite it. Then solve the equation by using the quadratic formula.

Directions: Use the quadratic formula to solve each equation. Compare your answers to the solutions that are provided. If a solution is correct, write "correct" on the line that follows. If a solution is incorrect, write the correct solution. Write the letters of the correct solutions only, and unscramble them to find a word that describes your work.

Problem	Solution	Correct or Incorrect
1. $4x^2 + 3x + 1 = 0$	$x = \frac{-3 \pm i\sqrt{7}}{8}$	U. _____
2. $x^2 + 2x + 4 = 0$	$x = -1 \pm \sqrt{3}$	I. _____
3. $x^2 + 2x + 8 = 0$	$x = -1 \pm i\sqrt{7}$	R. _____
4. $x^2 + 3x + 5 = 0$	$x = \frac{-3 \pm i\sqrt{11}}{2}$	E. _____
5. $-x^2 + x - 2 = 0$	$x = \frac{1 \pm \sqrt{7}}{-2}$	H. _____
6. $2x^2 + 2x + 1 = 0$	$x = -\frac{1}{2} \pm \frac{i}{2}$	S. _____
7. $3x^2 + 6x = -4$	$x = 4 \pm i\sqrt{2}$	A. _____
8. $-x^2 + 2x = 2$	$x = 1 \pm 2i$	N. _____
9. $2x^2 = -2x - 1$	$x = -\frac{1}{2} \pm i$	G. _____
10. $-x^2 + 3x = 7$	$x = \frac{-3 \pm i\sqrt{19}}{-2}$	P. _____

The unscrambled letters spell _____.

Basic Expressions, Equations, and Inequalities

Teaching Notes for the Activities of Section 3

3-1: (6.EE.1) WRITING AND EVALUATING NUMERICAL EXPRESSIONS WITH WHOLE-NUMBER EXPONENTS

For this activity, your students are to write and evaluate numerical expressions with whole-number exponents. They are also to describe the values they found.

Explain that a numerical expression contains only numbers and operations. To write a numerical expression, students should consider key terms that often (but not always) denote the indicated operation. Some of these terms are noted below:

Addition	Subtraction	Multiplication	Division
increased by	decreased by	times	quotient
more than	less than	multiplied by	divided by
plus	minus	product	
sum	difference		

Explain that to evaluate an expression means to find the value of the expression. Students should use the order of operations. If necessary, review the steps:

1. Simplify expressions within grouping symbols.

2. Simplify powers. (You may wish to review the meaning of exponents, such as 3 to the fourth power, which can be written as 3^4 or $3 \times 3 \times 3 \times 3$ or 81.)

3. Multiply and divide, in order from left to right.

4. Add and subtract, in order from left to right.

Discuss the examples on the worksheet with your students. Caution them to read the phrases of numerical expressions carefully; the phrases can be tricky. If necessary, include additional examples.

Go over the directions. If students find five different values, their work is likely to be correct.

ANSWERS

(1) 8^2, 64   (2) $9^2 \div 3$, 27   (3) $9 - 2^3$, 1   (4) $6^2 - 11$, 25   (5) $10 \div 2 - 2^2$, 1
(6) $7^2 - 6^2$, 13   (7) 1×3^3, 27   (8) $3^3 - 2$, 25   (9) $4^2 - 3$, 13   (10) $2^5 + 2^5$, 64

3-2: (6.EE.2) WRITING AND READING ALGEBRAIC EXPRESSIONS

For this activity, your students will be given phrases containing algebraic expressions. They are to determine if each expression is stated correctly. If it is incorrect, they are to correct the expression. Completing a statement at the end of the worksheet will enable students to check their work.

Explain that algebraic expressions contain variables. A variable is a letter that represents a number.

Discuss the examples on the worksheet. Emphasize that when writing an expression, order does not matter for addition and multiplication, but order does matter for subtraction and division. Grouping symbols indicate that a quantity must be treated as a unit. You might want to caution your students to be careful not to read the variable o as a zero.

Review the directions on the worksheet. Students must correct the incorrect expressions and use the variables of the corrected expressions to complete the statement at the end.

ANSWERS

Answers to incorrect problems are provided.　(2) $s - 2$　(5) $(t + 6) \div 12$　(7) $4^2 + u$
(8) $p(8 - 2)$　(11) $(e - 5) \div 6$　(13) $n - 15$　(16) $8d - 1$　(17) $6(o + 3)$　(19) $3u \div 3$
(20) $22s$　Your work with algebraic expressions is "stupendous."

3-3: (6.EE.2) EVALUATING ALGEBRAIC EXPRESSIONS

Your students will evaluate algebraic expressions in equations for this activity. By unscrambling the letters of their answers to find a math word, they can check their answers.

Explain that an equation is a mathematical sentence that expresses a relationship between two quantities. Formulas are a special type of equation.

Provide this example. The perimeter of a square is four times the length of a side. This can be written as an equation $P = 4s$. Students can find the value of P if they know the length, s, of a side. If $s = 12.5$ inches, students can substitute 12.5 for s into the expression $4s$ to find that $P = 50$ inches.

Go over the directions on the worksheet with your students. Note that some expressions involve two operations. If necessary, review the order of operations. Because some expressions contain exponents, your students might find a review of exponents helpful. Remind them that after completing the statements, they are to unscramble the letters of their answers to find a math word.

ANSWERS

(1) M, 12　(2) A, 16　(3) L, 64　(4) F, $\frac{1}{4}$　(5) R, 41　(6) S, $5\frac{1}{2}$　(7) O, $2\frac{1}{2}$　(8) U, $\frac{1}{2}$
The letters "malfrsou" can be unscrambled to spell "formulas."

3-4: (6.EE.3) APPLYING PROPERTIES OF OPERATIONS TO GENERATE EQUIVALENT EXPRESSIONS

This activity requires your students to write equivalent expressions. Answering a question at the end of the worksheet will enable them to check their work.

Review the definition of equivalent expressions and the properties that can be used to generate equivalent expressions, which are provided on the worksheet.

Provide this example. Ask your students to write an expression that is equivalent to $4(2x + 3y)$. Students should use the Distributive Property to write $8x + 12y$. Note that by using the Commutative Property for Addition students may also write this as $12y + 8x$. Caution them to pay close attention to the Commutative Property as they work on the problems on the worksheet.

Discuss the directions. Each expression can be written in another form, which can be matched with an expression in the Answer Bank. Students are to answer the question at the end.

ANSWERS

(1) U, $11x$ (2) N, $4x + 4$ (3) K, $12x$ (4) N, $4x + 4$ (5) O, 0   (6) W, $15x$
(7) N, $4x + 4$ (8) Q, x (9) U, $11x$ (10) A, $14x$ (11) N, $4x + 4$ (12) T, $2x + 6y$
(13) I, $3x + 6y$ (14) T, $2x + 6y$ (15) I, $3x + 6y$ (16) E, $3x$ (17) S, $6y + 6x$
Vowels were introduced to represent "unknown quantities."

3-5: (6.EE.4) IDENTIFYING EQUIVALENT EXPRESSIONS

For this activity, your students will determine if two expressions are equivalent. They can check their work by answering a question at the end of the worksheet.

Explain that equivalent expressions are always equal, no matter what values are substituted for the variables. Offer the following examples:

- Ask your students if $3y + 2y$ and $5y$ are equivalent expressions? It can easily be shown that they are by substituting the same number for the variables. If $y = 1$, both expressions are equal to 5. If $y = 3$, both expressions are equal to 15. Also note that if $3y$ and $2y$ are added, their sum is $5y$.

- Ask if $a + 1$ and $2a$ are equivalent expressions? Instruct your students to substitute a few different numbers for the variables into the equations, one number at a time. If $a = 1$, both expressions are equal to 2. But if $a = 3$, the first expression is equal to 4 and the second is equal to 6. Also note that when a and 1 are added, their sum is not $2a$. These expressions are not equivalent.

Go over the directions on the worksheet with your students. Suggest that they test to see if two expressions are equivalent by substituting numbers for the variables, similar to the examples you provided. Remind students to answer the question at the end.

3-6: (6.EE.5) IDENTIFYING SOLUTIONS OF EQUATIONS AND INEQUALITIES

For this activity, your students will determine if a given number makes an equation or inequality true. Finding the sum of answers will enable them to check their work.

Review the difference between equations and inequalities. Equations have an equal sign, denoting that both sides of the equation have the same value; inequalities may have a greater than sign, $>$, or a less than sign, $<$, indicating that the values on either side of the sign are not equal.

Discuss the directions on the worksheet. Note that for some problems students will need to use the order of operations. Review the steps, if necessary. After completing the problems, your students are to find the sum of the numbers that correspond to their yes answers, and then substitute the sum into the equation at the end to find their special score.

3-7: (6.EE.6) WRITING EXPRESSIONS IN WHICH VARIABLES REPRESENT NUMBERS

This activity provides your students with practice using variables to represent numbers and write expressions. In each problem, your students are to think of a number, do a series of numerical operations, and obtain an answer that the teacher can predict. To complete this activity successfully, your students must be able to write expressions.

Start this activity by reviewing the Distributive Property, $a(b + c) = ab + ac$, which students will need to use to complete some steps of the problems. Offer some examples, if necessary.

Go over the directions on the worksheet. Your students may find it helpful if you do the first problem as a class. Instruct them to write the number they choose to begin with in the first blank in column I, continuing and recording each resulting number in the blanks provided. (Students may choose any number they wish, but you may want to suggest that for these problems they choose a number between 1 and 9 to keep the math simple.) Next instruct them to complete column II, using a variable to represent a number.

Note that for problem 3, your students will be asked to use two numbers (one for their grade and the other for their age). They should choose a different variable for the second number.

Caution your students to pay close attention as they work through the problems. A careless mistake in one step will result in the following steps being incorrect. Depending on your class, you may decide to have students work with a partner to complete this activity.

ANSWERS

The expressions with the variables are shown. Problem 1: The final number is the same as the original number. n, $2n$, $2n + 8$, $2n + 6$, $n + 3$, $n + 3 - 3$, n.   Problem 2: The final number is 2. n, $n + 5$, $2n + 10$, $2n + 16$, $2n + 4$, $n + 2$, $n + 2 - n$, 2.   Problem 3: The final number is comprised of the grade followed by the age. n, $10n$, $10n + 6$, $100n + 60$, $100n + 48$, $100n + 48 + y$, $100n + 17 + y$, $100n + 17 - 17 + y$, $100n + y$. (Note: For problem 3, students may use their age in place of y. A variable is used in the answer because students in sixth grade may be 10, 11, or 12 years old.)

3-8: (6.EE.7) WRITING AND SOLVING EQUATIONS

For this activity, your students will be given information that they are to express in terms of an equation. All equations are of the form $x + p = q$ or $px = q$. After students have written an equation, they are to solve it.

Begin this activity by providing two examples: $P = 2l + 2w$ for finding the perimeter of a rectangle, and $P = 4s$ for finding the perimeter of a square. Substitute numbers for the variables and have students solve each equation. Encourage your students to volunteer examples of other equations, which the class can solve for practice.

Discuss the directions on the worksheet with your students. Remind them to be as accurate as possible in writing equations. Note that there may be more than one way to solve some problems.

ANSWERS

Equations may vary.   (1) $31 - 1 = s$; $s = 30$ days   (2) $c = 7 - 3$; $c = 4$ P.M.
(3) $l = 44 + 50$; $l = 94$ feet   (4) $2p = 16$; $p = 8$ pawns   (5) $\frac{1}{6}w = 4$; $w = 24$ time zones
(6) $r = \frac{1}{2} \times 70$; $r = 35$ mph   (7) $f = \frac{1}{4} \times 6$; $f = 1\frac{1}{2}$ feet   (8) $b = 350 - 206$; $b = 144$ bones
(9) $g = 2{,}600 - 400$; $g = 2{,}200$ calories   (10) $c = 9 \times 8$; $c = 72$ candies

3-9: (6.EE.8) USING INEQUALITIES

For this activity, your students are required to match each problem with an inequality or a number line that can be used to solve the problem. They can check if their answers are correct by answering a question at the end of the worksheet.

Explain that an inequality is a statement that one quantity is greater than or less than another. Discuss the symbols and key words on the worksheet.

Provide the following example: Children who are younger than 10 years old must be accompanied by a parent during their visit at the science exhibit. Ask students to write an inequality that represents the ages of children who must be accompanied by a parent. They should write $(x < 10)$, where x is the age of the child. Note that this includes children who are ages 1 through 9. Since children who are 10-years-old are not required to be accompanied by a parent, 10 is not a solution.

To show your students how to represent this solution on a number line, draw a number line with an open circle at 10 and shade to the left.

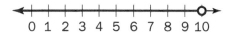

0 1 2 3 4 5 6 7 8 9 10

Discuss the directions on the worksheet. Make sure your students understand that they are to match each problem with an inequality or a number line. They are also to answer the question at the end.

ANSWERS

(1) D   (2) R   (3) A   (4) W   (5) R   (6) O   (7) F   (8) T   (9) S   (10) A   (11) F
The symbol represents "fast forward."

3–10: (6.EE.9) USING VARIABLES TO REPRESENT TWO QUANTITIES

For this activity, your students will write equations with variables that represent two quantities. They will then graph each equation. They will need rulers and graph paper.

Explain that when variables represent two quantities in an equation, one variable is the independent variable and the other is the dependent variable. The dependent variable "depends" on the independent variable.

Provide this example: The diameter, D, of a circle is twice the radius, r. This can be written as the equation $D = 2r$. No matter what value is substituted for r, the diameter is always two times the radius. r is the independent variable and D is the dependent variable. This relationship can be expressed in the following table:

r	0.5 inch	0.75 inch	1 inch	3.5 inches
D	1 inch	1.5 inches	2 inches	7 inches

Explain that to show this information in a graph, students must use the first quadrant because lengths are always positive. They should label the positive x-axis to graph the length of the radius and label the positive y-axis to graph the length of the diameter. Emphasize that independent variables are graphed along the x-axis and dependent variables are graphed along the y-axis.

Go over the directions on the worksheet with your students. For each problem, they are to write an equation, create a table of values that shows how the variables are related, and graph the values. Explain that in creating their tables, they must select values for the independent variables similar to the example you provided. They will also have to select the appropriate scales for their graphs.

ANSWERS

Following are the equations for each problem. Tables and graphs will vary, depending on the values students chose. (1) $E = \$15h$ (2) $P = 4s$ (3) $C = \$3p$ (4) $Y = \frac{1}{3}f$ (5) $s = \frac{1}{2}r$

3–11: (7.EE.1) ADDING, SUBTRACTING, FACTORING, AND EXPANDING LINEAR EXPRESSIONS

For this activity, your students will complete equations that require them to add, subtract, factor, and expand linear expressions. Answering a question at the end of the worksheet will enable them to check their work.

Discuss the properties provided on the worksheet. Explain that students will use these properties to complete the problems. Provide the following examples:

- Ask your students how they would complete this equation: $3x + 5 + x - 4 = 4x + $ _____. Students should use the Commutative Property for Addition to switch x and 5 to write $3x + x + 5 - 4$, which equals $4x + 1$. 1 belongs in the blank.

- Ask your students how they would complete this equation: $7x + 28 = $ _____ $(x + 4)$. Students should use the Distributive Property to a identify a factor that is common to $7x$ and 28. 7 belongs in the blank because 7 times x and 7 times 4 equals $7x + 28$.

- Ask your students how they would complete this equation: $3(2 - x) = $ ____ $- 3x$. Students should use the Distributive Property to multiply both 2 and x by 3. 6 belongs in the blank.

Go over the directions on the worksheet, noting that students should use the properties as they complete the equations. They should also complete the statement at the end.

ANSWERS

(1) R, 4   (2) P, $-x$ (3) F, 1   (4) E, 2   (5) O, -2 (6) E, 2   (7) S, $5x$ (8) C, x
(9) E, 2   (10) C, x (11) R, 4   (12) T, $2x$ You have a "perfect score."

3–12: (7.EE.2) REWRITING EXPRESSIONS IN DIFFERENT FORMS

For this activity, your students will identify expressions that are written in different forms. Completing a statement at the end of the worksheet will enable them to check their work.

Explain to your students that being able to rewrite expressions in different forms can help them to recognize equivalent values as well as the relationships between the quantities in an expression. When an expression is rewritten in a different form, values do not change. For example, $3a = 2a + a = a + a + a$.

Discuss the directions on the worksheet with your students. Caution them to pay close attention to each statement, and remind them to complete the final statement at the end.

ANSWERS

(1) A, 5   (2) I, 3   (3) N, $\frac{1}{x}$ (4) T, 3   (5) L, 0.85   (6) V, 100%   (7) U, $\frac{1}{4}x$ (8) E, $\frac{2}{3}$
(9) Q, 1.45   (10) E, 2   The two forms are "equivalent."

3-13: (7.EE.3) SOLVING MULTI-STEP PROBLEMS

This activity requires your students to solve multi-step word problems. Finding the correct answer to the last problem will verify that they have completed the other problems correctly.

Start the activity by presenting an example for which your students must write and solve an equation. Offer the following examples:

- 6 less than the product of a number and 3 is 21. What is the number? This can be represented by the equation $3n - 6 = 21$ and the solution is $n = 9$.

- An initial deposit of $100 and saving a specific amount of money for 22 weeks results in a balance of $562. How much money was saved each week? This can be represented by the equation $100 + 22n = \$562$ and the solution is $n = \$21$.

Discuss the guidelines for solving problems on the worksheet. Following these steps can help students to solve problems successfully.

Go over the directions on the worksheet. Suggest that to solve the problems students may find it helpful to write equations, similar to those in the examples you provided. Note that finding the correct answer to the last problem is contingent on finding the correct answers to the previous problems.

ANSWERS

(1) 15   (2) $17   (3) 8,000   (4) 5   (5) 96   (6) 10   (7) 13   (8) 524   (9) 29
(10) 2,828   If students found the correct answer to the last problem, it is likely that their work is correct.

3-14: (7.EE.4) SOLVING EQUATIONS AND INEQUALITIES

For this activity, your students will solve word problems by writing equations and inequalities. Completing a statement at the end of the worksheet will enable them to check their work.

Review the difference between an equation and an inequality. An equation is a mathematical statement showing that expressions on opposite sides of an equal sign are equivalent. An inequality is a mathematical statement showing that two expressions are not equivalent.

Discuss the directions on the worksheet. For each problem, students are to write and solve an equation or inequality. They should also complete the statement at the end.

ANSWERS

The equation or inequality is followed by the letter of the answer and the answer.

(1) $5n + 84 = 124$; X, $n = 8$ (2) $n - 7 < -6$; I, $n < 1$ (3) $n + (-4) > 15$; R, $n > 19$

(4) $7(n + 6) = 63$; P, $n = 3$ (5) $\frac{1}{2}n - 12 = 12$; N, $n = 48$ (6) $\frac{3}{4}n > -24$; C, $n > -32$

(7) $6 + 3n < 36$; A, $n < 10$ (8) $(n + 3)4 = 36$, T, $n = 6$ (9) $7n - 23 = 54$; E, $n = 11$

(10) $3n + 15 < 24$; L, $n < 3$ (11) $n(7 + 9) = 32$; O, $n = 2$ Your mathematical skills "are exceptional."

3-15: (8.EE.1) APPLYING PROPERTIES OF INTEGER EXPONENTS

For this activity, your students will apply the properties of integer exponents to identify equivalent expressions. Completing a statement at the end of the worksheet will enable them to check their work.

Discuss the properties of exponents that are included on the worksheet. Depending on your students, you may find it helpful to provide additional examples.

Go over the directions. Remind your students to complete the statement at the end.

ANSWERS

(1) A, 3^8 (2) G, $\frac{1}{4}$ (3) N, 7   (4) I, 1   (5) H, $\frac{1}{3^4}$ (6) N, 4^5 (7) A, 9×25 (8) N, 1

(9) E, $\frac{9}{16}$ (10) S, 18   (11) O, 3^{-3} (12) M, 5^6 Zero to the zero power "has no meaning."

3-16: (8.EE.2) USING SQUARE ROOTS AND CUBE ROOTS

This activity requires your students to solve equations that contain perfect squares and perfect cubes. Students can check if their work is correct by completing a statement at the end of the worksheet.

Explain that a perfect square is a whole number raised to the second power, such as $0 = 0^2$, $1 = 1^2$, $4 = 2^2$, $9 = 3^2$, $16 = 4^2, \ldots$, and so on. Finding the square root of a number is the opposite of squaring a number. Explain that the solution to $x^2 = p$ is $x = \pm\sqrt{p}$; emphasize the meaning of the $\pm$ sign. Note that numbers such as 2, 3, 5, 6, 7, $\ldots$, which are not perfect squares, also have two square roots but these square roots are irrational numbers.

Explain that a perfect cube is a whole number raised to the third power, such as $0 = 0^3$, $1 = 1^3$, $8 = 2^3$, $27 = 3^3$, $64 = 4^3$, ..., and so on. Finding the cube root of a number is the opposite of cubing a number. Explain that the solution to $x^3 = p$ is $x = \sqrt[3]{p}$; emphasize that the 3 outside the radical symbol indicates the cube root.

Discuss the examples and directions on the worksheet. Students should solve the equations and then complete the statement at the end.

ANSWERS

(1) W, $x = 5$ (2) E, $x = \pm 5$ (3) R, $x = \pm 11$ (4) T, $x = 3$ (5) Y, $x = \pm 2$ (6) L, $x = \pm 3$
(7) S, $x = 4$ (8) G, $x = \pm 7$ (9) A, $x = \pm 9$ (10) N, $x = \pm 8$ (11) I, $x = 1$ The square root of a perfect square is "always an integer."

3-17: (8.EE.3) USING NUMBERS EXPRESSED IN SCIENTIFIC NOTATION

This activity requires your students to write very large and very small numbers in scientific notation. Students will also be asked to determine how many times larger one number written in scientific notation is than another.

Explain that scientific notation is a way to write very large and very small numbers. It is a type of numerical shorthand in which a number is written in the form of $n \times 10^x$, where n is a number greater than or equal to 1 and less than 10 and x is an integer.

Explain that numbers written in scientific notation can be compared. Students can find how many times one number is larger than another by dividing the coefficients (first terms) and subtracting the exponents. For example, to find about how many times 5×10^4 is larger than 2×10^3, students should divide, $5 \div 2$, and subtract the exponents, $4 - 3$, to find 2.5×10 or 25 times.

Discuss the examples on the worksheet. Emphasize that when writing very small numbers less than 1, students must use a negative exponent.

Go over the directions on the worksheet. Students should use scientific notation to compare numbers when answering the questions.

ANSWERS

(1) Earth, 9.29×10^7 miles; Neptune, 2.8×10^9 miles. Neptune's distance from the sun is about 30 times the distance of Earth from the sun.   (2) Red blood cell, 8×10^{-3}; grain of pollen, 8.6×10^{-2}. A grain of pollen is about 11 times the size of a red blood cell.
(3) North America, 2.4474×10^7 square kilometers; Australia/Oceania, 8.112×10^6 square kilometers. The area of North America is about 3 times the area of Australia/Oceania.
(4) Staphylococcus bacterium, 2×10^{-3} millimeter; dust mite, 2.5×10^{-1} millimeter. A dust mite is about 125 times the size of a staphylococcus bacterium.   (5) Following is the correct order: (a) 370,000, (c) 99,000, (b) 64,500. 3.7×10^5 is about 6 times larger than 6.45×10^4.

3-18: (8.EE.4) OPERATIONS WITH SCIENTIFIC NOTATION

Your students will add, subtract, multiply, and divide numbers written in scientific notation for this activity. Completing a statement at the end of the worksheet will enable them to check their work.

Discuss the examples on the worksheet with your students. Note that in scientific notation the decimal must be greater than or equal to 1 and less than 10 and is referred to as the coefficient. Also note that when adding or subtracting, the exponents in each number must be the same. Make sure that your students understand how to rewrite one of the numbers so that the exponents are equal. Also make certain they understand that answers must be written in correct scientific notation form with the coefficient being less than or equal to 1 and less than 10. This may require rewriting some answers. Provide more examples, if necessary.

Go over the directions on the worksheet. After solving the problems, students are to complete the statement at the end.

ANSWERS

(1) N, 7.56×10^8 (2) G, 9.04×10^3 (3) E, 7.254×10^9 (4) S, 2.2×10^2
(5) T, 5.32×10^6 (6) R, 3.175×10^5 (7) O, 8.034×10^3 (8) W, 3.08×10^2
(9) I, 2.1655×10^8 (10) Z, 1.055×10^6 Scientific notation prevents making mistakes "writing zeroes."

3-19: (8.EE.5) GRAPHING PROPORTIONAL RELATIONSHIPS

For this activity, your students will be given pairs of proportional relationships in the form of $y = mx$, a verbal description, or a table. They will graph the proportional relationships and identify which one of each pair has the larger slope. Correct answers will reveal a math term at the end of the worksheet. Students will need rulers and graph paper.

Explain that a proportional relationship is a relationship between two equal ratios that can be written in the form of $y = mx$. Provide the following example that shows the various ways a proportional relationship may be described.

The relationship of a side of a square to the perimeter can be described by:

- An equation: $P = 4s$, where P is the perimeter and s is the length of a side.

- A verbal description: The perimeter of a square is four times the length of a side.

- A table of values:

s	1	2	3	4
P	4	8	12	16

- A graph:

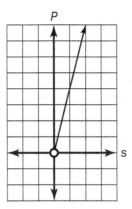

The slope, m, of the line is 4, which is the coefficient of s.

Note that although the graph of a proportional relationship is a straight line through the origin, in this context lengths are greater than 0 and the graph is in the first quadrant.

Explain that students may graph a proportional relationship in two ways:

- Make a table of values, express the values as ordered pairs, graph the points, and draw the graph.

- Start at the origin, then move up or down, then right or left depending on the slope.

Go over the directions on the worksheet with your students. Two proportional relationships are described in each problem. For each problem, students are to graph the relationships and identify the graph that has the larger slope. They are also to find the math term at the end.

ANSWERS

Each graph is in the first quadrant and includes the origin. The letter of the graph with the greater slope is followed by the slopes of the lines.   (1) O; T, $m = \$50$; O, $m = \$75$
(2) E; E, $m = \$1.99$; D, $m = \$1.75$ (3) S; R, $m = \$7$; S, $m = \$8$ (4) P; P, $m = 10$;
E, $m = 5$ (5) L; L, $m = \$8$; A, $m = \$5$ The math term is "slope."

3-20: (8.EE.6) DERIVING THE EQUATION $y = mx$

For this activity, your students will derive the equation of a line through the origin in the coordinate plane. Completing a statement at the end of the worksheet will enable students to check their work.

Explain that students will use similar triangles to derive the equation of a line through the origin of the coordinate plane. Discuss the diagram on the worksheet. Note that $\triangle ABC \sim \triangle DEF$, therefore corresponding sides have the same ratio. Also review that the lengths of vertical line segments can be found by subtracting the y-coordinates, and the lengths of horizontal line segments can be found by subtracting the x-coordinates.

Go over the directions with your students. They should refer to the diagram as they complete the statements. Caution them to work carefully because an incorrect answer may lead to another incorrect answer in subsequent problems. They are also to complete the statement at the end.

ANSWERS

(1) O, (x_1, y_1) (2) S, y (3) T, $x_2 - x_1$ (4) I, m (5) N, $\frac{y}{x} = m$ (6) C, $\frac{y}{x} = \frac{m}{1}$ (7) A, mx
The slope of a line "is constant."

3-21: (8.EE.7) IDENTIFYING EQUATIONS THAT HAVE ONE SOLUTION, NO SOLUTIONS, OR INFINITELY MANY SOLUTIONS

This activity requires your students to identify linear equations by their solutions or lack of a solution. After identifying the number of solutions, students are to solve the equations that have one solution. They are also to find relationships of solutions.

Explain that not all equations have a solution. It is possible for an equation to have no solutions or infinitely many solutions.

Discuss the examples on the worksheet. The last equation in example 1 shows a variable that is equivalent to a number. This number is the only solution to the original equation. The last equation in example 2 shows two numbers that are the same. Since this equation is true for all real numbers, there are an infinite number of solutions to the original equation. The last equation in example 3 shows a false statement. The original equation has no solution.

Go over the directions with your students. Emphasize that they are to identify the equations as having one solution, no solutions, or infinitely many solutions. If an equation has one solution, they are to find it. Then they are to describe relationships of the problem numbers to the types of solutions.

ANSWERS

(1) Infinitely many solutions   (2) $x = -17$ (3) $x = 3$ (4) No solutions   (5) $x = 2\frac{1}{3}$
(6) No solutions   The problem number that is neither a prime number nor a composite number has infinitely many solutions, the problem numbers that are prime numbers have one solution, and the problem numbers that are composite numbers have no solutions.

3-22: (8.EE.7) SOLVING EQUATIONS WITH VARIABLES ON BOTH SIDES

For this activity, your students will solve multi-step equations with variables on both sides of the equal sign. Completing a statement at the end of the worksheet will enable them to check their answers.

Begin the activity by explaining that students can use the Distributive Property to eliminate parentheses in order to add and subtract variable expressions in the same way they add or subtract numbers. The key to solving equations is to solve for a variable by simplifying each side of the equation, then isolating the variable.

Provide this example: $2(x + 5) = x + 5 + x$. Demonstrate the various steps for solving the problem. Also, make sure your students understand that $\varnothing$ is the notation for an empty set, indicating that this problem has no solution.

Go over the directions on the worksheet with your students. Mention that they will have to convert some fractions to decimals to complete the statement at the end.

ANSWERS

(P) −9   R) 1.5   (L) 4   (O) −0.5   (B) 27   (W) $\varnothing$ (N) 21   (K) −27   (U) −3   (H) 1
(A) −4   (F) 0   (V) 3   (T) −5   (E) −5.5   (S) −2.6   In 1637 René Descartes used the first letters of the "alphabet for known values."

3-23: (8.EE.8) SOLVING SYSTEMS OF LINEAR EQUATIONS ALGEBRAICALLY

For this activity, your students will solve systems of linear equations by using the methods of substitution, addition or subtraction, and multiplication with addition or subtraction. Completing a statement at the end of the worksheet will enable students to check their work.

Begin the activity by reviewing the following methods for solving systems of linear equations and provide examples if necessary.

- Substitution should be used if the coefficient of one variable is 1 or −1.

- Addition or subtraction should be used if the coefficients of one variable are opposites, or if the coefficients are the same.

- Multiplication with addition or subtraction should be used if the coefficient of a variable is a factor (other than 1) of the other, or if the coefficients of a variable are relatively prime (have a greatest common factor of 1).

Go over the directions on the worksheet with your students. Remind them to complete the statement at the end.

ANSWERS

(1) P, $x = 2$, $y = 4$ (2) N, $x = 5$, $y = 1$ (3) I, $x = -3$, $y = -1$ (4) S, $x = -5$, $y = -2$
(5) A, $x = 30$, $y = 6$ (6) O, $x = 5$, $y = -6$ (7) T, $x = -1$, $y = 7$ (8) U, $x = -22$, $y = -33$
(9) D, $x = -1$, $y = -5$ (10) H, $x = 2$, $y = 10$ "Diophantus" of Alexandria (c. 275) was a Greek mathematician who catalogued all of the algebra the Greeks understood.

3-24: (8.EE.8) SOLVING SYSTEMS OF EQUATIONS BY GRAPHING

For this activity, your students will graph systems of equations to find solutions. They will need rulers and enough graph paper to draw nine small graphs. To complete this activity successfully, your students should be able to graph the equation of a line. Completing a statement at the end of the worksheet will enable them to check their answers.

Start the activity by providing the following examples:

$$y = 3x + 1 \qquad 3x + y = 1$$

Instruct your students to graph the equations of each line on the same axes. The lines intersect at (0, 1). Explain that this is a solution to the system of equations. Students may verify this by substituting the values in both equations. Note that some systems have no solution, for example, those whose graphs are parallel lines, and that systems that have no solution are denoted by the $\varnothing$ symbol. Other systems have a solution set of all real numbers, an example being those whose graphs are the same line. The solutions to these systems are denoted by "R."

Go over the directions on the worksheet with your students. Remind them to draw accurate graphs and complete the statement at the end.

ANSWERS

(1) E, (4, −3)   (2) D, (−1, 2)   (3) I, (−3.5, 2.5)   (4) C, (−2.5, 5.5)   (5) S, (2, −5) (6) T, (−1, 6)   (7) N, (1, −2)   (8) O, $\varnothing$ (9) P, R   A system of equations of two or more parallel lines is called an "inconsistent" system, and a system of equations of the same line is called a "dependent" system.

Reproducibles for Section 3 follow.

3–1: WRITING AND EVALUATING NUMERICAL EXPRESSIONS WITH WHOLE-NUMBER EXPONENTS

A numerical expression has only numbers and operations. To evaluate an expression, follow the order of operations. Following are some examples:

Phrase	Numerical Expression	Value
Five more than four to the second power	$5 + 4^2 = 5 + 16$	21
Three to the second power times the sum of five and one	$3^2(5 + 1) = 3^2 \times 6 = 9 \times 6$	54
Four times the difference of two to the third power and seven	$4(2^3 - 7) = 4(8 - 7) = 4 \times 1$	4

Directions: Write a numerical expression for each phrase. Then find the value. After you have finished, check the values you found. You should find five different values.

1. Eight to the second power

2. Nine to the second power divided by three

3. Nine minus two to the third power

4. Six to the second power minus eleven

5. The quotient of ten and two, minus two to the second power

6. The difference of seven to the second power and six to the second power

7. One times three to the third power

8. The difference of three to the third power and two

9. Three less than four to the second power

10. Two to the fifth power plus two to the fifth power

Name _____ Date _____ Period _____

3–2: WRITING AND READING ALGEBRAIC EXPRESSIONS

An algebraic expression contains a variable. A variable is a letter that represents a number. For example, n, x, and y are often used as variables, but any letter can be used.

In an algebraic expression, order does not matter in addition or multiplication. For example, 2 more than a number can be expressed as $n + 2$ or $2 + n$. Three times a number can be expressed as $3n$, $n \times 3$, or $3 \times n$.

Order does matter in subtraction and division. 4 less than a number is $n - 4$. The quotient of 10 and x is $10 \div x$ and not $x \div 10$.

Grouping symbols are symbols such as parentheses and brackets. They must be included if numbers are to be grouped and then added, subtracted, multiplied, or divided. For example, 3 times the sum of a number and 5 is written as $3(n + 5)$. The sum is found first, then multiplied by 3. The sum of a number and 8 divided by 16 is written as $(n + 8) \div 16$.

Directions: Each phrase is followed by an algebraic expression. If the algebraic expression is correct, write *correct* on the line after the expression. If the expression is incorrect, correct it. Complete the statement at the end by writing the variables in each expression you corrected in order.

1. The sum of a number and 8: $a + 8$ _____

2. 2 less than a number: $2 - s$ _____

3. Twice a number: $2y$ _____

4. 4 more than a number: $r + 4$ _____

5. The sum of a number and 6 divided by 12: $t + 6 \div 12$ _____

6. 10 less than a number: $v - 10$ _____

7. 4 squared plus a number: $(4 + u)^2$ _____

8. A number multiplied by the difference of 8 and 2: $p \times 8 - 2$ _____

9. One-half times the sum of a number and 5: $\frac{1}{2}(z + 5)$ _____

10. 7 decreased by a number: $7 - c$ _____

11. The difference of a number and 5 divided by 6: $e - 5 \div 6$ _____

12. 6 more than twice a number: $2w + 6$ _____

13. A number decreased by 15: $15 - n$ _____

14. 5 times a number squared: $5 \times m^2$ _____

(*Continued*)

15. One-half of a number: $\frac{1}{2}k$ _____

16. One less than 8 times a number: $8(d - 1)$ _____

17. 6 times the sum of a number and 3: $6o + 3$ _____

18. The product of a number squared and 8: $8j^2$ _____

19. 3 times a number divided by 3: $3 \div 3u$ _____

20. The product of a number and 22: $22 + s$ _____

Your work with algebraic expressions is _____.

Name _____ Date _____ Period _____

3-3: EVALUATING ALGEBRAIC EXPRESSIONS

To find a missing quantity, substitute the value of the variable in an expression.

   Directions: Complete each statement and find your answers in the Answer Bank. Not all answers will be used. Then unscrambled the letters of your answers to reveal a math word.

1. $P = 3s$ can be used to find the perimeter of an equilateral triangle when you know s, the length of a side. If $s = 4$ inches, then $P =$ _____ inches.

2. $A = s^2$ can be used to find the area of a square when you know s, the length of a side. If $s = 4$ inches, then $A =$ _____ square inches.

3. $V = s^3$ can be used to find the volume of a cube when you know s, the length of a side. If $s = 4$ inches, then $V =$ _____ cubic inches.

4. $f = \frac{i}{12}$ can be used to find the number of feet when you know i, the number of inches. If $i = 3$ inches, then $f =$ _____ foot.

5. $F = 1.8C + 32$ can be used to find the temperature in degrees Fahrenheit when you know C, the temperature in degrees Celsius. If $C = 5°$ Celsius, then $F =$ _____ ° Fahrenheit.

6. $D = 2r$ can be used to find the diameter of a circle when you know r, the radius of the circle. If $r = 2\frac{3}{4}$ inches, then $D =$ _____ inches.

7. $G = \frac{q}{4}$ can be used to find the number of gallons when you know q, the number of quarts. If $q = 10$ quarts, then $G =$ _____ gallons.

8. $y = \frac{i}{36}$ can be used to find the number of yards if you know i, the number of inches. If $i = 18$ inches, then $y =$ _____ yard.

Answer Bank

A. 16	N. $3\frac{1}{4}$	E. 8	F. $\frac{1}{4}$	I. 32	L. 64
M. 12	O. $2\frac{1}{2}$	S. $5\frac{1}{2}$	R. 41	V. 4	U. $\frac{1}{2}$

The letters _____ can be unscrambled to spell _____.

Copyright © 2016 by Judith A. Muschla, Gary Robert Muschla, and Erin Muschla-Berry.

Name _____ Date _____ Period _____

3–4: APPLYING PROPERTIES OF OPERATIONS TO GENERATE EQUIVALENT EXPRESSIONS

Two expressions that represent the same number are called equivalent expressions. They can be generated by using the following properties:

- Distributive Property: $a(b + c) = ab + ac$. A product can be written as the sum of two products.

- Commutative Property for Addition: $a + b = b + a$. The order in which numbers are added does not affect the sum.

- Commutative Property for Multiplication: $a \times b = b \times a$. The order in which numbers are multiplied does not affect the product.

Directions: Write an equivalent expression for each expression below. Match each answer with an answer in the Answer Bank. Some answers will be used more than once. One answer will not be used. Then answer the question at the end by writing the letters of the answers in order, according to their problem numbers. You will need to divide the letters into words.

1. $4x + 7x$

2. $6x - 2x + 4$

3. $4 \times 3x$

4. $3x + x + 4$

5. $4x + 3x - 7x$

6. $3 \times 5x$

7. $4(x + 1)$

8. $2x - x$

9. $10x + x$

10. $7 \times 2x$

11. $2(2x + 2)$

12. $2(x + 3y)$

13. $3(x + 2y)$

14. $2(3y + x)$

15. $3(2y + x)$

16. $x + x + x$

17. $3(2y + 2x)$

Answer Bank

A. $14x$	E. $3x$	M. $6x$	I. $3x + 6y$	K. $12x$	N. $4x + 4$
O. 0	U. $11x$	W. $15x$	Q. x	S. $6y + 6x$	T. $2x + 6y$

In the late 1500s, vowels were introduced to represent something. What were vowels used to represent?

_____

Name_____ Date_____ Period_____

3–5: IDENTIFYING EQUIVALENT EXPRESSIONS

Two expressions are equivalent if they are always equal to each other. It does not matter what values are substituted for the variables.

Directions: Decide if each pair of expressions are equivalent. Circle *yes* if they are equivalent. Circle *no* if they are not equivalent. Then answer the question by writing the letters of your *yes* answers in order. You will need to reverse the order of the letters and divide them into words.

1. $x + y$	xy	Yes, R	No
2. $4x + x$	$x(4 + 1)$	Yes, E	No
3. $a(b + c)$	$ab + c$	Yes, K	No
4. $a + 3$	$1a + 3$	Yes, M	No
5. $3b$	$b + 3$	Yes, U	No
6. $3y$	$y \times y \times y$	Yes, O	No
7. x^1	x	Yes, A	No
8. $4a$	$a + a + a + a$	Yes, S	No
9. $2a + 5a$	$7a$	Yes, E	No
10. $3x + 7x$	$21x$	Yes, I	No
11. $2(x + y)$	$2x + 2y$	Yes, H	No
12. y^3	$y \times y \times y$	Yes, T	No

What are the values of equivalent expressions?

_____

81

Name _____ Date _____ Period _____

3–6: IDENTIFYING SOLUTIONS OF EQUATIONS AND INEQUALITIES

A solution of an equation or inequality is a number or numbers that make an equation or inequality true.

Directions: A number follows each equation or inequality. Decide if the number makes the equation or inequality true. Circle *yes* if it does or *no* if it does not. After you have finished all of the problems, find the sum of the numbers for the *yes* answers. Then substitute the sum for *x* in the final equation to find a special score.

1. $y - 4 = 3$	7	Yes	No
2. $4x - 12 = 8$	6	Yes	No
3. $15 < x + 6$	8	Yes	No
4. $4 - 3x = 1$	1	Yes	No
5. $36 \div x < 8$	9	Yes	No
6. $x + 8 = 21$	13	Yes	No
7. $3 + 7 > x - 5$	15	Yes	No
8. $x \div (2 + 3) > 7$	40	Yes	No
9. $6(3 + 1) - 2 < x$	20	Yes	No
10. $16 \div 4x < 4$	2	Yes	No
11. $21 \div (6 \div 2) + 5 < x - 3$	16	Yes	No
12. $x + 3 > 8(4 - 2)$	11	Yes	No

$188 - x = $ _____

Name _____ Date _____ Period _____

3-7: WRITING EXPRESSIONS IN WHICH VARIABLES REPRESENT NUMBERS

Algebra can be used to perform some mysterious tricks with numerical operations.

Directions: Follow the instructions for each problem. Write a number in Column I. Then complete Column II by using a variable for the number you are thinking of. Be sure to simplify expressions in Column II before you go to the next step. What do you notice about each answer?

Problem 1	**Column I**	**Column II**
1. Choose a number.	_____	_____
2. Multiply by 2.	_____	_____
3. Add 8.	_____	_____
4. Subtract 2.	_____	_____
5. Divide by 2.	_____	_____
6. Subtract 3.	_____	_____
7. The final number is:	_____	_____

Problem 2		
1. Choose a number.	_____	_____
2. Add 5.	_____	_____
3. Multiply by 2.	_____	_____
4. Add 6.	_____	_____
5. Subtract 12.	_____	_____
6. Divide by 2.	_____	_____
7. Subtract the original number.	_____	_____
8. The final number is:	_____	_____

Problem 3		
1. Start with your grade.	_____	_____
2. Multiply by 10.	_____	_____
3. Add 6.	_____	_____
4. Multiply by 10.	_____	_____
5. Subtract 12.	_____	_____
6. Add your age.	_____	_____
7. Subtract 31.	_____	_____
8. Subtract 17.	_____	_____
9. The final number is:	_____	_____

3–8: WRITING AND SOLVING EQUATIONS

An equation is a mathematical sentence which states that two quantities are equal. An equal sign, =, separates an equation into two parts, which are called sides of the equation. To solve an equation, find the values of the variable that make the equation true.

Directions: Write and solve an equation for each situation described below. Use the given variable. There may be more than one equation for each problem.

1. The number of days in September is one less than the number of days in October. Let s represent the number of days in September. There are 31 days in October.

   _____

2. The time in California is three hours earlier than the time in New York. It is 7 P.M. in New York. Let c represent the time in California.

   _____

3. The length of an NBA (National Basketball Association) court is 44 feet longer than the width, which is 50 feet. Let l stand for the length of the court.

   _____

4. Each player begins a chess game with a total of 16 chess pieces. This is twice the number of pawns. Let p stand for the number of pawns.

   _____

5. Forty-eight states of the United States are located in four time zones. This is $\frac{1}{6}$ of the number of time zones in the world. Let w represent the number of time zones in the world.

   _____

6. A rabbit can run half as fast as a cheetah at full speed. A cheetah can run 70 miles per hour. Let r stand for the speed of the rabbit.

   _____

7. The femur, or thighbone, of the average adult is $\frac{1}{4}$ of his or her height. A man is 6 feet tall. Let f stand for the length of his femur.

   _____

8. A newborn baby has more bones than an adult, because bones grow together as a person matures. The average baby has 350 bones, and the average adult has 206. Let b represent the difference in the number of bones.

   _____

(Continued)

9. The number of daily calories recommended for active boys, ages 11 to 13, is 2,600. The number of daily calories recommended for active girls, ages 11 to 13, is 400 calories less. Let g represent the number of calories recommended for active girls each day.

_____

10. The label on a bag of candy says there are about 9 servings per bag, and that the serving size is 8 pieces. Let c represent the number of candies in the bag.

_____

Name _____ Date _____ Period _____

3-9: USING INEQUALITIES

An inequality is a mathematical statement that one quantity is greater than or less than another quantity. Many real-world situations can be represented by writing inequalities.

The symbol > means "is greater than." Some other terms that can show that one quantity is greater than another are "more than," "older than," and "bigger than."

The symbol < means "is less than." Some other terms that show that one quantity is less than another are "fewer than," "younger than," and "smaller than."

The solutions of an inequality may be shown on a number line by using an open circle and shading part of the number line.

Directions: Find an inequality or a number line in the Answer Bank that can be used to solve each problem. Write the letter of the inequality or number line in the space after each question. Some answers will be used more than once. One answer will not be used. Then answer the question at the end by writing the letters of your answers in reverse order. You will need to divide the letters into words.

1. Selena needs to read more than 6 books to earn the reading award. How many books must she read to receive the award? _____

2. There are less than 6 seconds to the end of the quarter. How many seconds are left? _____

3. Mike scored more than 8 points in the first few minutes of the basketball game. How many points did he score? _____

4. There are less than 5 days until vacation. How many days are left? _____

5. The small cake serves fewer than 6 people. How many people will it serve? _____

6. There are more than 5 sports books in the classroom library. How many sports books are there? _____

7. The Little League team scored fewer than 3 runs, but they won the game. How many runs did they score? _____

8. Children must be taller than 4 feet to ride the Ferris wheel. How tall must they be? _____

9. More than 3 people are needed to play the board game. How many people are required to play? _____

10. At Brighton Middle School, there are more than 8 sixth grade teachers. How many sixth grade teachers are there at this school? _____

(Continued)

11. Children under the age of 3 can eat lunch for free at Tony's Diner. What are the ages of children that can eat lunch for free? _____

Answer Bank

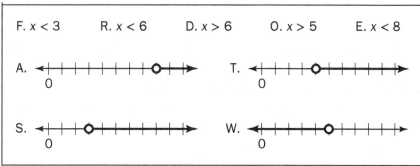

F. $x < 3$ R. $x < 6$ D. $x > 6$ O. $x > 5$ E. $x < 8$

This symbol on a remote control device resembles the greater than symbol. What command does this symbol represent?

_____

3–10: USING VARIABLES TO REPRESENT TWO QUANTITIES

Two different variables can represent two quantities in an equation. One variable is an independent variable, and the other is a dependent variable. The value of the dependent variable "depends" on the value of the independent variable.

The relationship between independent and dependent variables can be expressed in a table. The values in the table can be graphed.

Directions: For each problem, do the following:

- Write an equation.

- Create a table showing the values of the variables.

- Graph the values contained in the table.

1. The earnings, E, are \$15 per hour, h.

2. The perimeter, P, of a square is four times the length of a side, s.

3. The cost, C, of apples is \$3 per pound, p.

4. A yard, Y, is $\frac{1}{3}$ times the number of feet, f.

5. A store is having a going-out-of business sale. All items are to be sold at half of their regular price. Use r to represent the regular price and s to represent the sale price.

Name _____ Date _____ Period _____

3-11: ADDING, SUBTRACTING, FACTORING, AND EXPANDING LINEAR EXPRESSIONS

Understanding the properties of operations can help you add, subtract, factor, and expand expressions.

- When adding or subtracting expressions, use the Commutative Property for Addition, $a + b = b + a$, to change the order of the expressions.

- When factoring an expression, use the Distributive Property, $ab + ac = a(b + c)$, to write the sum of two products as a product.

- When expanding an expression, use the Distributive Property, $a(b + c) = ab + ac$, to write a product as the sum of two products.

Directions: Complete each equation. Find your answers in the Answer Bank. Some answers will be used more than once. Then complete the statement at the end by writing the letter of each answer in the space above its problem number. You will need to divide the letters into words.

1. $4x + 12 =$ _____ $(x + 3)$

2. $3x - 1 - 4x =$ _____ $- 1$

3. $-1(3x - 1) = -3x +$ _____

4. $6x + 8 =$ _____ $(3x + 4)$

5. $-2x + 4 =$ _____ $(x - 2)$

6. $\frac{1}{2}(2x + 4) = x +$ _____

7. $7x - (2x - 1) =$ _____ $+ 1$

8. $\frac{1}{5}(5 + 5x) + 1 =$ _____ $+ 2$

9. $-8x - 16 = -8(x +$ _____ $)$

10. $8 + (-2x) - (-3x) =$ _____ $+ 8$

11. $\frac{1}{4}(3x + 16) = \frac{3}{4}x +$ _____

12. $-6 + 7x - 5x + 3 =$ _____ $- 3$

Answer Bank

E. 2	P. $-x$	C. x	F. 1
O. -2	R. 4	S. $5x$	T. $2x$

You have a _____.

$\overline{2}$ $\quad$ $\overline{9}$ $\quad$ $\overline{11}$ $\quad$ $\overline{3}$ $\quad$ $\overline{4}$ $\quad$ $\overline{10}$ $\quad$ $\overline{12}$ $\quad$ $\overline{7}$ $\quad$ $\overline{8}$ $\quad$ $\overline{5}$ $\quad$ $\overline{1}$ $\quad$ $\overline{6}$

3–12: REWRITING EXPRESSIONS IN DIFFERENT FORMS

Rewriting an expression can help you to understand the relationship of its quantities.

Directions: Complete the statements. Choose your answers from the choices that follow each statement. Then complete the statement at the end by writing the letter of each answer in the space above its problem number.

1. Dividing x by $\frac{1}{5}$ is the same as multiplying x by _____. (E. $\frac{4}{5}$ A. 5   I. 0.5)

2. Adding $\frac{1}{3}x$ three times is the same as multiplying $\frac{1}{3}x$ by _____. (I. 3   E. 0.3   O. $\frac{2}{3}$)

3. Dividing $\frac{1}{4}$ by x is the same as multiplying $\frac{1}{4}$ by _____. (E. $4x$ N. $\frac{1}{x}$ E. x^2)

4. Adding $x + x + x$ is the same as multiplying x by _____. (T. 3   S. itself 3 times   N. $\frac{1}{3}$)

5. Decreasing x by 15% is the same as multiplying x by _____. (L. 0.85   R. 0.15   A. 8.5)

6. Adding $x + x$ is the same as increasing x by _____. (S. x^2 I. $2x$ V. 100%)

7. Multiplying 12 by $0.25x$ is the same as multiplying 12 by _____. (A. $\frac{1}{75}$ U. $\frac{1}{4}x$ S. 4)

8. Subtracting $4x$ from $12x$ is the same as multiplying $12x$ by _____. (E. $\frac{2}{3}$ U. 0.4   R. $\frac{3}{2}$)

9. Increasing x by 45% is the same as multiplying x by _____. (S. $\frac{9}{20}$ U. 0.45   Q. 1.45)

10. Multiplying x by $\frac{1}{2}$ is the same as dividing x by _____. (N. 0.2   E. 2   R. 5.0)

When an expression is written in a different form, the two forms are _____.

$\overline{8}$ $\overline{9}$ $\overline{7}$ $\overline{2}$ $\overline{6}$ $\overline{1}$ $\overline{5}$ $\overline{10}$ $\overline{3}$ $\overline{4}$

Copyright © 2016 by Judith A. Muschla, Gary Robert Muschla, and Erin Muschla-Berry.

Name _____ Date _____ Period _____

3–13: SOLVING MULTI-STEP PROBLEMS

To solve multi-step problems, do the following:

1. Read the problem carefully.

2. Identify what you are asked to find.

3. Determine the information needed to solve the problem.

4. Decide what operations to use to solve the problem.

5. Solve the problem.

6. Check your work and make sure your answer is reasonable.

Directions: Solve each problem.

1. How many boys are in a class of 35 students if the girls outnumber boys by 5?

2. Manuel opened a savings account with an initial deposit of $177. If he wants to have $500 (not counting interest) in the account after the next 19 weeks, how much must he save each week?

3. In a recent local election, the winning candidate had 2,700 more votes than the loser. If the total number of votes was 13,300, how many votes did the winner receive?

4. The sum of 10 times a number and −55 is −5. What is the number?

5. −6 and the sum of the quotient of a number and 4 decreased by 6 is 12. What is the number?

6. One number is $2\frac{1}{2}$ times another number. If the sum of the two numbers is 35, what is the smaller of the two numbers?

7. If the difference of a number and 18 is multiplied by −10, the product is 50. What is the number?

8. The Valley View High School has decided to print their own T-shirts for various teams and clubs. The equipment necessary to print the shirts costs $1,179. The shirts cost $4.75 each and will be sold for $7.00 each. How many shirts must be sold to cover the initial investment?

9. At a family reunion, three cousins were comparing their ages. Jennifer is 17 years younger than René, and René is 10 years older than Melissa. Their ages total 60 years. How old is René?

10. The sum of the answers to the odd-numbered problems decreased by the product of the answers to Problems 6 and 8 exceeds the product of the answers to Problems 2 and 4 by this amount. Find the amount.

3–14: SOLVING EQUATIONS AND INEQUALITIES

Writing and solving equations and inequalities requires clear thinking and accurate work.

Directions: Write and solve an equation or inequality for each problem. Let n represent the missing numbers. Find your answers in the Answer Bank. One answer will not be used. Then complete the statement at the end by writing the letter of each answer in the space above its problem number. You will need to divide the letters into words.

1. 5 times a number plus 84 equals 124.

2. A number decreased by 7 is less than −6.

3. The sum of a number and −4 is greater than 15.

4. 7 times the sum of a number and 6 equals 63.

5. The difference of $\frac{1}{2}$ of a number and 12 equals 12.

6. $\frac{3}{4}$ of a number is greater than −24.

7. 6 plus 3 times a number is less than 36.

8. The sum of a number and 3 multiplied by 4 equals 36.

9. 23 less than the product of 7 and a number equals 54.

10. 15 more than 3 times a number is less than 24.

11. The product of a number and the sum of 7 and 9 equals 32.

Answer Box

R. $n > 19$	X. $n = 8$	A. $n < 10$	N. $n = 48$	C. $n > -32$	T. $n = 6$
I. $n < 1$	P. $n = 3$	E. $n = 11$	O. $n = 2$	M. $n > 8$	L. $n < 3$

Your mathematical skills _____.

$\overline{7}$ $\quad$ $\overline{3}$ $\quad$ $\overline{9}$ $\quad$ $\overline{9}$ $\quad$ $\overline{1}$ $\quad$ $\overline{6}$ $\quad$ $\overline{9}$ $\quad$ $\overline{4}$ $\quad$ $\overline{8}$ $\quad$ $\overline{2}$ $\quad$ $\overline{11}$ $\quad$ $\overline{5}$ $\quad$ $\overline{7}$ $\quad$ $\overline{10}$

Name_____ Date_____ Period_____

3-15: APPLYING PROPERTIES OF INTEGER EXPONENTS

The properties of exponents as applied to integers are summarized below. Let x and y be real numbers and let m and n be integers.

- Product of Powers Property: $x^m x^n = x^{m+n}$; example: $2^4 \cdot 2^{-6} = 2^{-2} = \frac{1}{2^2} = \frac{1}{4}$
- Power of a Power Property: $(x^m)^n = x^{mn}$; example: $(3^2)^3 = 3^{2 \cdot 3} = 3^6 = 729$
- Power of a Product Property: $(xy)^m = x^m y^m$; example: $(2 \cdot 4)^2 = 2^2 \cdot 4^2 = 4 \cdot 16 = 64$
- Quotient of Powers Property: $\frac{x^m}{x^n} = x^{m-n}, x \neq 0$; example: $\frac{2^5}{2^{-2}} = 2^{5-(-2)} = 2^7 = 128$
- Power of a Quotient Property: $\left(\frac{x}{y}\right)^m = \frac{x^m}{y^m}, y \neq 0$; example: $\left(\frac{2}{3}\right)^3 = \frac{2^3}{3^3} = \frac{8}{27}$
- Zero Exponent Property: $x^0 = 1, x \neq 0$; examples: $5^0 = 1$ and $(-4)^0 = 1$
- Negative Exponent Property: $x^{-n} = \frac{1}{x^n}, x \neq 0$; examples: $3^{-2} = \frac{1}{3^2} = \frac{1}{9}$

Directions: Use the properties of exponents to match each expression with an equivalent expression from the choices that are provided. Then complete the statement at the end by writing the letter of each answer in the space above its problem number. You will need to divide the letters into words.

1. $(3^4)^2$ (A. 3^8 C. 3^6)   2. $4^{-2} \times 4^1$ (G. $\frac{1}{4}$ E. 4)

3. $\frac{1}{7^{-1}}$ (O. $\frac{1}{7}$ N. 7)   4. $\frac{1}{5^0}$ (I. 1   H. $\frac{1}{5}$)

5. 3^{-4} (T. $\frac{3}{4}$ H. $\frac{1}{3^4}$)   6. $\frac{4^2}{4^{-3}}$ (S. 4^{-1} N. 4^5)

7. $(3 \times 5)^2$ (C. 8^3 A. 9×25)   8. 7^0 (R. 7   N. 1)

9. $\left(\frac{3}{4}\right)^2$ (Y. $\frac{9}{4}$ E. $\frac{9}{16}$)   10. $3^2 \times 2^1$ (S. 18   R. 6^2)

11. $\frac{3^{-2}}{3}$ (O. 3^{-3} R. 3^{-1})   12. $(5^2)^3$ (M. 5^6 Y. 5^5)

Zero to the zero power _____.

$\overline{5}$ $\overline{7}$ $\overline{10}$ $\overline{3}$ $\overline{11}$ $\overline{12}$ $\overline{9}$ $\overline{1}$ $\overline{6}$ $\overline{4}$ $\overline{8}$ $\overline{2}$

3–16: USING SQUARE ROOTS AND CUBE ROOTS

To solve equations containing perfect squares and perfect cubes of integers, follow these guidelines:

- If $x^2 = p$, take the square root of each side to find $x = \pm\sqrt{p}$. For example, if $x^2 = 16$, take the square root of each side to find $x = \pm\sqrt{16}$. To solve for x, find a number that can be multiplied by itself to equal 16. There are two solutions: $4 \times 4 = 16$ and $-4 \times (-4) = 16$; $x = \pm 4$.

- If $x^3 = p$, take the cube root of each side to find $x = \sqrt[3]{p}$. For example, if $x^3 = 8$, take the cube root of each side to find $x = \sqrt[3]{8}$. To solve for x, find a number that can be multiplied by itself three times to equal 8. There is only one solution: $2 \times 2 \times 2 = 8$; $x = 2$.

Directions: Solve each problem and find your answers in the Answer Bank. One answer will not be used. Then complete the statement at the end by writing the letter of each answer in the space above its problem number. You will need to divide the letters into words.

1. $x^3 = 125$ 2. $x^2 = 25$ 3. $x^2 = 121$ 4. $x^3 = 27$

5. $x^2 = 4$ 6. $x^2 = 9$ 7. $x^3 = 64$ 8. $x^2 = 49$

9. $x^2 = 81$ 10. $x^2 = 64$ 11. $x^3 = 1$

Answer Bank

E. $x = \pm 5$	Y. $x = \pm 2$	H. $x = 8$	A. $x = \pm 9$	I. $x = 1$	R. $x = \pm 11$
T. $x = 3$	W. $x = 5$	N. $x = \pm 8$	S. $x = 4$	G. $x = \pm 7$	L. $x = \pm 3$

The square root of a perfect square is _____.

$\overline{9}$ $\overline{6}$ $\overline{1}$ $\overline{9}$ $\overline{5}$ $\overline{7}$ $\overline{9}$ $\overline{10}$ $\overline{11}$ $\overline{10}$ $\overline{4}$ $\overline{2}$ $\overline{8}$ $\overline{2}$ $\overline{3}$

Name _____ Date _____ Period _____

3–17: USING NUMBERS EXPRESSED IN SCIENTIFIC NOTATION

Scientific notation is a convenient way to write extremely large or extremely small numbers by using powers of 10. Use the form $n \times 10^x$, where n is a number greater than or equal to 1 and less than 10 and x is an integer, and follow these guidelines:

- To write 51,000 in scientific notation, move the decimal point four places to the left. $51,000 = 5.1 \times 10^4$

- To write 0.000034 in scientific notation, move the decimal point five places to the right. $0.000034 = 3.4 \times 10^{-5}$.

- To write 3.6×10^3 as a standard number, move the decimal point three places to the right. $3.6 \times 10^3 = 3,600$.

- To write 8.2×10^{-6} as a standard number, move the decimal point six places to the left. $8.2 \times 10^{-6} = 0.0000082$.

Directions: Solve each problem and answer the questions.

1. Write the distances of the Earth, 92,900,000 miles, and Neptune, 2,800,000,000 miles, from the sun in scientific notation. About how many times farther is the distance of Neptune from the sun than the distance of Earth from the sun?

2. Write the diameters of a red blood cell, 0.008 millimeter, and a grain of pollen, 0.086 millimeter, in scientific notation. About how many times larger is a grain of pollen than a red blood cell?

3. Write the areas of North America, 24,474,000 square kilometers, and Australia/Oceania, 8,112,000 square kilometers, in scientific notation. About how many times larger is the area of North America than the area of Australia/Oceania?

4. Write the size of a staphylococcus bacterium, 0.002 millimeter, and the size of a dust mite, 0.25 millimeter, in scientific notation. About how many times larger is a dust mite than a staphylococcus bacterium?

5. Write the following numbers in order from largest to smallest. About how many times larger is the largest number than the smallest? Verify your answers by converting them from scientific notation to standard numbers.

    a. 3.7×10^5 b. 6.45×10^4 c. 9.9×10^4

Name _____ Date _____ Period _____

3–18: OPERATIONS WITH SCIENTIFIC NOTATION

Use the following guidelines to add, subtract, multiply, and divide numbers written in scientific notation:

- To add or subtract, the exponents in each number must be the same. Then add or subtract the coefficients of each expression and keep the exponent. Example: $(3.1 \times 10^3) + (2.5 \times 10^3) = 5.6 \times 10^3$. If the exponents are not the same, you must rewrite one of the numbers so that the exponents are the same. Example: $(4.9 \times 10^4) - (3.8 \times 10^3) = (4.9 \times 10^4) - (0.38 \times 10^4) = 4.52 \times 10^4$

- To multiply, multiply the coefficients and add the exponents. Example: $(4.5 \times 10^3) \times (2.1 \times 10^6) = 9.45 \times 10^9$

- To divide, divide the coefficients and subtract the exponents. Example: $\frac{8.6 \times 10^5}{2 \times 10^3} = \frac{8.6}{2} \times 10^{5-3} = 4.3 \times 10^2$

Remember that scientific notation requires that all answers be expressed in the form of $n \times 10^x$, with n being a number greater than or equal to 1 and less than 10 and x being an integer. For example, if after performing any of the operations, you find an answer of 15.4×10^5, you must rewrite the answer as 1.54×10^6 so that it is expressed in scientific notation.

Directions: Solve each problem and find your answers in the Answer Bank. Then complete the statement at the end by writing the letter of each answer in the space above its problem number. You will need to divide the letters into words.

1. $(1.89 \times 10^5) \times (4 \times 10^3)$

2. $(6.94 \times 10^3) + (2.1 \times 10^3)$

3. $(3.1 \times 10^3) \times (2.34 \times 10^6)$

4. $(4.4 \times 10^6) \div (2 \times 10^4)$

5. $(9.7 \times 10^6) - (4.38 \times 10^6)$

6. $(3.75 \times 10^4) + (2.8 \times 10^5)$

7. $(8.47 \times 10^3) - (4.36 \times 10^2)$

8. $(9.24 \times 10^7) \div (3 \times 10^5)$

9. $(7.1 \times 10^4) \times (3.05 \times 10^3)$

10. $(6.3 \times 10^5) + (4.25 \times 10^5)$

Answer Bank

O. 8.034×10^3	N. 7.56×10^8	T. 5.32×10^6	G. 9.04×10^3	R. 3.175×10^5
W. 3.08×10^2	S. 2.2×10^2	Z. 1.055×10^6	I. 2.1655×10^8	E. 7.254×10^9

When writing very large or very small numbers, using scientific notation helps to prevent making mistakes _____.

$\overline{8}$ $\overline{6}$ $\overline{9}$ $\overline{5}$ $\overline{9}$ $\overline{1}$ $\overline{2}$ $\overline{10}$ $\overline{3}$ $\overline{6}$ $\overline{7}$ $\overline{3}$ $\overline{4}$

3–19: GRAPHING PROPORTIONAL RELATIONSHIPS

A proportional relationship can be described by an equation in the form of $y = mx$, a verbal description, a table of values, or as the graph of a line through the origin that has a slope of m. A proportional relationship is also called a direct variation.

Directions: Two proportional relationships are described in each problem. Graph each relationship. Then circle the letter of the proportional relationship whose graph has the greater slope. Write the letters you have circled above the problem numbers to reveal a math term at the end of the worksheet.

1. Two electricians have different hourly rates. C is the total cost, and h is the number of hours worked.

   T. $C = \$50h$

   O.

h	1	2	3	4
C	\$75	\$150	\$225	\$300

2. The price of a pound of apples varies.

   E. Apples cost \$1.99 a pound.

   D. $C = \$1.75p$, where p is the number of pounds, and C is the total cost.

3. Two friends charge different rates for babysitting.

   R. Rachael charges \$7 per hour.

   S. Sally's rate is \$1 per hour more than Rachael charges.

4. The amount deducted for each incorrect answer varies with each quiz. T is the total number of points deducted, and a is the number of incorrect answers. (The values of a are integers.)

   P.

a	0	1	2	4
T	0	10	20	40

   E. $T = 5a$

5. Two theaters charge different amounts for movie tickets to a matinee. T stands for the total charge, and a stands for the number of tickets purchased. (The values of a are integers.)

   L. $T = 8a$

   A. The cost of each ticket is half of the original price of \$10 per ticket.

$$\overline{3} \qquad \overline{5} \qquad \overline{1} \qquad \overline{4} \qquad \overline{2}$$

Name _____ Date _____ Period _____

3–20: DERIVING THE EQUATION $y = mx$

You can use similar triangles to derive the equation of a line through the origin in the coordinate plane. In the diagram, $\triangle ABC \sim \triangle DEF$.

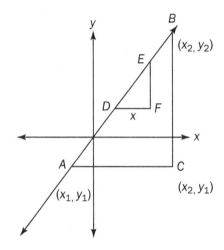

Directions: Consider the diagram and complete each statement. Find your answers in the Answer Bank. Some answers will not be used. Then complete the statement at the end by writing the letter of each answer in the space above its problem number. You will need to divide the letters into words.

1. The coordinates of A are _____.

2. $\overline{DF} = x$, therefore $\overline{EF} =$ _____.

3. Because the triangles are similar, $\frac{y}{x} = \frac{y_2 - y_1}{\rule{1cm}{0.4pt}}$.

4. The letter that is used to represent the slope is _____.

5. Substitute m for $\frac{y_2 - y_1}{x_2 - x_1}$ in Problem 3 to get _____.

6. Rewrite the ratio in problem 5 so that the denominator of the slope is 1 to get

   _____.

7. Use cross-multiplication in problem 6 to solve for y. $y =$ _____.

Answer Bank

E. (x_2, y_1)	O. (x_1, y_1)	S. y	R. $x_1 - x_2$	T. $x_2 - x_1$
I. m	N. $\frac{y}{x} = m$	A. mx	C. $\frac{y}{x} = \frac{m}{1}$	P. $\frac{y}{1} = \frac{m}{x}$

The slope of a line _____.

$\overline{4}$ $\quad$ $\overline{2}$ $\quad$ $\overline{6}$ $\quad$ $\overline{1}$ $\quad$ $\overline{5}$ $\quad$ $\overline{2}$ $\quad$ $\overline{3}$ $\quad$ $\overline{7}$ $\quad$ $\overline{5}$ $\quad$ $\overline{3}$

3-21: IDENTIFYING EQUATIONS THAT HAVE ONE SOLUTION, NO SOLUTIONS, OR INFINITELY MANY SOLUTIONS

Linear equations may have one solution, no solutions, or infinitely many solutions, depending on the equation. To identify the number of solutions or if there are no solutions, write equivalent equations, following these steps:

1. Use the Distributive Property to eliminate all parentheses.

2. Simplify each side, if possible.

3. Add or subtract the same term or terms to or from each side of the equation.

4. Multiply or divide both sides of the equation by the same nonzero number.

Here are some examples:

1. $7x = x - 48$
   $6x = -48$
   $x = -8$
   One solution

2. $3(1 - x) + 2 = 5 - 3x$
   $3 - 3x + 2 = 5 - 3x$
   $5 - 3x = 5 - 3x$
   $0 = 0$
   Infinitely many solutions

3. $2(x - 1) = 2x + 5$
   $2x - 2 = 2x + 5$
   $-2 = 5$
   No solutions

Directions: Identify which equations have one solution, no solution, or infinitely many solutions. If an equation has one solution, state the solution. Describe the relationships between the problem numbers and the types of solutions. (Hint: Think about prime and composite problem numbers.)

1. $\frac{1}{3}(12x + 2) = 4x + 1 - \frac{1}{3}$

2. $2x = 51 + 5x$

3. $45 - 4x = 11x$

4. $2x - 7 = 7 + 2x$

5. $2(3x - 2) = 3(x + 1)$

6. $7x - 1 = 7(x - 1)$

Copyright © 2016 by Judith A. Muschla, Gary Robert Muschla, and Erin Muschla-Berry.

Name_____ Date_____ Period_____

3–22: SOLVING EQUATIONS WITH VARIABLES ON BOTH SIDES

Sometimes equations are written with variables on both sides of the equal symbol. To solve these types of equations, you must rewrite the equations so that the variables are on the same side of the equation.

Directions: Solve each equation. Write the letter of the problem above its solution to complete the statement at the end. You will need to divide the letters into words.

P. $7x = x - 54$

U. $-8x - x = 24 - x$

R. $4x - 9 = 3 - 4x$

H. $-8 + 5x = 3x - 11 + 5x$

L. $x - 10 = -2x + 2$

A. $-13 + x = 4x + 23 + 6x$

O. $-1 + x = 7x + 2$

F. $3(2x - 1) + \frac{1}{2}x = \frac{1}{2}x - 3$

B. $\frac{2}{3}x + 7 = x - 2$

V. $4(3x - 5) - x = -x + 16$

W. $4x - 9 = 3 + 4x$

T. $2(1 - x) = 3(x + 9)$

N. $3(x - 7) = 2x$

E. $2(3 - 4x) = 4 + 4(6 - x)$

K. $7 = -\frac{1}{3}(x + 6)$

S. $9(2x + 3) = -36 - 27(x + 2)$

In 1637, René Descartes used the first letters of the _____.

$\overline{-4}$ $\quad$ $\overline{4}$ $\quad$ $\overline{-9}$ $\quad$ $\overline{1}$ $\quad$ $\overline{-4}$ $\quad$ $\overline{27}$ $\quad$ $\overline{-5.5}$ $\quad$ $\overline{-5}$ $\quad$ $\overline{0}$ $\quad$ $\overline{-0.5}$ $\quad$ $\overline{1.5}$

$\overline{-27}$ $\quad$ $\overline{21}$ $\quad$ $\overline{-0.5}$ $\quad$ $\overline{\varnothing}$ $\quad$ $\overline{21}$ $\quad$ $\overline{3}$ $\quad$ $\overline{-4}$ $\quad$ $\overline{4}$ $\quad$ $\overline{-3}$ $\quad$ $\overline{-5.5}$ $\quad$ $\overline{-2.6}$

Name _____ Date _____ Period _____

3-23: SOLVING SYSTEMS OF LINEAR EQUATIONS ALGEBRAICALLY

A system of linear equations is a group of two or more equations with two or more variables. Three methods for solving systems of linear equations include: substitution, addition or subtraction, and multiplication with addition or subtraction.

   Directions: Solve each system of equations and find the answers in the Answer Bank. Some answers will not be used. Complete the statement at the end by writing the letter of each answer in the space above its problem number.

1. $y = x + 2$ $x =$ _____ $y =$ _____
   $y = 3x - 2$

2. $x + y = 6$ $x =$ _____ $y =$ _____
   $x - 4 = y$

3. $8x + 3y = -27$ $x =$ _____ $y =$ _____
   $2x - 3y = -3$

4. $2x = 5y$ $x =$ _____ $y =$ _____
   $3y + x = -11$

5. $x - 4y = 6$ $x =$ _____ $y =$ _____
   $x - 2y = 18$

6. $3x - y = 21$ $x =$ _____ $y =$ _____
   $2x + y = 4$

7. $8x + 3y = 13$ $x =$ _____ $y =$ _____
   $3x + 2y = 11$

8. $8x - 5y = -11$ $x =$ _____ $y =$ _____
   $3y = 4x - 11$

9. $y = 3x - 2$ $x =$ _____ $y =$ _____
   $x - y = 4$

10. $x - y = -8$ $x =$ _____ $y =$ _____
    $x + y = 12$

Answer Bank

S. $x = -5, y = -2$	P. $x = 2, y = 4$	U. $x = -22, y = -33$	N. $x = 5, y = 1$
A. $x = 30, y = 6$	O. $x = 5, y = -6$	H. $x = 2, y = 10$	D. $x = -1, y = -5$
R. $x = -4, y = 6$	T. $x = -1, y = 7$	X. $x = -2, y = -4$	I. $x = -3, y = -1$

_____ of Alexandria (c. 275) was a Greek mathematician who catalogued all of the algebra the Greeks understood.

$\overline{9}$ $\overline{3}$ $\overline{6}$ $\overline{1}$ $\overline{10}$ $\overline{5}$ $\overline{2}$ $\overline{7}$ $\overline{8}$ $\overline{4}$

Name _____ Date _____ Period _____

3–24: SOLVING SYSTEMS OF EQUATIONS BY GRAPHING

Graphing can be used to solve systems of equations. Follow these steps:

- Graph the equations of two or more lines on the same axes.

- Find the point where the lines intersect.

The ordered pair at the point of intersection is a solution of all the equations in the system. If the graphs of the equations do not intersect, then the system has no solution and is denoted by $\varnothing$. If the graphs of the equations are the same line, the solution is all real numbers and is denoted by "R."

Directions: Solve each system of equations by graphing. Find your answers in the Answer Bank. One answer will not be used. Then complete the statement at the end by writing the letter of each answer in the space above its problem number.

1. $x + 4y = -8$
   $3x + 2y = 6$

2. $2x + 3y = 4$
   $3x - y = -5$

3. $y = x + 6$
   $y = -x - 1$

4. $3x + y = -2$
   $x - y = -8$

5. $3x + y = 1$
   $2x + 3y = -11$

6. $2x + y = 4$
   $3x + 2y = 9$

7. $y = -2$
   $x = 1$

8. $2x + y = 5$
   $y = -2x + 1$

9. $x + y = 2$
   $3x + 3y = 6$

Answer Bank

O. $\varnothing$	S. (2, −5)	I. (−3.5, 2.5)	E. (4, −3)	K. (6, −4)
T. (−1, 6)	N. (1, −2)	P. R	C. (−2.5, 5.5)	D. (−1, 2)

A system of equations of two or more parallel lines is called an _____ system, and a system of equations of the same line is called a _____ system.

$\overline{3}$ $\overline{7}$ $\overline{4}$ $\overline{8}$ $\overline{7}$ $\overline{5}$ $\overline{3}$ $\overline{5}$ $\overline{6}$ $\overline{1}$ $\overline{7}$ $\overline{6}$

$\overline{2}$ $\overline{1}$ $\overline{9}$ $\overline{1}$ $\overline{7}$ $\overline{2}$ $\overline{1}$ $\overline{7}$ $\overline{6}$

Polynomial, Rational, Exponential, and Radical Expressions, Equations, and Inequalities

Teaching Notes for the Activities of Section 4

4-1: (A-SSE.1) INTERPRETING EXPRESSIONS

For this activity, your students will write expressions, following step-by-step instructions. They will then answer questions about the expressions they wrote. Because each answer is dependent upon the previous answer being correct, finding the correct answer for problem 8 indicates that your students most likely completed the activity correctly.

Review the information on the worksheet, noting that terms may be combined only when they are identical, except for their coefficients. For example, $a + a = 2a$, but when $6a$ is added to $2b + c$, the sum is $6a + 2b + c$.

Go over the directions with your students. Students should refer to the definitions on the worksheet to help them write the expressions and answer the questions. Caution your students to work carefully because an error in one problem will lead to subsequent errors. Also note that problem 5 requires students to use the Distributive Property. For example, when $e + f$ is doubled, the product should be expressed as $2(e + f)$. Students should not expand the expression.

ANSWERS

(1) a, b, c (2) abc (3) $-8abc$ (4) $-8abc + 4d$ (5) $2(-8abc + 4d)$
(6) $2, (-8abc + 4d)$ (7) $-8abc$ (four factors)   (8) -8

4-2: (A-SSE.2) USING THE STRUCTURE OF AN EXPRESSION TO IDENTIFY WAYS TO REWRITE IT

For this activity, your students will rewrite expressions as sums, differences, and products. Completing a statement at the end of the worksheet will enable them to check their answers.

Start by reviewing the following vocabulary:

- Term—an expression using numbers, variables, or both numbers and variables to indicate a product or quotient.

- Polynomial—the sum of monomials.

- Monomial—an expression that is either a number, a variable, or a product of a number and one or more variables.

- Square—a number or variable raised to the second power.

- Cube—a number or variable raised to the third power.

Discuss the equations and properties listed on the worksheet. Explain that to complete the worksheet, students will need to identify the terms of expressions and select the appropriate property to rewrite the expressions. For example, to rewrite $10x - 10$ as the product of a number and a polynomial, students must identify 10 as the common factor and use the Distributive Property to write $10(x - 1)$. To rewrite $x^3 - 125$ as the product of two polynomials, students should recognize that this is the difference of cubes and then use the formula $a^3 - b^3 = (a - b)(a^2 + ab + b^2)$ to write $(x - 5)(x^2 + 5x + 25)$.

Review the directions with your students. Emphasize that most of the problems have answers with multiple parts.. To complete the statement at the end, students should write the letters of their answers starting with the first problem and, if necessary, unscramble the letters.

ANSWERS

(1) C, $x + 2$; A, $x - 2$; N, $x^2 + 4$ (2) H, 7; E, x^2 (3) L, $1 + 9$ (4) P, $4 - 1$ (5) Y, $x + 4$; O, $x - 4$ (6) R, $x - 1$; U, $x^2 + x + 1$ (7) W, 16; E, x^2 (8) R, $x - 1$; I, $x + 1$ (9) T, 4; E, x^2 (10) I, $x + 1$; T, 4   Seeing the structure of an expression "can help you rewrite it."

4–3: (A-SSE.3) FACTORING QUADRATIC EXPRESSIONS TO REVEAL ZEROES

This activity requires your students to factor quadratic expressions to find the zeroes of the function they define. Completing a statement at the end of the worksheet will enable them to check their answers.

Begin the activity by reviewing the definition of a quadratic equation, which is a polynomial equation of degree two. Emphasize that a polynomial of degree two means that the polynomial is simplified and the highest degree of any term is two. Also note that the zeroes of a function, f, are the solutions to the equation $f(x) = 0$. Graphically, these are the values of x where the graph of the function intersects the x-axis.

Review the procedures for factoring and discuss the Zero Product Property, which states that if a product is zero, then one of the factors or both of the factors are zero. Explain the example on the worksheet and offer additional examples if necessary.

Go over the directions with your students. Remind them that some letters in some problems may need to be reversed when completing the statement at the end.

ANSWERS

(1) O, 0; F, 10   (2) T, −5; H, −3   (3) E, 2; T, −5   (4) Y, 3; P, $\frac{1}{2}$ (5) E, 2; I, $-\frac{1}{2}$

(6) S, $2\frac{1}{2}$; O, 0   (7) N, −1; T, −5   (8) H, −3; E, 2   (9) S, $2\frac{1}{2}$; A, 4   (10) M, $-\frac{3}{4}$; E, 2

(11) L, −2; I, $-\frac{1}{2}$ (12) N, −1; E, 2   Although René Descartes first used raised numbers for powers in 1637, he continued to write x^2 as xx because xx uses the same amount of space as x^2 yet all "of the type is on the same line."

4-4: (A-SSE.3) COMPLETING THE SQUARE TO REVEAL MAXIMUM OR MINIMUM VALUES

This activity requires your students to complete the square to write equations in the form of $y = ax^2 + bx + c$, $a \neq 0$, as $y - k = a(x - h)^2$. Completing a statement at the end of the worksheet will enable your students to check their work.

Explain that when an equation is expressed in the form of $y - k = a(x - h)^2$, $a \neq 0$, students can determine whether the graph opens upward or downward as well as determine the maximum or minimum value of the parabola. Discuss the information on the worksheet with your students, particularly the procedure for completing the square. Note that the reasons for each step of the process are provided on the right in the table.

Go over the directions with your students. Some equations will be matched with an equation obtained by completing the square, while others will be matched with their maximum or minimum value. Students should also complete the statement at the end.

ANSWERS

(1) I, minimum value, $(-3, 1)$ (2) T, $y - 1 = (x + 2)^2$ (3) O, maximum value, $(2, 9)$
(4) C, minimum value, $(-2, -13)$ (5) E, $y - 11.5 = -2(x + 2.5)^2$ (6) N, minimum value,
$\left(-\dfrac{1}{3}, \dfrac{2}{3}\right)$ (7) S, $y + 4\dfrac{1}{16} = \left(x + \dfrac{1}{4}\right)^2$ (8) A, $y + 7 = 2(x - 1)^2$ A parabola is "a conic
section."

4-5: (A-SSE.4) FINDING SUMS OF FINITE GEOMETRIC SERIES

This activity has two parts. The first part requires students to fill in blanks to derive the formula for finding the sum of a finite geometric series. The second part requires students to use this formula to find the sum of finite geometric series. Completing a statement at the end of the worksheet will enable students to check their answers.

Review the definitions of sequence and series that are summarized below and discuss the examples on the worksheet.

- A sequence is a group of numbers (called terms) arranged in a pattern.

- Each term of a geometric sequence is formed by multiplying the preceding term by a nonzero constant called the common ratio.

- A series is the sum of the terms of a sequence.

- A geometric series is the sum of the terms of a geometric sequence.

- The formula for finding the sum of a finite geometric series is $S_n = \dfrac{a_1(1 - r^n)}{1 - r}$, $r \neq 1$.

Discuss the directions, noting the two parts of the assignment. Remind students to complete the statement at the end.

4–6: (A-APR.1) ADDING, SUBTRACTING, AND MULTIPLYING POLYNOMIALS

For this activity, your students will add, subtract, and multiply polynomials, using the answer of each problem to start the next problem. Finding the correct answer to problem 9 will verify that their other answers are most likely to be correct.

Begin the activity by reviewing the steps and examples for adding, subtracting, and multiplying polynomials on the worksheet. If necessary, provide more examples.

Go over the directions with your students. Make sure they understand that they are to use the answer of each problem to begin the next problem. They should then perform the indicated operation. Caution them to be accurate in their work because a mistake in any of the problems will result in not finding the correct answer for the last problem. They should recognize the answer to the last problem.

ANSWERS

(1) $(8x + 1)$ (2) $(16x^2 - 6x - 1)$ (3) $(2x^2 - 4x - 6)$ (4) $(x^2 - 9)$
(5) $(x^3 - 3x^2 - 9x + 27)$ (6) $(x^2 + 2)$ (7) $(x^4 + 3x^3 + 6x^2 + 6x + 8)$ (8) $(-x^2 + 6x + 12)$
(9) $(3x + 2)$ The last answer is the same as the first polynomial in problem 1.

4–7: (A-APR.2) APPLYING THE REMAINDER THEOREM

For this activity, your students will apply the Remainder Theorem to answer specific questions about given polynomials. Unscrambling letters of the polynomials that are the answers to these questions will reveal math terms and enable students to verify their answers.

Explain that students can find the factors of a polynomial by factoring or by using the Remainder Theorem. Discuss the Remainder Theorem that is explained on the worksheet, noting that it is the more efficient way to determine if a binomial is a factor of a polynomial, especially if the polynomial is of a degree greater than 3, which is difficult to factor.

Go over the directions with your students. For the first question, they are to list the letters of the polynomials that have a factor of $x - 1$, and for the second question they are to list the letters of the polynomials that have a factor of $x + 2$. Note that some of the polynomials have factors of both $x - 1$ and $x + 2$. Unscrambling the letters they listed for each question will reveal two math terms.

(1) T, $x^2 + x - 2$; F, $2x^2 - x - 1$; R, $x^4 + x^3 - 3x^2 - x + 2$; O, $x^3 + 2x^2 - x - 2$;
C, $x^3 + 4x^2 + x - 6$; A, $x^2 - 3x + 2$ (2) T, $x^2 + x - 2$; U, $x^3 + 2x^2 + 4x + 8$; P,
$x^3 + x^2 + 3x + 10$; R, $x^4 + x^3 - 3x^2 - x + 2$; D, $x^2 - 3x - 10$; O, $x^3 + 2x^2 - x - 2$; C,
$x^3 + 4x^2 + x - 6$ (3) The math terms are "factor" and "product."

4–8: (A-APR.3) USING ZEROES TO CONSTRUCT A ROUGH GRAPH OF A POLYNOMIAL FUNCTION

For this activity, your students will construct six rough graphs by using the zeroes of polynomial functions. They will need graph paper and rulers.

Discuss the procedure for using zeroes to construct graphs of polynomial functions, which is described on the worksheet. Your students may find it helpful if you review the degree of a polynomial, which is the greatest degree of the terms of the polynomial after it has been simplified, as well as review the zeroes of a polynomial, which are the points where the graph intersects the x-axis. If necessary, also review factoring polynomials.

Explain the figures on the worksheet, noting that students should refer to these figures to select the correct shape of the graphs. Provide the following example:

Construct a rough graph of $f(x) = 3x^2 - 8x - 3$. The degree of the polynomial is degree 2 and the coefficient of x^2 is 3. The shape of the graph will resemble figure C on the worksheet. Since $3x^2 - 8x - 3 = (3x + 1)(x - 3)$, the zeroes are $-\frac{1}{3}$ and 3. The graph is shown below.

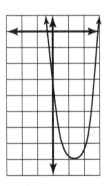

Emphasize that when students use zeroes to construct the graphs, the graphs will be rough sketches. To be accurate, the y-intercepts, maximum and minimum values, and relative maximum and relative minimum values must be determined. (Note: This standard requires only a rough sketch of the graph.)

Discuss the directions with your students. They should follow the procedure provided on the worksheet to graph each equation.

The zeroes are listed above a rough graph.

(1) −1, 0, 1

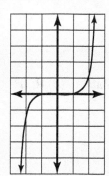

(2) 2, −2

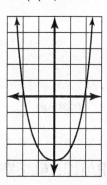

(3) −1, 1, 3

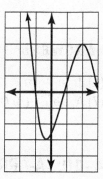

(4) −2, 0, 3

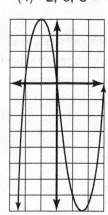

(5) −3, 1

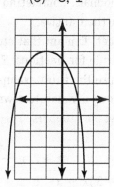

(6) −1, 0, 1

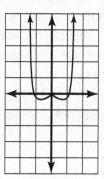

4-9: (A-APR.4) PROVING POLYNOMIAL IDENTITIES

For this activity, your students will be given proofs of four polynomial identities. Some expressions in the proofs are missing but are provided in the Answer Bank. Students are to determine the missing expressions and complete the proofs. Completing a statement at the end of the worksheet will enable students to check their answers.

Explain that polynomial identities are true for every value of the variable. To prove that an identity is true, students must show that both sides of the equation have the same value. They may show this by factoring, expanding, or simplifying expressions. Provide the following example:

$$\text{Prove } (a - b)^2 = a^2 - 2ab + b^2$$

$$(a - b)^2 = (a - b)(a - b)$$

$$(a - b)^2 = a^2 - 2ab + b^2$$

Note that the first step shows the expansion of $(a - b)^2$. The second step shows the product of $(a - b)^2$, which proves the identity.

Discuss the directions on the worksheet with your students. Note that the proofs are labeled A through D and that spaces in the proofs indicate missing expressions. The spaces are numbered 1 through 8. After finding the missing expressions, students are to complete the statement at the end.

ANSWERS

(1) J, $(a + b)$ (2) T, a^2b (3) G, $(a - b)$ (4) E, $(a^2 - 2ab + b^2)$ (5) B, $2ab^2$ (6) R, a^3
(7) A, ab^2 (8) O, $(a^2 - b^2)$ You did a "great job."

4–10: (A-APR.6) REWRITING RATIONAL EXPRESSIONS

For this activity, your students will rewrite rational expressions that are the quotient of two monomials or the quotient of two polynomials. Completing a statement at the end of the worksheet will enable students to check their answers.

Discuss the examples on the worksheet. Explain that students must factor each expression, if possible, and then use the cancellation rule for fractions. The first two examples on the worksheet can be factored and are rewritten. Because the third example, the quotient of two polynomials, cannot be factored, students must use long division to rewrite the expression. Explain that the steps are similar to long division with whole numbers.

$$x - 3 \overline{\smash{)}\, x^2 - x - 5} \quad \Big(x + 2 + \frac{1}{x - 3} \Big)$$
$$\underline{x^2 - 3x}$$
$$2x - 5$$
$$\underline{2x - 6}$$
$$1$$

Review the directions on the worksheet with your students. Note that all of the expressions can be rewritten either by factoring or using long division. Remind your students to complete the statement at the end.

ANSWERS

(1) T, $\dfrac{12}{x}$ (2) E, $x + 2$ (3) D, $x - 1 - \dfrac{9}{x - 3}$ (4) F, $\dfrac{x - 5}{x - 1}$ (5) A, $x + 2 + \dfrac{11}{x - 3}$
(6) O, $\dfrac{x - 4}{x + 4}$ (7) R, $\dfrac{25}{x}$ (8) C, $x + 2 + \dfrac{14}{x - 5}$ Some rational expressions cannot be "factored."

4-11: (A-CED.1) WRITING AND SOLVING EQUATIONS AND INEQUALITIES IN ONE VARIABLE

For this activity, your students will write equations and inequalities that they will use to solve problems. To complete the activity successfully, they must be familiar with linear, quadratic, rational, and exponential equations and inequalities.

Review that equations show that quantities on either side of the equation sign are equal. However, there are four different inequality signs that show four different relationships. Discuss the meanings of these symbols:

- $<$ means "is less than."

- $>$ means "is greater than."

- $\leq$ means "is less than or equal to."

- $\geq$ means "is greater than or equal to."

Extend these descriptions to include other meanings. For example, $\leq$ can also mean "cannot exceed," "is at most," or "is no more than," and $\geq$ can also mean "is at least" and "is no less than."

Go over the directions on the worksheet with your students. Emphasize that they are to identify the variable and write and solve an equation or inequality for each problem.

ANSWERS

Equations and inequalities may vary; possible answers follow: (1) w = the number of calories in a half cup of watermelon; $2w = 56$; $w = 28$ calories   (2) t = the number of years; $46t = 506$; $t = 11$ years   (3) m = the number of miles; $180 + 0.20m \leq 300$; $m \leq 600$
(4) d = Dad's age; $14 = \frac{1}{3}d$; $d = 42$ years   (5) A = area; $30 \times 20 > A$; $A < 600$ square feet   (6) s = score on the fourth test; $(87 + 91 + 86 + s) \div 4 \geq 90$; $s \geq 96$
(7) s = length of a side; $s^2 \leq 49$; $s \leq 7$ inches   (8) n = the number; $\frac{1}{n}$ = the reciprocal; $n + \frac{1}{n} = 2\frac{1}{2}$; $n = 2$ or $n = \frac{1}{2}$ (9) r = walking rate; $1.5r$ = jogging rate; $\frac{3}{r} + \frac{3}{1.5r} < 1$; $r > 5$ kilometers per hour   (10) x = the exponent; $64 = 2^x$; $x = 6$

4-12: (A-CED.2) WRITING AND GRAPHING EQUATIONS IN TWO VARIABLES

For this activity, your students are to write equations and graph them in the coordinate plane. Completing a statement at the end of the worksheet will enable them to verify that their equations are correct. They will need rulers and graph paper.

Discuss the procedure outlined on the worksheet, using the following example:

Suzanna purchased notebooks for $2 each and small notepads for $0.50 each. She spent a total of $12.50. Let x = the number of notebooks she purchased and y = the number of notepads she purchased.

1. Create an equation to represent the relationship between the quantities, using the variables x and y. $2x + 0.5y = 12.50$

2. Express the equation $2x + 0.5y = 12.50$ as $y = -4x + 25$. (This equation is in slope-intercept form.)

3. Label the axes and select a scale. The x-axis shows the number of notebooks she purchased, and the y-axis shows the number of notepads she purchased. An appropriate scale may be 1 unit on the x-axis represents 1 notebook, while 1 unit on the y-axis represents 5 notepads.

4. Graph the equation. Start at the y-intercept and move up or down and right or left, depending on the slope of the line, which is the coefficient of x.

Review the directions, noting that all equations in the Equation Bank are expressed as $y = mx + b$. Remind your students to complete the statement at the end.

ANSWERS

The graphs may be checked by using the y-intercept and the slope. (1) T, $y = -\frac{4}{5}x + 316$

(2) N, $y = x - 2$ (3) S, $y = -x + 40$ (4) A, $y = x - 18$ (5) E, $y = \frac{3}{5}x$

(6) G, $y = -\frac{2}{3}x + 12$ (7) C, $y = -\frac{2}{5}x + 3$ (8) I, $y = \frac{1}{10}x$ (9) L, $y = \frac{1}{3}x$ An important

step to consider when graphing equations is "selecting a scale."

4–13: (A-CED.3) REPRESENTING CONSTRAINTS AND INTERPRETING SOLUTIONS

For this activity, your students will be given four scenarios. They are to write equations, inequalities, systems of equations, and systems of inequalities, noting constraints on the variables. They will then determine if given solutions are viable or nonviable. Completing a statement at the end of the worksheet will enable them to verify their answers.

Explain that solutions to equations, inequalities, systems of equations, and systems of inequalities may not be viable options (make sense) when they are applied to some problems, even though the solutions are correct. Constraints or limits on the variable must be provided so that the solution is a viable option.

Present this scenario to your students: Jefferson High School requires that at least one chaperone accompany every group of ten students on a field trip. How many chaperones are required if 32 students go on a field trip? Ask your students to write an inequality that models this situation, identify the variable, represent constraints on the variable, and solve the inequality. Finally, they are to provide a solution that is nonviable and a solution that is viable.

The solution follows: $C \geq \frac{32}{10}$, where C stands for the number of chaperones and C is a positive integer. Although 3.2 is the solution to the inequality, $C \geq 3.2$, 3.2 is a nonviable option because there cannot be a partial chaperone. $C = 4$ is a viable option.

Review the directions on the worksheet. Note that the scenarios are labeled A through D and the numbers of the problems are labeled 1 through 9. Remind your students that they are to complete the statement at the end.

ANSWERS

Scenario A: $20A + 15S = \$1{,}500$ where A and S are whole numbers. (1) A, Yes   (2) E, No
Scenario B: $4s < 18$ where $s > 0$.   (3) E, No   (4) S, Yes   Scenario C: $2l + 2w < 24$ and $lw < 27$ where $l > 0$ and $w > 0$ in each equation.   (5) M, No   (6) N, Yes   (7) K, Yes
Scenario D) $5^x = y$ and $5x = y$. In the second equation, y is a positive integer.   (8) S, No
(9) E, Yes   The solutions "make sense."

4–14: (A-CED.4) HIGHLIGHTING QUANTITIES OF INTEREST IN FORMULAS

For this activity, your students will work with various common formulas, highlighting different quantities. Completing a statement at the end of the worksheet will enable them to check their work.

   Explain that formulas are rules expressed in algebraic form. Formulas provide a method that can be applied to solving specific problems. For example, distance traveled can be found using the formula $d = rt$, where d represents the distance, r represents the rate, and t represents the time. In solving some problems, it may be helpful to highlight a different quantity by rearranging the formula. Using the distance formula, if we knew the distance and time and wanted to find the rate, we could rearrange the formula as $r = \frac{d}{t}$ and solve for r.

   Discuss the directions on the worksheet with your students. Emphasize that they are to rearrange each formula so that a specific variable is highlighted; they are not solving problems. They should complete the statement at the end.

ANSWERS

(1) S, $A = \dfrac{F}{p}$ (2) M, $d = \dfrac{W}{F}$ (3) I, $e = \sqrt{\dfrac{S}{6}}$ (4) E, $B = \dfrac{3V}{h}$ (5) O, $l = \dfrac{S - \pi r^2}{\pi r}$ (6) V,

$T = \dfrac{D}{S}$ (7) L, $h = \dfrac{A}{b}$ (8) A, $m = \dfrac{E}{c^2}$ (9) B, $l = \dfrac{S - 2wh}{2w + 2h}$ (10) R, $r = \sqrt[3]{\dfrac{3V}{4\pi}}$ A formula is an equation that relates two "or more variables."

4–15: (A-REI.1) JUSTIFYING SOLUTIONS TO EQUATIONS

For this activity, your students will provide explanations for the steps leading to the solutions of equations. Completing a statement at the end of the worksheet will enable them to check their answers.

Explain that even the most complicated equations can be solved by following a procedure based on mathematical properties and rules. A sound understanding of these properties and rules can help students to solve equations effectively.

Discuss the directions on the worksheet with your students. The steps for solving equations are provided; students are to provide the reason for each step. Your students might find it helpful if you do the first one or two steps of the first equation as a class to demonstrate what they are to do. After providing a reason for the steps of all of the equations, they are to complete the statement at the end.

ANSWERS

(1) Add 10 to each side, M. Divide each side by 3, E.   (2) Distribute 2, T. Subtract 6 from each side, H. Divide each side by 2, O.   (3) Distribute −3, D. Subtract 12 from each side, I. Divide each side by −3, C.   (4) Distribute 3, A. Simplify the expression on the left, L. Add 6 to each side, R. Divide each side by 3, E.   (5) Distribute 3, A. Add 3x to each side, S. Divide each side by 2, O.   (6) Combine like terms, N. Subtract 12 from each side, I. Combine like terms, N. Subtract 6x from each side, G.   Solving equations is a process that requires "methodical reasoning."

4–16: (A-REI.2) SOLVING RATIONAL AND RADICAL EQUATIONS

For this activity, your students will solve rational and radical equations and also explain how extraneous solutions may occur. By answering a question at the end of the worksheet, they will be able to check their answers.

Review the difference between a rational equation and a radical equation. A rational equation is an equation in which one or more of the terms is a fraction. A radical equation contains a variable in the radicand.

Discuss the examples on the worksheet. Emphasize that for both rational and radical equations, students must substitute their solution or solutions into the original equation to see whether the solution they found is a solution to the original equation. Values that are not solutions to the original equation are extraneous solutions.

Go over the directions. Note that after answering the question at the end students are to explain how extraneous solutions may occur.

ANSWERS

(1) C, $x = -3$ (2) I, $x = 20$ (3) O, $x = 1\frac{1}{4}$ or $x = -1$ (4) H, $x = 4$ (5) A, $x = 0$ (6) N, $x = 6$ or $x = -1$ (7) L, $x = 12$ (8) Z, $x = 2$ (9) B, $x = \pm 6$ (10) R, $x = 5$ (11) T, $x = 9$ (12) F, $x = \pm 2$ Leonardo of Pisa was the first European mathematician to use a "horizontal fraction bar." Extraneous solutions may occur when you multiply both sides of a rational equation by an expression that may represent zero, or when you square both sides of a radical equation, producing an equation that is not equivalent to the original equation.

4-17: (A-REI.3) SOLVING MULTI-STEP LINEAR EQUATIONS IN ONE VARIABLE

This activity requires your students to solve linear equations involving more than one step. Some of the problems require your students to combine like terms, use the Distributive Property, and/or add or subtract variable expressions. Some problems have coefficients represented by variables. Answering a question at the end of the worksheet will enable students to check their answers.

Introduce this activity by providing the following equation as an example: $2x - 1 = -15$. Instruct your students to isolate the variable by adding 1 to each side. The result is a one-step equation that your students may then solve to find that $x = -7$. You may wish to extend this line of reasoning to combining like terms and using the Distributive Property. (The steps are provided on the worksheet.)

Present the following example of a problem that has a coefficient of x represented by a variable and discuss the steps that lead to the solution:

$$ax - 3 = 3(ax - 4)$$
$$ax - 3 = 3ax - 12$$
$$ax = 3ax - 9$$
$$-2ax = -9$$
$$x = \frac{9}{2a}, a \neq 0$$

Go over the directions on the worksheet. Remind your students that after they solve the equations, they must answer the question at the end.

ANSWERS

(T) $x = -6$ (O) $x = \frac{22}{a}$ (L) $x = \frac{75}{a}$ (H) $x = -105$ (S) $x = \frac{-5}{a}$ (G) $x = -1$
(M) $x = -16$ (A) $x = -12$ (R) $x = -7$ (I) $x = -25$ The step-by-step methods of problem solving developed by al-Khwarizmi are called "algorithms."

4-18: (A-REI.3) SOLVING MULTI-STEP LINEAR INEQUALITIES IN ONE VARIABLE

This activity requires your students to solve inequalities that have several steps. A few of the inequalities on the worksheet have coefficients represented by letters. Answering a question at the end of the worksheet will enable your students to check their answers.

Start the activity by reviewing the rules for solving inequalities as noted on the worksheet. Emphasize that if both sides of an inequality are multiplied or divided by a negative number, the direction of the inequality symbol must be changed.

Go over the directions with your students. Remind them that once they have solved the inequalities they are to answer the question at the end.

(1) S, $x < -20$ (2) T, $x > -1$ (3) M, $x > -2$ (4) I, $x \geq 1$ (5) O, $x \leq -6$ (6) A, $x < \dfrac{1}{a}$

(7) H, $x < \dfrac{7}{a}$ (8) R, all real numbers   (9) A, $x < \dfrac{1}{a}$ (10) O, $x \leq -6$ (11) T, $x > -1$

(12) H, $x < \dfrac{7}{a}$ (13) R, all real numbers   The mathematician was "Thomas Harriot."

4-19: (A-REI.4) SOLVING A QUADRATIC EQUATION BY COMPLETING THE SQUARE

This activity requires your students to complete the square in order to solve quadratic equations. To complete the activity successfully, students should be able to simplify square roots, factor trinomials, and work with polynomials. Completing a statement at the end of the worksheet will enable students to check their answers.

Discuss the example on the worksheet, making certain that your students understand the procedure for completing the square. Note that they will always add $a\left(\dfrac{b}{2a}\right)^2$ to both sides of the equation. Doing so creates a perfect square.

Go over the directions with your students. Note that the Value Bank contains the number that is added in each problem and that the Answer Bank contains the solution to each problem. Remind your students to complete the statement at the end.

ANSWERS

(1) A, 16; R, $4 \pm \sqrt{3}$ (2) E, 4; K, $2 \pm \sqrt{3}$ (3) N, $\dfrac{1}{4}$; O, $\dfrac{-1 \pm \sqrt{5}}{2}$ (4) W, 9; N, $-3 \pm 3\sqrt{2}$

(5) V, 12; A, $2 \pm \dfrac{\sqrt{21}}{3}$ (6) L, 3; U, $1 \pm \dfrac{\sqrt{39}}{3}$ (7) E, 4; S, $-2 \pm 2\sqrt{5}$ Thanks to Francois Viète (1540–1603), equations such as $ax^2 + bx + c = 0$, $a \neq 0$, can be solved by writing a formula if a, b, and c "are known values."

4-20: (A-REI.4) SOLVING QUADRATIC EQUATIONS IN A VARIETY OF WAYS

For this activity, your students will solve quadratic equations, using four different methods: inspection, completing the square, factoring, and the quadratic formula. Completing a statement at the end of the worksheet will enable students to check their work.

Discuss the examples of the four methods that students can use to solve quadratic equations on the worksheet. If necessary, provide additional examples.

Go over the directions. Students may solve the equations using the methods they prefer. They are to also complete the statement at the end.

(1) I, $x = \pm 10$ (2) T, $x = 3$ or $x = 2$ (3) U, $x = \pm i$ (4) V, $x = 2 \pm \sqrt{5}$ (5) O, $x = 3$ (6) C,

$x = -1 \pm \sqrt{13}$ (7) L, $x = \pm 5$ (8) N, $x = \dfrac{2 \pm i\sqrt{2}}{2}$ (9) E, $x = 4$ or $x = 3$ (10) S, $x = 8$ or

$x = -5$ (11) Q, $x = 0$ or $x = -1$ (12) A, $x = -\dfrac{1}{2}$ or $x = 3$ You "can solve equations."

4–21: (A-REI.5) SOLVING SYSTEMS OF EQUATIONS

For this activity, your students will solve eight systems of equations. Completing a statement at the end of the worksheet will enable them to check their answers.

Explain that one way to solve a system of equations is to replace one equation by the sum of that equation and a nonzero multiple of the other equation. This will result in an equation that has the same solutions as the original system.

Discuss the example on the worksheet, which is solved by the method described above. Note the reasons for each step.

This Standard requires a proof of why this method may be used to solve systems of equations. To prove this method, show that replacing the first equation with the sum of the first equation and a nonzero multiple of the second equation results in an equation that is equivalent to the first equation.

Write a system of two general equations as an example:

$$Ax + By = C$$

$$Dx + Ey = G$$

- Multiply the second equation by k, where $k \neq 0$, to obtain $k(Dx + Ey) = kG$. This equation is equivalent to $Dx + Ey = G$ by the Multiplication Property of Equality.

- Add this equation to the first equation to obtain $Ax + By + k(Dx + Ey) = C + kG$. This equation is equivalent to the first equation by the Addition Property of Equality.

This method could also be proven by replacing the second equation with the sum of the second equation and a nonzero multiple of the first equation to obtain an equation that is equivalent to the second equation.

Go over the directions on the worksheet with your students. Note that they should solve each system of equations using the method that was proven above. They should also complete the statement at the end.

(1) C, $x = 2$, $y = -3$ (2) W, $x = 4$, $y = 1$ (3) K, $x = 3$, $y = -1$ (4) N, $x = 1$, $y = 2$
(5) R, $x = 3$, $y = 4$ (6) I, $x = 4$, $y = 2$ (7) E, $x = -2$, $y = -3$ (8) O, $x = 2$, $y = -1$ You did "nice work."

4-22: (A-REI.6) SOLVING SYSTEMS OF LINEAR EQUATIONS

For this activity, your students will solve systems of linear equations in a variety of ways. Completing a statement at the end of the worksheet will enable them to check their answers. They will need rulers and graph paper.

Begin the activity by reviewing the methods for solving systems of linear equations, including the following:

- Emphasize that all of the methods may be used for solving any system of linear equations; however, some methods are more efficient than others for particular systems.

- Graphing is practical when the solutions are close to the origin.

- Substitution is practical if the coefficient of one variable is 1 or −1.

- Addition or subtraction is practical if the coefficients of one of the variables are the same or if the coefficients are opposite.

- Multiplication with addition or subtraction is practical if the coefficient of a variable is a factor (other than 1) of the other, or if the coefficients of a variable are relatively prime (have a greatest common factor of 1).

Discuss the directions on the worksheet with your students. They must solve each system, using whichever method they prefer, and record the value of x first. Remind them to complete the statement at the end.

ANSWERS

(1) T, (−2, 3)   (2) U, (0, 0)   (3) M, $\varnothing$ (4) L, (−2, −2)   (5) W, (6, 9)   (6) V, (−3, −3)
(7) O, (−5, 3)   (8) Y, (0.5, 0.25)   (9) E, (−2, 4)   (10) S, (2, −2)   The statement is "You solve systems well."

4-23: (A.REI.7) SOLVING A SYSTEM OF A LINEAR AND A QUADRATIC EQUATION

This activity requires your students to solve a system of a linear equation and a quadratic equation in two variables, algebraically and graphically. By answering a question at the end of the worksheet, your students will be able to verify their answers. They will need rulers and graph paper.

Explain that for this activity the systems of equations consist of a linear equation of the form $y = mx + b$ and a quadratic equation of the form $y = ax^2 + bx + c$, where $a \neq 0$. Both of these types of equations are classified as polynomial equations. A linear equation has degree 1, because the exponent of x is 1. A quadratic equation has degree 2, because 2 is the largest exponent of x. Other types of polynomial equations have different degrees.

Discuss the methods for solving systems of equations included on the worksheet. Note that the solutions are expressed as ordered pairs.

Go over the directions on the worksheet and emphasize that students must solve three systems algebraically and two graphically. They may decide which method to use on which system. Each system has two solutions. Remind your students to answer the question at the end.

4-24: (A-REI.10) RELATING GRAPHS TO THE SOLUTIONS OF EQUATIONS

For this activity, your students will be provided with tables listing some solutions to equations. They will use these points to graph the solutions and then identify other points that are also solutions. Completing a statement at the end of the worksheet will enable students to verify their answers. They will need rulers and graph paper.

Explain that the graph of an equation in two variables is the set of points that are solutions to the equation. Provide the following example:

$y = 2x + 1$ is an equation whose solutions include $(−1, −1)$, $(1, 3)$, and $(0, 1)$. There are several other solutions, such as $\left(\frac{1}{2}, 2\right)$ and $(5, 11)$. Show the graph of this equation as sketched below.

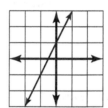

Explain that each solution of this equation lies on the graph of $y = 2x + 1$. Many other pairs of numbers, such as $(0, −1)$, $(5, 10)$, and $(−3, 9)$, are not solutions to the equation and are not on the graph.

Go over the directions on the worksheet. Students should create a separate graph for each problem, using the values in each table. They should draw 10 graphs. For each graph, they are to select another pair of values from the Answer Bank that are solutions to the equation and therefore lie on the graph. They should also complete the statement at the end.

4-25: (A-REI.11) USING GRAPHS AND TABLES TO FIND SOLUTIONS TO SYSTEMS OF EQUATIONS

This activity requires your students to use graphing calculators to graph and to create a table of values in order to find the solutions to pairs of equations. The equations include linear, rational, absolute value, exponential, and logarithmic functions. Completing a statement at the end of the worksheet will enable students to verify their answers.

Discuss the information on the worksheet, using the example that follows:

Find the point or points of $\begin{matrix} f(x) = 3x \\ g(x) = x^2 - x - 12 \end{matrix}$ by graphing each equation on a graphing calculator. Students should rewrite the equations and enter them as $y_1 = 3x$ and $y_2 = x^2 - x - 12$. Show your students how to graph these equations and how to adjust the viewing window so that the maximum value of y is at least 20. Next, demonstrate how to calculate the points of intersection. Students will find that the graphs intersect at $(-2, -6)$ and $(6, 18)$.

You may use the same example and show your students how to find the points of intersection by using the table of values. First, they should rewrite the equations and enter them as $y_1 = 3x$ and $y_2 = x^2 - x - 12$. Demonstrate how to set up and view the table of values.

Show your students how to scroll up and down. Note that when $x = -2$, both y_1 and y_2 each equal -6, and when $x = 6$, both y_1 and y_2 each equal 18. This shows that $(-2, -6)$ and $(6, 18)$ are both solutions to the equations.

Review the directions on the worksheet with your students. Emphasize that students must solve each system of equations either by graphing or creating a table of values. Some systems have two solutions. Students are to also complete the statement at the end.

ANSWERS

(1) V, $(-1, -1)$ and $(2, 2)$ (2) D, $(-1, -1)$ and $(1, 1)$ (3) E, $(-1, -1)$ and $(1, -1)$
(4) C, $(0, 1)$ (5) N, $(10, 1)$ (6) R, $(2, 8)$ (7) O, $(-0.\overline{3}, -1.\overline{3})$ (8) I, $\varnothing$
The graphs of different types of functions will "never coincide."

4-26: (A-REI.12) SOLVING SYSTEMS OF INEQUALITIES BY GRAPHING

For this activity, your students will be asked to match the solutions of systems of inequalities with a tan or combination of tans (shapes of a tangram) pictured on the worksheet. When your students find the solution of the systems of inequalities, the solution will match one of the tans or a combination of tans. To complete this activity successfully, your students should be able to graph the solution of a linear inequality and the solution of systems of equations. They will need rulers and graph paper.

Introduce the activity by providing the graph of the solution of a linear inequality, such as $x + y > 5$. First graph the line $y = -x + 5$. Then graph $y > -x + 5$ by making the line dashed or broken. Choose any point not on the line and shade that portion of the coordinate plane that makes the inequality true. Extend this concept to graphing the solution of a system of inequalities by graphing the inequalities on the same axes. The overlap of the regions is the solution to the system.

Review the directions on the worksheet with your students. Note that they must draw the graphs and then match their solutions with a tan or tans.

ANSWERS

(1) VI   (2) IV   (3) VI, VII   (4) I   (5) II   (6) VII   (7) II, III

Reproducibles for Section 4 follow.

4–1: INTERPRETING EXPRESSIONS

Understanding the following is necessary for interpreting expressions.

- An expression is a variable or a combination of numbers, symbols, and/or variables. Examples include $4x$, x, $a + b$, ab, $4(2a + b)$, and $\frac{x}{4}$.

- A term is an expression using numbers or variables, or both numbers and variables, to indicate a product or quotient. Examples include $4x$, x, ab, and $\frac{x}{4}$.

- A factor is two or more numbers to be multiplied. Each number is a factor of the product. For example, a and b are factors of ab.

- A coefficient is a number multiplied by a variable. For example, 7 is the coefficient of $7ab$.

Directions: Do the following.

1. Write the three terms of $a + b + c$.

2. Use every term in problem 1 to create a product.

3. Multiply the product in problem 2 by −8.

4. Add $4d$ to the product found in problem 3.

5. Use the Distributive Property to show how to double the sum you found in problem 4.

6. Write two factors of the expression you found in problem 5.

7. Write the term that has the most factors in problem 6.

8. What is the coefficient of the term you wrote in problem 7?

Name _____ Date _____ Period _____

4–2 USING THE STRUCTURE OF AN EXPRESSION TO IDENTIFY WAYS TO REWRITE IT

An expression may be written in equivalent forms, for example, as sums, differences, and products. Following are some equations and properties you may use to rewrite expressions:

- Difference of squares: $a^2 - b^2 = (a + b)(a - b)$.
- Sum of cubes: $a^3 + b^3 = (a + b)(a^2 - ab + b^2)$.
- Difference of cubes: $a^3 - b^3 = (a - b)(a^2 + ab + b^2)$.
- Distributive Property: $ab + ac = a(b + c)$.
- Power of a Product Property: $(ab)^x = a^x b^x$.

Directions: Rewrite each of the following expressions as indicated. Find the answers in the Answer Bank. Some answers will be used more than once, and one answer will not be used. Then complete the statement at the end by writing the letters of your answers, starting with the first problem. If necessary, unscramble the letters to form five words.

1. Rewrite $x^4 - 16$ as the product of three polynomials.

2. Rewrite $7x^2$ as the product of a number and a term.

3. Rewrite 10 as the sum of two squares.

4. Rewrite 3 as the difference of two squares.

5. Rewrite $x^2 - 16$ as the product of two polynomials.

6. Rewrite $x^3 - 1$ as the product of two polynomials.

7. Rewrite $(4x)^2$ as the product of a number and a term.

8. Rewrite $x^2 - 1$ as the product of two polynomials.

9. Rewrite $(2x)^2$ as the product of a number and a term.

10. Rewrite $4x + 4$ as the product of a number and a polynomial.

Answer Bank

C. $x + 2$	H. 7	O. $x - 4$	L. $1 + 9$	T. 4
R. $x - 1$	U. $x^2 + x + 1$	W. 16	N. $x^2 + 4$	Y. $x + 4$
I. $x + 1$	S. $5 + 5$	A. $x - 2$	E. x^2	P. $4 - 1$

Seeing the structure of an expression _____.

Name _____ Date _____ Period _____

4–3: FACTORING QUADRATIC EXPRESSIONS TO REVEAL ZEROES

You can find the zeroes of a quadratic expression by factoring. If the product of two factors is equal to 0, then one or both factors must equal 0. Write an equation stating that one or both factors is equal to zero and then solve for x. The values of x are the zeroes of the function. For example:

$$x^2 - 2x - 15 = 0$$

$$(x - 5)(x + 3) = 0$$

$$(x - 5) = 0 \text{ or } (x + 3) = 0$$

$$x = 5 \text{ or } x = -3$$

The zeroes are 5 and -3.

Directions: Solve each equation and find your answers in the Answer Bank. Write the letters of the answers in the spaces after the values of x for each problem. Some of the answers will be used more than once, and one answer will not be used. When you are done, write the letters, starting with the first problem, to complete the statement at the end. You may have to reverse the order of some letters in each problem. You will need to divide the letters into words.

1. $x^2 - 10x = 0$ The zeroes are $x =$ _____ and $x =$ _____. _____ _____

2. $x^2 + 8x + 15 = 0$ The zeroes are $x =$ _____ and $x =$ _____. _____ _____

3. $x^2 + 3x - 10 = 0$ The zeroes are $x =$ _____ and $x =$ _____. _____ _____

4. $2x^2 - 7x + 3 = 0$ The zeroes are $x =$ _____ and $x =$ _____. _____ _____

5. $2x^2 - 3x - 2 = 0$ The zeroes are $x =$ _____ and $x =$ _____. _____ _____

6. $2x^2 - 5x = 0$ The zeroes are $x =$ _____ and $x =$ _____. _____ _____

7. $x^2 + 6x + 5 = 0$ The zeroes are $x =$ _____ and $x =$ _____. _____ _____

8. $x^2 + x - 6 = 0$ The zeroes are $x =$ _____ and $x =$ _____. _____ _____

9. $2x^2 - 13x + 20 = 0$ The zeroes are $x =$ _____ and $x =$ _____. _____ _____

10. $4x^2 - 5x - 6 = 0$ The zeroes are $x =$ _____ and $x =$ _____. _____ _____

11. $2x^2 + 5x + 2 = 0$ The zeroes are $x =$ _____ and $x =$ _____. _____ _____

12. $x^2 - x - 2 = 0$ The zeroes are $x =$ _____ and $x =$ _____. _____ _____

(Continued)

Copyright © 2016 by Judith A. Muschla, Gary Robert Muschla, and Erin Muschla-Berry.

Answer Bank

E. 2	P. $\frac{1}{2}$	L. −2	T. −5	I. −$\frac{1}{2}$	F. 10	R. −10
M. −$\frac{3}{4}$	A. 4	S. $2\frac{1}{2}$	H. −3	N. −1	O. 0	Y. 3

Although René Descartes first used raised numbers for powers in 1637, he continued to write x^2 as xx, because xx uses the same amount of space as x^2 yet all

_____.

— — — — — — — — — — — —

— — — — — — — — — — — —

Copyright © 2016 by Judith A. Muschla, Gary Robert Muschla, and Erin Muschla-Berry.

Name _____ Date _____ Period _____

4–4: COMPLETING THE SQUARE TO REVEAL MAXIMUM OR MINIMUM VALUES

The graph of a quadratic equation in the form of $y - k = a(x - h)^2$ is a parabola with the vertex (h, k). If $a > 0$, the parabola opens upward, and the vertex is the minimum value. If $a < 0$, the parabola opens downward, and the vertex is the maximum value.

The most common form of a quadratic equation is $y = ax^2 + bx + c$, $a \neq 0$. You can rewrite this as $y - k = a(x - h)^2$ by completing the square. Following is an example for completing the square to find the maximum or minimum value of $y = 2x^2 + 18x + 5$.

$y = 2x^2 + 18x + 5$	$a = 2, b = 18, c = 5$
$y - 5 = 2x^2 + 18x$	Addition or Subtraction Property of Equality
$y - 5 = 2(x^2 + 9x)$	Factor the coefficient of x^2.
$y - 5 + \frac{81}{2} = 2\left(x^2 + 9x + \frac{81}{4}\right)$	Add $a\left(\frac{b}{2a}\right)^2$ to both sides.
$y + \frac{71}{2} = 2\left(x^2 + 9x + \frac{81}{4}\right)$	Simplify.
$y + \frac{71}{2} = 2\left(x + \frac{9}{2}\right)^2$	Express the trinomial as a perfect square.

The vertex is $\left(-\frac{9}{2}, -\frac{71}{2}\right)$. Because $a > 0$, the parabola opens upward and the vertex is the minimum value.

Directions: Rewrite the quadratic equations by completing the square. Find the equivalent equations or the maximum or minimum values in the Answer Bank. One answer will not be used. Complete the statement at the end by writing the letter of each answer in the space above its problem number. You will need to divide the letters into words.

1. $y = x^2 + 6x + 10$ 2. $y = x^2 + 4x + 5$

3. $y = -x^2 + 4x + 5$ 4. $y = 3x^2 + 12x - 1$

5. $y = -2x^2 - 10x - 1$ 6. $y = 3x^2 + 2x + 1$

7. $y = x^2 + \frac{1}{2}x - 4$ 8. $y = 2x^2 - 4x - 5$

(Continued)

Answer Bank

A. $y + 7 = 2(x - 1)^2$

T. $y - 1 = (x + 2)^2$

S. $y + 4\frac{1}{16} = \left(x + \frac{1}{4}\right)^2$

E. $y - 11.5 = -2(x + 2.5)^2$

I. minimum value, $(-3, 1)$

C. minimum value, $(-2, -13)$

N. minimum value, $\left(-\frac{1}{3}, \frac{2}{3}\right)$

U. maximum value, $(3, -2)$

O. maximum value, $(2, 9)$

A parabola is _____.

$\overline{8}$ $\overline{4}$ $\overline{3}$ $\overline{6}$ $\overline{1}$ $\overline{4}$ $\overline{7}$ $\overline{5}$ $\overline{4}$ $\overline{2}$ $\overline{1}$ $\overline{3}$ $\overline{6}$

Copyright © 2016 by Judith A. Muschla, Gary Robert Muschla, and Erin Muschla-Berry.

Name _____ Date _____ Period _____

4–5: FINDING SUMS OF FINITE GEOMETRIC SERIES

A geometric sequence can be expressed as a_1, a_1r, a_1r^2, ... where $r \neq 1$. Each term is found by multiplying the preceding term by a common ratio, r. To find the value of r, divide any term by the term preceding it. For example, 10, 30, 90, 270, ... is a geometric sequence. The first term, a_1, is 10 and the common ratio, r, is 3. (The common ratio can be found by dividing 30 by 10 or by dividing 90 by 30 and so on.)

A geometric series can be expressed as $S_n = a_1 + a_1r + a_1r^2 + ... + a_1r^{n-1}$. The sum of the terms can be found by using the formula $S_n = \frac{a_1(1-r^n)}{1-r}$, $r \neq 0$, where n stands for the number of terms to be added, a_1 stands for the first term in the series, and r stands for the common ratio. For example, $10 + 30 + 90 + 270 + ...$ is a geometric series. To find the sum of the first seven terms, use the formula $S_n = \frac{a_1(1-r^n)}{1-r}$, substituting 7 for n, 10 for a_1, and 3 for r. $S_7 = \frac{10(1-3^7)}{1-3} = 10,930$.

Directions:

Part One: Fill in the blanks to derive the formula for finding the sum of a finite geometric series, $S_n = \frac{a_1(1-r^n)}{1-r}$. The first two steps are completed for you. Assume $r \neq 1$.

1. Write the general geometric series: $S_n = a_1 + a_1r + a_1r^2 + ... + a_1r^{n-1}$

2. Multiply by r: $rS_n = a_1r + a_1r^2 + a_1r^3 + ... + a_1r^{n-1} + a_1r^n$

3. Subtract rS_n from S_n: $S_n - rS_n =$ _____

4. Factor both sides: _____ = _____

5. Solve for S_n: _____ = _____

Part Two: Use the formula $S_n = \frac{a_1(1-r^n)}{1-r}$ to find the indicated sum of each geometric series. Write the letter of the problem in the space above its sum to complete the statement at the end. You will need to divide the letters into words.

O. $3 + 9 + 27 + 81 + ...$ Find S_{10}.
H. $50 + 25 + 12.5 + 6.25 + ...$ Find S_5.
R. $0.5 + 1.5 + 4.5 + 13.5 + ...$ Find S_{12}.
F. $\frac{1}{8} + \frac{1}{4} + \frac{1}{2} + 1 + ...$ Find S_{15}.
E. $-2 + 4 - 8 + 16 - ...$ Find S_8.

S. $-1 - 2 - 4 - 8 - ...$ Find S_5.
P. $-10 - 20 - 40 - 80 - ...$ Find S_8.
T. $-5 - 30 - 180 - 1,080 - ...$ Find S_5.
W. $-\frac{1}{16} + \frac{1}{8} - \frac{1}{4} + \frac{1}{2} - ...$ Find S_5.

_____ are a geometric sequence.

$\overline{-7,775}$ $\overline{96.875}$ $\overline{170}$ $\overline{-2,550}$ $\overline{88,572}$ $\overline{-0.6875}$ $\overline{170}$ $\overline{132,860}$ $\overline{-31}$

$\overline{88,572}$ $\overline{4,095\frac{7}{8}}$ $\overline{-7,775}$ $\overline{-0.6875}$ $\overline{88,572}$

Name_____ Date_____ Period_____

4–6: ADDING, SUBTRACTING, AND MULTIPLYING POLYNOMIALS

Polynomials may be added, subtracted, and multiplied according to the following procedures:

- To add polynomials, simplify by adding similar terms. $(3x + 7) + (5x - 2) = 8x + 5$

- To subtract polynomials, add the opposite of each term. Then simplify by adding similar terms. $(3x + 7) - (5x + 2) = (3x + 7) + (-5x - 2) = -2x + 5$

- To multiply two polynomials, use the Distributive Property twice. Then combine similar terms. $(2x + 3)(8x^2 + x + 4) = 2x(8x^2 + x + 4) + 3(8x^2 + x + 4) = 16x^3 + 26x^2 + 11x + 12$

Directions. Add the first polynomial and write the sum in the space after problem 1. Write this sum to start problem 2 and multiply the sum by $(2x - 1)$. Find the product and continue this process to complete the remaining problems. Refer back to problem 1 and explain why the answer to problem 9 looks familiar.

1. $(3x + 2) + (5x - 1) =$ _____

2. _____ $\times (2x - 1) =$ _____

3. _____ $- (14x^2 - 2x + 5) =$ _____

4. _____ $- (x^2 - 4x + 3) =$ _____

5. _____ $\times (x - 3) =$ _____

6. _____ $+ (-x^3 + 4x^2 + 9x - 25) =$ _____

7. _____ $\times (x^2 + 3x + 4) =$ _____

8. _____ $+ (-x^4 - 3x^3 - 7x^2 + 4) =$ _____

9. _____ $+ (x^2 - 3x - 10) =$ _____

4–7: APPLYING THE REMAINDER THEOREM

The Remainder Theorem states that if $x - a$ is a factor of polynomial $p(x)$, then $p(a) = 0$, and if $p(a) = 0$, then $x - a$ is a factor of $p(x)$.

Following are two examples:

- To find if $x - 5$ is a factor of $x^2 - 9x + 20$, find $p(5)$. $p(5) = 5^2 - 9 \cdot 5 + 20 = 0$, therefore $x - 5$ is a factor of $x^2 - 9x + 20$.

- To find if $x + 4$ is a factor of $x^2 - 9x + 20$, find $p(-4)$. $p(-4) = (-4)^2 - 9(-4) + 20 \neq 0$, therefore $x + 4$ is not a factor of $x^2 - 9x + 20$.

Directions: Use the Remainder Theorem to answer the questions.

1. Which polynomials below have a factor of $x - 1$?

2. Which polynomials below have a factor of $x + 2$?

3. Unscramble the letters of the polynomials you found for question 1. Then unscramble the letters of the polynomials you found for question 2. Which two mathematical terms are revealed?

T. $x^2 + x - 2$	U. $x^3 + 2x^2 + 4x + 8$	F. $2x^2 - x - 1$
P. $x^3 + x^2 + 3x + 10$	R. $x^4 + x^3 - 3x^2 - x + 2$	D. $x^2 - 3x - 10$
O. $x^3 + 2x^2 - x - 2$	C. $x^3 + 4x^2 + x - 6$	A. $x^2 - 3x + 2$

Name _____ Date _____ Period _____

4–8: USING ZEROES TO CONSTRUCT A ROUGH GRAPH OF A POLYNOMIAL FUNCTION

To use zeroes to construct a rough graph of a polynomial function, follow these steps:

1. Find the degree of the polynomial.

2. Identify the coefficient of the variable that has the highest degree.

3. Determine the shape of the graph by considering the information below.

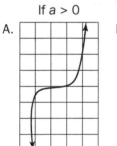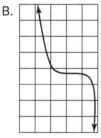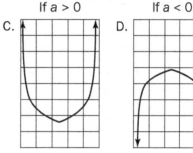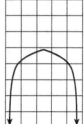

$f(x) = ax^n$ when n is odd $f(x) = ax^n$ when n is even

If $a > 0$ If $a < 0$ If $a > 0$ If $a < 0$

A.   B.   C.   D.

4. Factor the polynomial.

5. Find the zeroes.

6. Draw a coordinate plane and graph the zeroes on the x-axis.

7. Sketch the graph using the information on this worksheet as a guide.

Directions: Use zeroes to construct a rough graph of each polynomial function.

1. $f(x) = x^5 - x^3$ 2. $g(x) = x^2 - 4$ 3. $h(x) = -x^3 + 3x^2 + x - 3$

4. $F(x) = x^3 - x^2 - 6x$ 5. $G(x) = -x^2 - 2x + 3$ 6. $H(x) = x^4 - x^2$

Name _____ Date _____ Period _____

4–9: PROVING POLYNOMIAL IDENTITIES

A polynomial equation is an equation whose sides are both polynomials. A polynomial identity is a polynomial equation that is true for all values of a variable. To prove that an identity is true for all values of the variables, write equivalent equations by expanding, factoring, or simplifying expressions.

   Directions: Some expressions are missing from the proofs of four polynomial identities below. The missing expressions are indicated by the spaces in the proofs and are numbered 1 through 8. Find the missing expressions in the Answer Bank. Some expressions will not be used. Then complete the statement at the end by writing the letter of each answer in the space above its number. You will need to reverse the order of the letters and divide them into words.

A. Prove $(a + b)^3 = a^3 + 3a^2b + 3ab^2 + b^3$

$(a + b)^3 = (a + b)(a + b)(a + b)$

$(a + b)^3 = (a^2 + 2ab + b^2)$ ___1___

$(a + b)^3 = a^3 +$ ___2___ $+ 2a^2b + 2ab^2 + ab^2 + b^3$

$(a + b)^3 = a^3 + 3a^2b + 3ab^2 + b^3$

B. Prove $(a - b)^3 = a^3 - 3a^2b + 3ab^2 - b^3$

$(a - b)^3 = (a - b)(a - b)$ ___3___

$(a - b)^3 =$ ___4___ $(a - b)$

$(a - b)^3 = a^3 - a^2b - 2a^2b +$ ___5___ $+ ab^2 - b^3$

$(a - b)^3 = a^3 - 3a^2b + 3ab^2 - b^3$

C. Prove $(a + b)(a^2 - ab + b^2) = a^3 + b^3$

$(a + b)(a^2 - ab + b^2) =$ ___6___ $- a^2b +$ ___7___ $+ a^2b - ab^2 + b^3$

$(a + b)(a^2 - ab + b^2) = a^3 + b^3$

D. Prove $(a - b)(a + b)(a^2 + b^2) = a^4 - b^4$

$(a - b)(a + b)(a^2 + b^2) =$ ___8___ $(a^2 + b^2)$

$(a - b)(a + b)(a^2 + b^2) = a^4 - b^4$

Answer Bank

O. $(a^2 - b^2)$	R. a^3	S. $a^2 + b^2$	J. $(a + b)$	N. $(a^3 + b^2)$
E. $(a^2 - 2ab + b^2)$	T. a^2b	G. $(a - b)$	A. ab^2	B. $2ab^2$

You did a _____ .

$\overline{5}$ $\overline{8}$ $\overline{1}$ $\overline{2}$ $\overline{7}$ $\overline{4}$ $\overline{6}$ $\overline{3}$

Name_____ Date_____ Period_____

4-10: REWRITING RATIONAL EXPRESSIONS

A rational expression is another name for a fraction. To rewrite a quotient of monomials or polynomials, factor the numerator and/or denominator and apply the cancellation rule for fractions.

If k, x, and y are real numbers, $k \neq 0$ and $y \neq 0$, then $\frac{kx}{ky} = \frac{x}{y}$.

If the cancellation rule for fractions cannot be applied to the quotient of polynomials, divide using the same process as dividing whole numbers: divide, multiply, subtract, compare the difference with the divisor, and bring down the next digit or term.

Following are examples of rational expressions that are rewritten. Assume that the denominators do not equal zero.

- $\frac{3x^2}{6x} = \frac{3 \cdot x \cdot x}{3 \cdot 2 \cdot x} = \frac{x}{2}$
- $\frac{x^2+4x-5}{x^2+3x-4} = \frac{(x+5)(x-1)}{(x+4)(x-1)} = \frac{x+5}{x+4}$
- $\frac{x^2-x-5}{x-3} = x + 2 + \frac{1}{x-3}$

Directions: Rewrite the expressions and find your answers in the Answer Bank. Some answers will not be used. Complete the statement at the end of the worksheet by writing the letter of each answer in the space above its problem number. Assume that the denominators do not equal zero.

1. $\frac{12x}{x^2}$ 2. $\frac{x^2-4}{x-2}$ 3. $\frac{x^2-4x-6}{x-3}$ 4. $\frac{x^2-3x-10}{x^2+x-2}$

5. $\frac{x^2-x+5}{x-3}$ 6. $\frac{x^2-6x+8}{x^2+2x-8}$ 7. $\frac{25x^2}{x^3}$ 8. $\frac{x^2-3x+4}{x-5}$

Answer Bank

F. $\frac{x-5}{x-1}$ N. $\frac{x}{12}$ A. $x + 2 + \frac{11}{x-3}$ D. $x - 1 - \frac{9}{x-3}$

O. $\frac{x-4}{x+4}$ E. $x + 2$ S. $\frac{4-x}{3+x}$ C. $x + 2 + \frac{14}{x-5}$

U. $x - 4$ R. $\frac{25}{x}$ T. $\frac{12}{x}$ I. $x - 1 + \frac{3}{x}$

Some rational expressions cannot be_____.

$\overline{4}$　$\overline{5}$　$\overline{8}$　$\overline{1}$　$\overline{6}$　$\overline{7}$　$\overline{2}$　$\overline{3}$

Name _____ Date _____ Period _____

4–11: WRITING AND SOLVING EQUATIONS AND INEQUALITIES IN ONE VARIABLE

Various relationships can be described in terms of equations and inequalities.

Directions: Identify the variable and write and solve an equation or inequality for each problem.

1. A half cup of grapes contains 56 calories. This is twice the number of calories in a half cup of watermelon. How many calories are in a half cup of watermelon?

2. By installing two storm doors that cost a total of $506, the Smiths estimate that they will save $46 per year on heating bills. In how many years will the savings equal the cost of the doors?

3. A local car rental agency charges $180 per week plus $0.20 per mile. How far can a person drive in a week if the weekly charge is at most $300?

4. Sue is 14 years old, which is $\frac{1}{3}$ of her dad's age. How old is her dad?

5. The Simons are planning to build a deck running 30 feet along the side of their house. The width must be less than 20 feet. What is the area of the largest deck they can build?

6. Aly needs a test average of at least 90 to get an "A" this marking period in math. Her three test scores are 87, 91, and 86. What score must she get on her fourth test to receive at least a 90 test average for the marking period?

7. The area of a square cannot exceed 49 square inches. What is the length of a side?

8. The sum of a number and its reciprocal is $2\frac{1}{2}$. What is the number?

9. Angelo lives near a jogging trail that is 3 kilometers long. He can jog 1.5 times as fast as he can walk. He began working out by walking the entire trail and then jogging the entire trail. He covered a total of 6 kilometers. His workout took less than 1 hour. How fast did he walk? (Hint: Use the distance formula, $d = rt$, expressed as $\frac{d}{r} = t$ to find his walking time.)

10. 64 is the number of squares on a checkerboard and can be represented as 2^x. Find the value of x.

Name _____ Date _____ Period _____

4–12: WRITING AND GRAPHING EQUATIONS IN TWO VARIABLES

Writing an equation requires you to translate a word sentence into a mathematical statement about the relationship between two quantities. After you write an equation, you can graph it in the coordinate plane. Follow these steps:

1. Create an equation using the variables to show how the quantities are related.

2. Express the equation as $y = mx + b$.

3. Label the axes and select a scale.

4. Graph the equation.

Directions: Write an equation for each situation described below, using the variables that are given. Find each equation, expressed as $y = mx + b$, in the Answer Bank. Some answers will not be used. Then complete the statement at the end by writing the letter of each equation in the space above its problem number. You will need to divide the letters into words. Finally, graph each equation.

1. Movie tickets at a local theater cost $10 for adults and $8 for students. Ticket sales for a matinee totaled $3,160. Let x = the number of student tickets that were sold and y = the number of adult tickets that were sold.

2. The difference of two numbers is 2. Let x = the larger number and y = the smaller number.

3. A 40-foot rope is cut into 2 pieces. Let x = the length of one piece and y = the length of the other piece.

4. One integer is 18 more than another integer. Let x = the larger integer and y = the smaller integer.

5. The ratio of boys to girls at a school dance was 3:5. Let x = the number of girls and y = the number of boys.

6. A chemistry lab can be used by 36 students. The lab has workstations, some set up for two students and the others set up for three students. Let x = the number of workstations set up for two students and y = the number of workstations set up for three students.

7. The cost of five hamburgers and two sodas is $15. Let x = the cost of the sodas and y = the cost of the hamburgers.

8. There is one chaperone for each group of 10 students. Let x = the number of students and y = the number of chaperones.

(Continued)

9. In Nan's garden, there are three times as many red roses as there are white roses. Let $x =$ the number of red roses and $y =$ the number of white roses.

Answer Bank

G. $y = -\frac{2}{3}x + 12$	R. $y = x + 2$	T. $y = -\frac{4}{5} + 316$	I. $y = \frac{1}{10}x$
S. $y = -x + 40$	E. $y = \frac{3}{5}x$	P. $y = \frac{10}{x}$	N. $y = x - 2$
C. $y = -\frac{2}{5}x + 3$	J. $y = -x - 185$	L. $y = \frac{1}{3}x$	A. $y = x - 18$

An important step to consider when graphing equations is _____.

$\overline{3}$ $\overline{5}$ $\overline{9}$ $\overline{5}$ $\overline{7}$ $\overline{1}$ $\overline{8}$ $\overline{2}$ $\overline{6}$ $\overline{4}$ $\overline{3}$ $\overline{7}$ $\overline{4}$ $\overline{9}$ $\overline{5}$

Copyright © 2016 by Judith A. Muschla, Gary Robert Muschla, and Erin Muschla-Berry.

Name _____ Date _____ Period _____

4–13: REPRESENTING CONSTRAINTS AND INTERPRETING SOLUTIONS

When solving some word problems, even though the solution is correct, the solution may not make sense given the context of the problem. Constraints or limits on the variable must be provided so that the solution is a viable option.

Directions: Read each scenario and solve each problem. Write equations, inequalities, systems of equations, and systems of inequalities, noting constraints on the variables. Then answer each question *Yes* or *No*. Complete the statement at the end by unscrambling the letters of your answers.

A. The Student Council collected $1,500 for a school concert. Adult tickets sold for $20 each, and student tickets sold for $15 each. Let A = the number of adult tickets that were sold, and let S = the number of student tickets that were sold. Find the number of adult tickets and the number of students tickets that may have been sold.

1. Is $A = 48$ and $S = 36$ a viable option?   (A. Yes   R. No)
2. Is $A = 52.5$ and $S = 30$ a viable option?   (C. Yes   E. No)

B. The perimeter of a square is less than 18 inches. What is the length of a side? Let s = the length of a side.

3. Is $s = 4.5$ a viable option?   (T. Yes   E. No)
4. Is $s = 3.5$ a viable option?   (S. Yes   F. No)

C. The perimeter of a rectangle is less than 24 inches, and the area is less than 27 square inches. Find the length and width of the rectangle. Let l = the length and w = the width.

5. Is $w = 3$ inches and $l = 9$ inches a viable option?   (P. Yes   M. No)
6. Is $w = 2.5$ inches and $l = 9$ inches a viable option?   (N. Yes   H. No)
7. Is $w = 2$ inches and $l = 2$ inches a viable option?   (K. Yes   R. No)

D. 5^x generates powers of 5. $5x$ may generate multiplies of 5. For one value of x, a power of 5 equals a multiple of five. Find the value of x. Let x = the missing value and y = the power of 5 and the multiple of 5.

8. Is $x = -1$ a viable option?   (H. Yes   S. No)
9. Is $x = 1$ a viable option?   (E. Yes   I. No)

The solutions _____.

4–14: HIGHLIGHTING QUANTITIES OF INTEREST IN FORMULAS

Formulas are useful to many applications in mathematics and science. When applying a formula, it is sometimes helpful to rearrange the formula to express a variable in terms of other variables.

Directions: Rearrange each formula to highlight the required variable. Choose your answers from the choices that are provided. Then complete the statement at the end by writing the letter of each answer in the space above its problem number. You will need to divide the letters into words.

1. Pressure: $P = \frac{F}{A}$; solve for A. $\left(\text{S. } A = \frac{F}{P} \quad \text{N. } A = FP \right)$

2. Work: $W = Fd$; solve for d. $\left(\text{R. } d = \frac{F}{W} \quad \text{M. } d = \frac{W}{F} \right)$

3. Surface area of a cube: $S = 6e^2$; solve for e. $\left(\text{A. } e = \frac{S^2}{6^2} \quad \text{I. } e = \sqrt{\frac{S}{6}} \right)$

4. Volume of a pyramid: $V = \frac{Bh}{3}$; solve for B. $\left(\text{U. } B = \frac{Vh}{3} \quad \text{E. } B = \frac{3V}{h} \right)$

5. Surface area of a right cone: $S = \pi r^2 + \pi r l$; solve for l.
$\left(\text{O. } l = \frac{S - \pi r^2}{\pi r} \quad \text{K. } l = \frac{S - \pi}{\pi r} \right)$

6. Speed: $S = \frac{D}{T}$; solve for T. $\left(\text{V. } T = \frac{D}{S} \quad \text{N. } T = SD \right)$

7. Area of a parallelogram: $A = bh$; solve for h. $\left(\text{L. } h = \frac{A}{b} \quad \text{I. } h = \frac{b}{a} \right)$

8. Energy: $E = mc^2$; solve for m. $\left(\text{O. } m = \sqrt{\frac{E}{c^2}} \quad \text{A. } m = \frac{E}{c^2} \right)$

9. Surface area of a rectangular prism: $S = 2lw + 2lh + 2wh$; solve for l.
$\left(\text{M. } l = \frac{S + 2wh}{2w + 2h} \quad \text{B. } l = \frac{S - 2wh}{2w + 2h} \right)$

10. Volume of a sphere: $V = \frac{4\pi r^3}{3}$; solve for r. $\left(\text{R. } r = \sqrt[3]{\frac{3V}{4\pi}} \quad \text{E. } r = \frac{\sqrt{3V}}{4\pi r^3} \right)$

A formula is an equation that relates two _____.

$\overline{5} \quad \overline{10} \quad \overline{2} \quad \overline{5} \quad \overline{10} \quad \overline{4} \quad \overline{6} \quad \overline{8} \quad \overline{10} \quad \overline{3} \quad \overline{8} \quad \overline{9} \quad \overline{7} \quad \overline{4} \quad \overline{1}$

Copyright © 2016 by Judith A. Muschla, Gary Robert Muschla, and Erin Muschla-Berry.

Copyright © 2016 by Judith A. Muschla, Gary Robert Muschla, and Erin Muschla-Berry.

4-15: JUSTIFYING SOLUTIONS TO EQUATIONS

Understanding the steps necessary for solving equations is an important mathematical skill.

Directions: Six equations are solved below. Provide the reason for each step. Reasons are listed in the Answer Bank. Some reasons will be used more than once and one reason will not be used. Then complete the statement at the end by writing the letters of your answers in order, starting with the first reason of equation 1.

1. $3x - 10 = 14$
   $3x = 24$ Reason: _____
   $x = 8$ Reason: _____

2. $2(x + 3) = -2$
   $2x + 6 = -2$ Reason: _____
   $2x = -8$ Reason: _____
   $x = -4$ Reason: _____

3. $-3(x - 4) = 0$
   $-3x + 12 = 0$ Reason: _____
   $-3x = -12$ Reason: _____
   $x = 4$ Reason: _____

4. $3(x - 4) + 6 = 0$
   $3x - 12 + 6 = 0$ Reason: _____
   $3x - 6 = 0$ Reason: _____
   $3x = 6$ Reason: _____
   $x = 2$ Reason: _____

5. $-x = 3(-x - 2)$
   $-x = -3x - 6$ Reason: _____
   $2x = -6$ Reason: _____
   $x = -3$ Reason: _____

6. $3x + 4x + 12 = 3x + 3x$
   $7x + 12 = 3x + 3x$ Reason: _____
   $7x = 3x + 3x - 12$ Reason: _____
   $7x = 6x - 12$ Reason: _____
   $x = -12$ Reason: _____

(Continued)

Divide each side by 2, O.	Add 6 to each side, R.	Add 3x to each side, S.
Divide each side by 3, E.	Distribute 2, T.	Subtract 6 from each side, H.
Add 10 to each side, M.	Distribute −3, D.	Divide each side by −3, C.
Subtract 12 from each side, I.	Distribute 3, A.	Subtract 6x from each side, G.
Distribute −2, U.	Combine like terms, N.	Simplify the expression on the left, L.

Solving equations is a process that requires _____.

Name _____ Date _____ Period _____

4-16: SOLVING RATIONAL AND RADICAL EQUATIONS

To solve a rational equation, cross-multiply or multiply by the least common denominator (LCD). To solve a radical equation, isolate the term that contains the radical on one side of the equation and square both sides. Then solve for the variable. Following are examples:

Rational Equation

$$\frac{1+x}{8x} = \frac{1}{x}$$
$$x + x^2 = 8x$$
$$x^2 - 7x = 0$$
$$x(x - 7) = 0$$
$$x = 0 \text{ or } x = 7$$

$x = 0$ is an extraneous solution.
$x = 7$ is the only solution.

Radical Equation

$$\sqrt{5x^2 - 16} - x = 0$$
$$\sqrt{5x^2 - 16} = x$$
$$5x^2 - 16 = x^2$$
$$4x^2 = 16$$
$$x^2 = 4$$
$$x = \pm 2$$

$x = -2$ is an extraneous solution.
$x = 2$ is the only solution.

All solutions should be checked to see if extraneous solutions have been found.

Directions. Solve each equation and find your answers in the Answer Bank. One answer will not be used. Answer the question at the end by writing the letter of each answer in the space above its problem number. You will need to divide the letters into words. Then explain how extraneous solutions may occur.

1. $\sqrt{x + 4} = 1$

2. $\sqrt{5x} + 2 = 12$

3. $2x = \frac{x+5}{2x}$

4. $\frac{x+2}{x-1} = \frac{x}{x-2}$

5. $\sqrt{x^2} = 3x$

6. $\frac{x-5}{2} = \frac{3}{x}$

7. $\frac{3x+5}{6} - \frac{10}{x} = \frac{x}{2}$

8. $\sqrt{x - 2} + 1 = 1$

9. $\frac{9}{x} = \frac{x}{4}$

10. $\sqrt{2x^2 - 25} = x$

11. $\frac{6-x}{4-x} = \frac{3}{5}$

12. $\sqrt{x^2 - 3} = 1$

Answer Bank

A. $x = 0$	C. $x = -3$	F. $x = \pm 2$	R. $x = 5$
I. $x = 20$	L. $x = 12$	N. $x = 6$ or $x = -1$	T. $x = 9$
O. $x = 1\frac{1}{4}$ or $x = -1$	H. $x = 4$	B. $x = \pm 6$	Z. $x = 2$

Leonardo of Pisa was the first European to use this. What was it?

$\overline{}$ $\overline{}$ $\overline{}$ $\overline{}$ $\overline{}$ $\overline{}$ $\overline{}$ $\overline{}$ $\overline{}$ $\overline{}$ $\overline{}$
5   4   3   10   2   8   3   6   11   5   7

$\overline{}$ $\overline{}$ $\overline{}$ $\overline{}$ $\overline{}$ $\overline{}$ $\overline{}$ $\overline{}$ $\overline{}$ $\overline{}$ $\overline{}$
12   10   5   1   11   2   3   6   9   5   10

Name _____ Date _____ Period _____

4–17: SOLVING MULTI-STEP LINEAR EQUATIONS IN ONE VARIABLE

To solve multi-step equations, do the following:

1. Simplify first by using the Distributive Property and combining like terms.

2. Add or subtract the same number or variable to or from each side of the equation.

3. Multiply or divide both sides of the equation by the same nonzero number.

Directions: Solve each equation for x. Answer the question at the end by writing the letter of each problem in the space above its solution. Assume that $a \neq 0$.

T. $4x + 43 = 19$

L. $\frac{ax}{5} - 25 = -10$

S. $5ax - ax = -20$

M. $8(x + 7) = -72$

R. $2(x + 8) = x + 9$

O. $ax - 9 = 13$

H. $\frac{3}{7}x + 45 = 0$

G. $x - 4x + 4 = 7$

A. $-\frac{3}{2}(x - 2) = 21$

I. $4(x + 6) = -76$

In the 1100s, al-Khwarizmi, an Islamic mathematician, developed step-by-step problem-solving methods that came to be known by a Latinized form of his name. What are these step-by-step methods for problem solving called?

$\overline{}_{-12}$ $\overline{}_{\frac{75}{a}}$ $\overline{}_{-1}$ $\overline{}_{\frac{22}{a}}$ $\overline{}_{-7}$ $\overline{}_{-25}$ $\overline{}_{-6}$ $\overline{}_{-105}$ $\overline{}_{-16}$ $\overline{}_{\frac{-5}{a}}$

Name _____ Date _____ Period _____

4–18: SOLVING MULTI-STEP LINEAR INEQUALITIES IN ONE VARIABLE

The rules that apply to solving equations apply to solving inequalities as well. Follow these steps:

1. Simplify each side of the inequality.

2. Add or subtract the same number or expression to or from both sides.

3. Multiply or divide both sides by the same nonzero number or expression.

If you multiply or divide both sides of the inequality by a negative number, you must change the direction of the inequality sign.

Directions: Solve each inequality for x and find its solution in the Answer Bank. Some answers will be used more than once. Some answers will not be used. Answer the question at the end by writing the letter of each answer in the space above its problem number.

1. $5x - 7x > 40$

2. $2x - 3 < 3x - 2$

3. $-5x + 6 < 16$

4. $4(3x - 1) \geq 2(x + 3)$

5. $7 - 2x \geq 19$

6. $ax - 4 > 2ax - 5,\ a > 0$

7. $ax - 1 < 2(ax - 4),\ a < 0$

8. $2(4 - x) - 2 \leq -2x + 6$

9. $3(ax - 1) < 2(ax - 1),\ a > 0$

10. $4x + 6 \leq 2x - 6$

11. $3x - 2(x - 4) > 7$

12. $3ax - 1 > 2(ax + 3),\ a < 0$

13. $3(5 - x) - 7 \geq -3x + 8$

Answer Bank

T. $x > -1$	A. $x < \frac{1}{a}$	M. $x > -2$	B. $x \leq 6$	L. $x > 21$
I. $x \geq 1$	S. $x < -20$	O. $x \leq -6$	H. $x < \frac{7}{a}$	R. all real numbers

This mathematician was the first to use inequality symbols in a work published posthumously in 1631. Who was he?

$\overline{11}$ $\overline{12}$ $\overline{5}$ $\overline{3}$ $\overline{9}$ $\overline{1}$ $\overline{7}$ $\overline{6}$ $\overline{13}$ $\overline{8}$ $\overline{4}$ $\overline{10}$ $\overline{2}$

4–19: SOLVING A QUADRATIC EQUATION BY COMPLETING THE SQUARE

One way to solve a quadratic equation expressed as $ax^2 + bx + c = 0$, $a \neq 0$, is by completing the square. The example below shows the steps necessary when solving for x.

$x^2 + 6x - 12 = 0$	$a = 1$, $b = 6$, $c = -12$.
$x^2 + 6x = 12$	Write variables only on one side.
$x^2 + 6x + 9 = 12 + 9$	Add $a\left(\dfrac{b}{2a}\right)^2$ to both sides.
$x^2 + 6x + 9 = 21$	Simplify.
$(x + 3)^2 = 21$	Rewrite the trinomial as a perfect square.
$x + 3 = \pm\sqrt{21}$	Take the square root of both sides.
$x = -3 \pm \sqrt{21}$	Isolate the variable.

Directions: Solve each equation by completing the square. Match the value you add to each equation with the values in the Value Bank, and match your answers with the answers in the Answer Bank. For each problem, write the corresponding letter of the value you added in the first space after the problem number, then write the corresponding letter of the answer in the space directly before the problem. When you are done, write the letters in order, starting with the first problem, to complete the statement at the end of the activity. One value will be used twice, and one answer will not be used.

1. _____ _____ $x^2 - 8x + 13 = 0$

2. _____ _____ $x^2 - 4x + 1 = 0$

3. _____ _____ $x^2 + x - 1 = 0$

4. _____ _____ $x^2 + 6x - 9 = 0$

5. _____ _____ $3x^2 - 12x + 5 = 0$

6. _____ _____ $3x^2 - 6x - 10 = 0$

7. _____ _____ $x^2 + 4x - 16 = 0$

Value Bank

V. 12	N. $\frac{1}{4}$	E. 4	L. 3	W. 9	A. 16

Answer Bank

N. $-3 \pm 3\sqrt{2}$	K. $2 \pm \sqrt{3}$	U. $1 \pm \frac{\sqrt{39}}{3}$	O. $\frac{-1 \pm \sqrt{5}}{2}$
R. $4 \pm \sqrt{3}$	S. $-2 \pm 2\sqrt{5}$	B. $7 \pm \sqrt{3}$	A. $2 \pm \frac{\sqrt{21}}{3}$

Thanks to Francois Vietè (1540–1603), equations such as $ax^2 + bx + c = 0$, $a \neq 0$, can be solved by writing a formula if a, b, and c _____.

Name_____ Date_____ Period_____

4-20: SOLVING QUADRATIC EQUATIONS IN A VARIETY OF WAYS

Quadratic equations may be solved by inspection, completing the square, factoring, and using the quadratic formula. An example of each method follows:

Inspection	Completing the Square	Factoring	Using the Quadratic Formula
$x^2 = 36$ $x = \pm 6$	$x^2 + 6x = 12$ $x^2 + 6x + 9 = 12 + 9$ $(x+3)^2 = 21$ $x + 3 = \pm\sqrt{21}$ $x = -3 \pm \sqrt{21}$	$x^2 - 3x - 4 = 0$ $(x-4)(x+1) = 0$ $x = 4$ or $x = -1$	$x^2 - 5x = -7$ $x = \frac{5 \pm \sqrt{25 - 4 \cdot 7 \cdot 1}}{2}$ $x = \frac{5 \pm \sqrt{-3}}{2}$ $x = \frac{5 \pm i\sqrt{3}}{2}$

Directions: Solve each equation using any of the methods above and match each answer with an answer in the Answer Bank. Write the letter of each answer in the space above its problem number to complete the statement at the end. You will need to divide the letters into words.

1. $x^2 = 100$ 2. $x^2 - 5x + 6 = 0$ 3. $x^2 + 1 = 0$ 4. $x^2 - 4x = 1$

5. $x^2 - 6x + 9 = 0$ 6. $x^2 + 2x = 12$ 7. $x^2 - 25 = 0$ 8. $2x^2 - 4x = -3$

9. $x^2 - 7x + 12 = 0$ 10. $x^2 - 3x - 40 = 0$ 11. $x^2 + x = 0$ 12. $2x^2 - 5x = 3$

Answer Bank

C. $x = -1 \pm \sqrt{13}$	V. $x = 2 \pm \sqrt{5}$	A. $x = -\frac{1}{2}$ or $x = 3$	T. $x = 3$ or $x = 2$
S. $x = 8$ or $x = -5$	U. $x = \pm i$	Q. $x = 0$ or $x = -1$	O. $x = 3$
I. $x = \pm 10$	N. $x = \frac{2 \pm i\sqrt{2}}{2}$	L. $x = \pm 5$	E. $x = 4$ or $x = 3$

You _____.

$\overline{6}$ $\overline{12}$ $\overline{8}$ $\overline{10}$ $\overline{5}$ $\overline{7}$ $\overline{4}$ $\overline{9}$ $\overline{9}$ $\overline{11}$ $\overline{3}$ $\overline{12}$ $\overline{2}$ $\overline{1}$ $\overline{5}$ $\overline{8}$ $\overline{10}$

Name_____ Date_____ Period_____

4-21: SOLVING SYSTEMS OF EQUATIONS

One method for solving systems of equations is to replace one equation by the sum of that equation and a nonzero multiple of the other equation. This will result in an equation that has the same solution as the original system.

Using this method, solve the following system of equations:

$$3x - 4y = -6$$

$$x - 3y = -7$$

$x - 3y = -7 \rightarrow -3x + 9y = 21$ Multiply the second equation by -3 so that the sum of this equation and the first equation will not contain the variable x.

$3x - 4y - 3x + 9y = -6 + 21$ Add the multiple of the second equation and the original equation.

$5y = 15$ Simplify both sides of the equation.

$y = 3$ Divide both sides of the equation by 5. (Division Property of Equality).

$x - 3(3) = -7$ Substitute 3 for y in the second equation.

$x - 9 = -7$ Simplify.

$x = 2$ Add -9 to both sides of the equation. (Addition Property of Equality).

The solution may be checked by substituting 2 for x and 3 for y in each of the original equations.

Directions: Solve each system of equations by multiplying an equation by a nonzero number and adding it to the other equation. Find your solutions in the Answer Bank, and then complete the statement at the end by writing the letter of each answer in the space above its problem number. You will need to reverse the order of the letters and break them into words.

1. $3y + 4x = -1$
   $y - x = -5$

2. $2x - y = 7$
   $x + 2y = 6$

3. $3x - y = 10$
   $x + 2y = 1$

4. $3y - x = 5$
   $-y + 3x = 1$

5. $-2x + y = -2$
   $3x + 2y = 17$

6. $3x - 2y = 8$
   $x - y = 2$

7. $-3x - y = 9$
   $x - 3y = 7$

8. $4x - 3y = 11$
   $2x - y = 5$

(Continued)

O. $x = 2, y = -1$	R. $x = 3, y = 4$	C. $x = 2, y = -3$	N. $x = 1, y = 2$
E. $x = -2, y = -3$	I. $x = 4, y = 2$	K. $x = 3, y = -1$	W. $x = 4, y = 1$

You did _____.

$\overline{3}$ $\overline{5}$ $\overline{8}$ $\overline{2}$ $\overline{7}$ $\overline{1}$ $\overline{6}$ $\overline{4}$

4–22: SOLVING SYSTEMS OF LINEAR EQUATIONS

You can use different methods to solve systems of linear equations, including substitution, addition or subtraction, multiplication with addition or subtraction, and graphing.

Directions: Solve each system of equations, using whichever method you prefer. Record the value for *x* first, and then record the value for *y*. Match each answer with an answer in the Answer Bank. Some answers will not be used. Write a statement at the end by writing the letter of each answer in the space above its problem number. You will need to divide the letters into words.

1. $5x = -2y - 4$
   $-5x - 2y = 4$

2. $5x = 15y$
   $x = 2y$

3. $5x = 10y$
   $3x - 6y = 7$

4. $\frac{4}{3}x - 5y = 7\frac{1}{3}$
   $x - y = 0$

5. $x - \frac{2y}{3} = 0$
   $\frac{x}{6} - \frac{y}{18} = \frac{1}{2}$

6. $\frac{5}{2}x - 3y = \frac{3}{2}$
   $8x - 10y = 6$

7. $x + y = -2$
   $\frac{3}{5}x - \frac{1}{5}y = -3\frac{3}{5}$

8. $x + 4y = -0.5 + 4x$
   $2x + 3y = 0.5x + 2y + 1$

9. $7x - 2y = -22$
   $4x - 4y = -24$

10. $5x = 2 - 4y$
    $-3x + 10 = -2y$

Answer Bank

Y. (0.5, 0.25)	W. (6, 9)	U. (0, 0)	S. (2, −2)
T. (−2, 3)	M. ∅	E. (−2, 4)	O. (−5, 3)
N. (0.25, 2)	D. (10.7, −6.8)	V. (−3, −3)	L. (−2, −2)

$\overline{8}$ $\overline{7}$ $\overline{2}$ $\overline{10}$ $\overline{7}$ $\overline{4}$ $\overline{6}$ $\overline{9}$

$\overline{10}$ $\overline{8}$ $\overline{10}$ $\overline{1}$ $\overline{9}$ $\overline{3}$ $\overline{10}$ $\overline{5}$ $\overline{9}$ $\overline{4}$ $\overline{4}$

Name _____ Date _____ Period _____

4-23: SOLVING A SYSTEM OF A LINEAR AND A QUADRATIC EQUATION

You can solve a system of equations algebraically or by graphing.

To solve a system algebraically, follow these steps:

1. Rewrite one equation so that y equals an expression.

2. Substitute and solve for x.

3. Place this value in one of the original equations and solve for y.

4. Check your solutions by substituting both values in each of the original equations.

5. Express your answer as an ordered pair.

To solve a system graphically, follow these steps:

1. Graph each equation on the same graph.

2. Find the points of intersection and express them as ordered pairs.

Directions: Solve three systems of equations algebraically, and solve two systems of equations by graphing. Each system of equations will have two solutions. Match each solution with a solution in the Answer Bank. Some solutions may be used more than once. Some solutions will not be used. Answer the question at the end by writing the letters of the solutions, starting with problem 1. You may have to switch the order of the letters in some problems.

1. $\begin{array}{l} x^2 + y^2 = 5 \\ y = 2x \end{array}$ _____ _____

2. $\begin{array}{l} y + 4 = \frac{1}{2}x^2 \\ y = x \end{array}$ _____ _____

3. $\begin{array}{l} y + 3 = x^2 \\ y = 2x \end{array}$ _____ _____

4. $\begin{array}{l} y + 1 = x^2 \\ y - 2 = 2x \end{array}$ _____ _____

5. $\begin{array}{l} y = -3x^2 + 10 \\ y = -3x - 8 \end{array}$ _____ _____

Answer Bank

N. (3, 6)	I. (3, 8)	O. (−1, −2)	S. (2, −2)	M. (−1, 0)
A. (3, −17)	U. (−3, 5)	L. (−2, −2)	P. (1, 2)	Y. (4, 4)

What type of equation is often used in algebra? _____

149

Name _____ Date _____ Period _____

4–24: RELATING GRAPHS TO THE SOLUTIONS OF EQUATIONS

The graph of an equation in two variables is the set of all the points that are solutions to the equation. Conversely, the points that are not on the graph are not solutions to the equation.

Directions: Following are tables containing some solutions to the equations above them. Graph each equation using the points in its table. Then locate another point in the Answer Bank that is also a solution to the equation. Some points will be used twice. Complete the statement at the end by writing the letter of each point in the space above its equation number. You will need to divide the letters into words.

1. $y = -3x$

x	y
0	0
-1	3
3	-9
4	-12

2. $y = x^2 - 3$

x	y
-2	1
1	-2
3	6
2	1

3. $y = x^3 - 1$

x	y
2	7
1	0
0	-1
-2	9

4. $y = -x$

x	y
4	-4
-4	4
3	-3
0	0

5. $y = 3|x|$

x	y
-2	6
1	3
0	0
-3	9

6. $y = \frac{1}{2}x - 1$

x	y
0	-1
4	1
2	0
6	2

7. $y = -x^2$

x	y
-3	-9
-1	-1
2	-4
1	-1

8. $y = -x - 1$

x	y
1	-2
-1	0
-4	3
0	-1

9. $y = x$

x	y
-1	-1
0	0
3	3
2	2

10. $y = 4x$

x	y
-2	-8
1	4
-1	-4
0	0

Answer Bank

L. (2, 8)	I. (5, −5)	B. (−5, 4)	Y. (2, 6)
A. (−1, −2)	M. (−2, −4)	N. (2, −6)	E. (−2, −2)

The graph of an equation in two variables _____.

$\overline{7}$ $\quad$ $\overline{2}$ $\quad$ $\overline{5}$ $\quad$ $\overline{8}$ $\quad$ $\overline{6}$ $\quad$ $\overline{3}$ $\quad$ $\overline{10}$ $\quad$ $\overline{4}$ $\quad$ $\overline{1}$ $\quad$ $\overline{9}$

Name _____ Date _____ Period _____

4–25: USING GRAPHS AND TABLES TO FIND SOLUTIONS TO SYSTEMS OF EQUATIONS

You can use graphing calculators to graph and to create a table of values in order to find the solutions of a system of equations.

To find the solutions to a system of equations using a graphing calculator to graph the equations, follow these steps:

1. Rewrite each function as y is equal to an expression.

2. Enter the equations.

3. Graph the equations.

4. Adjust the view window to show the intersection of the graphs, if the graphs intersect.

5. Find the point or points of intersections of the graphs.

To find the solutions to a system of equations by making a table of values, follow these steps:

1. Rewrite each function as y is equal to an expression.

2. Enter the equations.

3. Set up the table so that the first column shows the values of x, the second column shows the values of y_1, and the third column shows the values of y_2.

4. View the table.

5. Scroll up or down the table to find a value of x that is paired with two values of y_1 and y_2 that are the same.

Directions: Solve each system of equations either by graphing or creating a table of values. Find your answers in the Answer Bank. Some answers will not be used. Complete the statement by writing the letter of each answer in the space above its problem number. You will need to divide the letters into words.

1. $f(x) = x$
   $h(x) = x^2 - 2$

2. $g(x) = x$
   $l(x) = \frac{1}{x}$

3. $h(x) = x^2 - 2$
   $H(x) = -|x|$

4. $k(x) = 2^x$
   $K(x) = -x + 1$

5. $F(x) = \log x$
   $b(x) = x - 9$

6. $b(x) = x^3$
   $G(x) = 2x + 4$

7. $j(x) = x - 1$
   $G(x) = 4x$

8. $F(x) = \log x$
   $J(x) = 10^x$

(Continued)

Answer Bank

D. (−1, −1) (1, 1)	C. (0, 1)	I. ∅	N. (10, 1)	V. (−1, −1) (2, 2)
M. (1, −1)	E. (−1, −1) (1, −1)	T. (1.$\overline{3}$, 1.$\overline{4}$)	R. (2, 8)	O. (−0.$\overline{3}$, −1.$\overline{3}$)

The graphs of different types of functions will _____.

$\overline{5}$ $\quad$ $\overline{3}$ $\quad$ $\overline{1}$ $\quad$ $\overline{3}$ $\quad$ $\overline{6}$ $\quad$ $\overline{4}$ $\quad$ $\overline{7}$ $\quad$ $\overline{8}$ $\quad$ $\overline{5}$ $\quad$ $\overline{4}$ $\quad$ $\overline{8}$ $\quad$ $\overline{2}$ $\quad$ $\overline{3}$

Name_____ Date_____ Period_____

4-26: SOLVING SYSTEMS OF INEQUALITIES BY GRAPHING

To solve systems of inequalities by graphing, follow these guidelines:

- Graph each inequality on the same axes.
- Find the overlap of the regions of the graphs, including portions of the boundary lines. This is the solution.

Directions: Pictured below are the seven shapes of a tangram. Each shape is called a tan. Graph the solutions of the systems of inequalities, then match your solutions with a shape or shapes identified by a Roman numeral. Write the Roman numerals in the spaces provided. The first one is done for you.

1. __VI__ $y \geq -2$
$y < x + 3$
$y \leq -x + 1$

2. _____ $y < 4$
$y \geq -x + 1$
$y > x + 3$

3. _____ $y < x + 3$
$y \geq -2$
$x \leq 3$

4. _____ $x > -5$
$y \geq x + 7$
$y \leq 6$

5. _____ $y > x + 3$
$x > -5$
$y \leq -x - 3$

6. _____ $y \geq -x + 1$
$y < x + 3$
$x \leq 3$

7. _____ $x > -5$
$y > x + 3$
$y \geq x + 7$
$y < -x + 1$

(Continued)

153

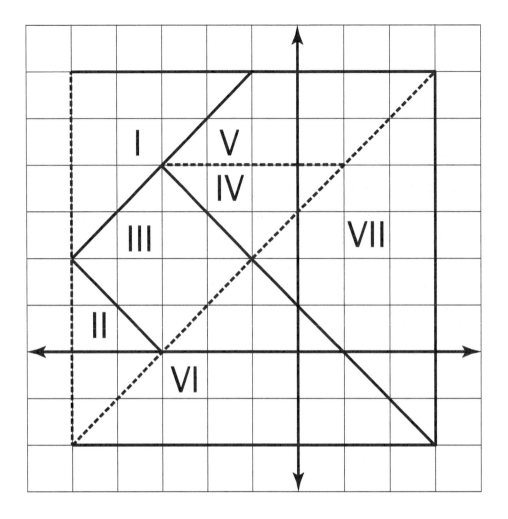

Functions

Teaching Notes for the Activities of Section 5

5-1: (8.F.1) IDENTIFYING FUNCTIONS

For this activity, your students are to complete tables to determine whether or not ordered pairs represent a function. At the end of the worksheet, they are to state which problems do not represent functions and explain why.

Begin this activity by writing the following tables on the board:

Table 1

x	y
8	−2
2	−1
0	0
2	1
8	2

Table 2

x	Y
−2	−6
−1	−3
0	0
1	3
2	6

Ask your students to compare and contrast the tables. Note that in the first table some values of x have two different values of y. For example, 8 is paired with −2 and 2, and 2 is paired with −1 and 1. This set of data does not represent a function. In the second table, each value of x is paired with only one value of y. This set of data is a function.

Go over the opening information and directions on the worksheet with your students. Note that they should complete the tables and then determine which ones are functions. They are to answer the question at the end.

ANSWERS

The missing values for x and y are provided.   (1) y: −4, −1, 2, 5, 8   (2) y: 2, 1, 0, −1, −2
(3) y: 8, 2, 0, 2, 8   (4) y: 2, 1, 0, 1, 2   (5) x: 12, 3, 0, 3, 12   (6) y: −8, −1, 0, 1, 8
(7) x: 2, 1, 0, 1, 2   (8) y: −1, $-\frac{1}{2}$, 0, $\frac{1}{2}$, 1   (9) y: 3, 3, 3, 3, 3   (10) x: 5, 5, 5, 5, 5   The
set of points in tables 5, 7, and 10 do not represent functions, because in each case at least one value of x is paired with two different values of y.

5-2: (8.F.2) COMPARING FUNCTIONS

For this activity, your students will compare the properties of pairs of functions that are represented in different ways. The focus will be on identifying the greater rate of change, but you can adapt this activity to include other important characteristics of functions such as the y-intercept or determining if the function is increasing or decreasing. Completing a statement at the end of the worksheet will enable your students to verify their answers.

Explain that functions can be represented in a variety of ways: algebraically, graphically, numerically in tables, or verbally. Discuss the information and examples on the worksheet with your students. Also discuss the rate of change and the y-intercept.

Go over the directions with your students. Students are to compare each pair of functions by determining which function has the greater rate of change. Remind them to complete the statement at the end.

ANSWERS

(1) L   (2) O   (3) S   (4) P   (5) E   Another word for the rate of change is "slope."

5-3: (8.F.3) DETERMINING WHETHER DATA LIES ON A LINE

For this activity, your students are required to graph data and find whether the points result in a line. Graph paper and rulers are needed for the activity.

Explain that the equation $y = mx + b$ is a linear equation whose graph is a line. m represents slope and b represents the y-intercept.

Discuss the directions on the worksheet with your students. Remind them to graph each set of data on a separate graph and to write an equation that represents each line.

ANSWERS

The following data sets lie on a line; the equations follow.   (1) $y = 50x$, where y represents the distance traveled and x represents the hours.   (4) $y = \$8.25$, where y represents the cumulative weekly earnings and x represents the number of hours worked.

5-4: (8.F.4) FINDING THE SLOPE AND Y-INTERCEPT OF A LINE

This activity has three parts and requires your students to write a function rule and find the slope and y-intercept of a line from tables, graphs, equations, and descriptions. Completing two statements at the end of the worksheet will enable your students to check their answers.

Discuss the information on the worksheet, focusing on the slope, y-intercept, and equation $y = mx + b$. This equation is written in slope-intercept form, where m represents the slope of a line and b represents the y-intercept. When writing a function rule, students will find it easiest to use this form.

Discuss the directions for each part on the worksheet with your students. Note that part one contains numbers 1 to 4, part two contains numbers 5 to 7, and part three contains numbers 8 to 10. Students are to also complete the two statements at the end.

(1) G, 2   (2) R, −2   (3) E, 6   (4) U, −4   (5) N, 3   (6) T, −3   (7) H, −1
(8) I, $y = 12x + 100$ (9) D, $y = x + 20$ (10) O, $y = 2x - 5$ William "Oughtred" was the person to use the symbol for parallel. Pierre "Herigone" was the first person to use the symbol for perpendicular.

5-5: (8.F.5) ANALYZING AND GRAPHING FUNCTIONS

This activity has two parts. For part one, your students will analyze graphs and compare the relationship between two quantities. For part two, they will be given relationships between two quantities and draw graphs. Your students will need rulers and graph paper to complete the activity.

Explain that graphs show a relationship between two quantities. Provide some examples of relationships with which your student are familiar. For example: The perimeter of a square is four times the length of a side. Ask your students to explain how this relationship would be graphed. Students could make a table of values as shown below and then graph the points to draw a line in the first quadrant that has a slope of 4.

s	0.5	1	1.5
P	2	4	6

Discuss the graphs on the worksheet, noting that each describes a relationship between two quantities. Focus your students' attention on the first graph and explain that it shows the cumulative points scored by a professional football team during the first quarter of a game. Ask your students what the horizontal lines show. (There is no change in the number of points scored.)

Go over the directions. After students complete part one, discuss their answers before they go on to part two.

ANSWERS

Explanation may vary.   (1) 7 points were scored after 10 minutes of play. 7 more points were scored after about 12.5 minutes of play. 14 total points were scored in the first quarter. (2) The shipping cost is a percentage of the cost of an item that costs $50 or less. Shipping is free on items that cost more than $50.   (3) It took three hours to travel 120 miles. They stopped traveling for a little less than two hours, after which they resumed their trip, traveling at a slower rate than they did the first three hours.

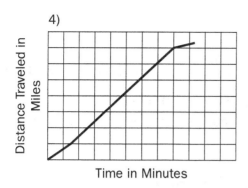

4)

Distance Traveled in Miles (vertical axis)

Time in Minutes (horizontal axis)

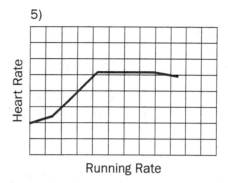

5)

Heart Rate (vertical axis)

Running Rate (horizontal axis)

5-6: (F-IF.1) UNDERSTANDING FUNCTIONS

For this activity, your students will determine if statements about functions are true or false. Completing a sentence at the end of the worksheet will enable your students to check their answers.

Review the following concepts of functions:

- A function assigns every element in the domain to exactly one element in the range. Note that "exactly one" means *one and only one*.

- If x is an element in the domain of function f, then $f(x)$ denotes the output that is paired with x.

- The graph of function f is the graph of the equation $y = f(x)$.

Go over the directions on the worksheet with your students. Remind them to complete the statement at the end.

ANSWERS

(1) I, true   (2) P, false   (3) S, true   (4) R, true   (5) R, true   (6) O, true   (7) E, false
(8) U, false   Your work is "superior."

5-7: (F-IF.2) FINDING THE VALUES OF FUNCTIONS

This activity requires your students to find the values of functions. To complete the activity successfully, they should be familiar with the use of the arrow notation and the meaning of $f(x)$. Completing a statement at the end of the worksheet will enable them to check their answers.

Begin the activity by reviewing the concept of a function. A function is a set of points and a rule that pairs each value of x with exactly one value of y. Note that sometimes a function cannot be evaluated, because the denominator is zero. In this case, a function is undefined, and the value is $\emptyset$. (Note: A function that has a negative number under the radical symbol cannot be evaluated as a real number, but this skill is not a part of this activity.)

Review the instructions on the worksheet with your students. After completing the problems, students are to complete the statement.

(1) U, $\frac{1}{25}$ (2) B, $-\frac{1}{2}$ (3) C, 6   (4) E, 0   (5) A, $2\frac{1}{2}$ (6) L, –20   (7) F, –3   (8) S, –7

(9) R, 20   (10) Y, –1   (11) T, $\frac{1}{4}$ (12) N, 2   (13) I, $\varnothing$ (14) G, –13   (15) D, 1   In

mathematics, a function "is defined by a rule indicating" what operations must be performed.

5-8: (F-IF.3) DEFINING SEQUENCES RECURSIVELY

For this activity, your students will be given sequences that are defined recursively. They are to find the indicated term of the sequence. Answering a question at the end of the worksheet will enable them to verify their answers.

Discuss the information that is provided on the worksheet, using the multiples of 5. Then provide this example: Find $f(4)$ for the sequence defined as $f(1) = 1$, $f(n) = 3f(n - 1)$ where $n > 1$. Explain that $f(1) = 1$, $f(2) = 3f(1) = 3 \times 1 = 3$, $f(3) = 3f(2) = 3 \times 3 = 9$, $f(4) = 3f(3) = 3 \times 9 = 27$.

Go over the directions on the worksheet. Remind your students to answer the question at the end.

ANSWERS

(1) G, 3   (2) L, 16   (3) A, 6.4   (4) T, 126   (5) R, 5   (6) I, 2.5   (7) N, 1   (8) U, 13   The numbers are known as "triangular" numbers.

5-9: (F-IF.4) IDENTIFYING KEY FEATURES OF GRAPHS

This activity requires your students to sketch graphs of functions and describe the key features of the graphs. Completing a statement at the end of the worksheet will enable students to check their answers. Your students will need graphing calculators or graph paper (if they are sketching the graphs by hand).

Begin this activity by reviewing how to graph a function, either by making a table of values or using a graphing calculator. Discuss the key features of graphs listed on the worksheet. If necessary, illustrate these features by sketching graphs.

Go over the directions with your students. Remind them to complete the statement at the end.

ANSWERS

(1) C, decreasing in (–2, 0); A, the y-intercept is –4; N, the x-intercept is 1.   (2) B, there are two relative minimums; E, positive in (–∞, ∞); G, $x = 0.5$ is the axis of symmetry; R, the relative maximum is (0.5, 40.0625).   (3) A, the y-intercept is –4; P, $y \to -\infty$ as $x \to \infty$.
(4) H, increasing in (1, ∞); E, positive in (–∞, ∞); D, $x = 1$ is the axis of symmetry.   Every function "can be graphed."

5-10: (F-IF.5) RELATING THE DOMAIN OF A FUNCTION TO ITS GRAPH OR DESCRIPTION

For this activity, your students will be given a graph or a verbal description of the quantities that a function describes. They are to find the domain of the function. Completing a statement at the end of the worksheet will enable them to verify their answers.

Review interval notation that is summarized on the worksheet. If your students are not familiar with the concepts of negative infinity and infinity, review these concepts as well.

Sketch the following graphs and discuss the domains with your students.

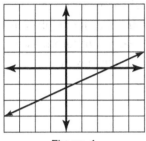 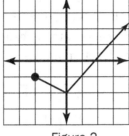 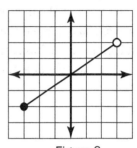

| Figure 1 | Figure 2 | Figure 3 |

The domain of the function in figure 1 is all real numbers, which can be written as $(-\infty, \infty)$. The arrows on the graph indicate that the graph continues indefinitely in both directions.

The domain of the function in figure 2 is all real numbers greater than or equal to -2, which can be written as $[-2, \infty)$. Note that the closed circle on the graph indicates that -2 is in the domain. The arrow on the graph indicates that the graph continues indefinitely in one direction.

The domain of the function in figure 3 is all real numbers that are greater than or equal to -3 and less than 3. This can be expressed as $[-3, 3)$.

To find the domain of a function, given a verbal description of the quantities it describes, students should determine the values of x for which the description makes sense. For example, the domain of a function that relates the side of a square to its area is all real numbers that are greater than 0. This can be expressed as $(0, \infty)$.

Go over the directions on the worksheet. Note that the first six functions are represented by graphs. Remind your students to complete the statement at the end.

ANSWERS

(1) T, $(-\infty, -1]$ (2) F, $[-1, \infty)$ (3) O, $(0, \infty)$ (4) R, $(-\infty, \infty)$ (5) M, $[-2, \infty)$
(6) P, $(-3, 3)$ (7) O, $(0, \infty)$ (8) E, the positive integers (9) R, $(-\infty, \infty)$ Function is taken from the Latin term "functio," which means "to perform."

5–11: (F-IF.6) FINDING THE AVERAGE RATE OF CHANGE OVER SPECIFIED INTERVALS

For this activity, your students will find the average rate of change over specified intervals for linear and nonlinear functions. The functions are described in tables and graphs, and the intervals are provided. Completing a statement at the end of the worksheet will enable students to check their work.

Explain that the same formula, $m = \frac{y_2 - y_1}{x_2 - x_1}$, that is used to find the slope of a line can be used to find the average rate of change of any function. The average rate of change describes the average rate that one quantity changes with respect to another. If a function is linear, the average rate of change is the slope of the line that is the graph of the function. If the function is nonlinear, the average rate of change is the slope of the line through the two points on the graph whose x-values are the endpoints of the interval. The average rate of change will vary in other intervals.

Provide this example of a nonlinear function $f(x)$ described by the values in the table.

x	−2	0	2
y	−9	5	7

To find the average rate of change of the function in the interval [−2, 2], find the slope of the line through (−2, −9) and (2, 7). $m = \frac{y_2 - y_1}{x_2 - x_1} = \frac{7 - (-9)}{2 - (-2)} = \frac{16}{4} = 4$ This means that for every 1-unit change in x, there is a 4-unit change in the value of $f(x)$ in this interval. Note that if students are provided with a graph, they should follow the same procedure and select the x-values on the graph that are the same values of x that are the endpoints of the interval.

Go over the directions on the worksheet. Remind your students to complete the statement at the end.

ANSWERS

(1) O, 1   (2) T, 3   (3) N, 2   (4) E, $\frac{4}{3}$ (5) A, −3   (6) L, 0   (7) P, $-\frac{5}{4}$ (8) C, −1   (9) S, $\frac{3}{2}$
The graphs of linear functions have a "constant slope."

5–12: (F-IF.7) GRAPHING LINEAR AND QUADRATIC FUNCTIONS

For this activity, your students will graph linear and quadratic functions, and then identify the intercepts and/or maximum and minimum values. They will use this information to match graphs with specific descriptions. Completing a statement at the end of the worksheet will enable them to verify their answers. Students will need rulers and graph paper to complete the activity.

Discuss the information on the worksheet for graphing linear and quadratic functions. Provide this example of a quadratic function: $f(x) = x^2 - 7x + 6$. Then explain the following.

- To find the y-intercept, find $f(0)$. $f(0) = 0^2 - 7 \cdot 0 + 6 = 6$

- To find the x-intercept, let $f(x) = 0$ and solve for x. $0 = x^2 - 7x + 6 = (x - 6)(x - 1) \rightarrow x = 1$ or $x = 6$. The x-intercepts are 1 and 6. Note that there are two x-intercepts in this example.

Graphs of quadratic functions may have two, one, or no x-intercepts. Graphs of linear functions will always have one x-intercept.

- To find the vertex, write the equation in the form of $y = ax^2 + bx + c$, where $a \neq 0$. Note that $a = 1$, $b = -7$, and $c = 6$. The x-coordinate of the vertex is $\frac{-b}{2a}$ or $\frac{7}{2} = 3.5$. The y-coordinate of the vertex is $f(3.5) = 3.5^2 - 7 \cdot 3.5 + 6 = -6.25$. Because $a > 0$, the parabola opens upward and the vertex is the minimum value.

- Create a table of values, including the vertex, y-intercept, and x-intercept.

- Use these values to draw the graph.

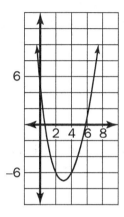

Go over the directions. Note that the functions are labeled by letters. Remind your students to complete the statement at the end.

ANSWERS

The intercepts and maximum and/or minimum values are included in the table. The letters of the functions are listed across the top.

	Y	S	A	I	E	N	W	L
y-intercept	3	3	4	−5	−3	−6	7	4
x-intercept	−0.75	–	1 and 4	–	3	−6	–	2
Maximum Value	–	–	–	(0, −5)	–	–	–	–
Minimum Value	–	(0, 3)	(2.5, −2.25)	–	–	–	(−1, 6)	(2, 0)

The answers to the descriptions follow: (1) A, L   (2) W   (3) A   (4) Y, S   (5) A   (6) L   (7) I   (8) N   (9) E   The graph of a linear function is "always a line."

5–13: (F-IF.7) GRAPHING POLYNOMIAL FUNCTIONS

For this activity, your students will match polynomial functions with the zeroes and end behavior of the functions and then sketch the graphs. Completing a statement at the end of the worksheet will enable them to check their answers.

Explain that a polynomial function is of the form $f(x) = a_n x^n + a_{n-1} x^{n-1} + \ldots + a_1 x + a_0$, where n is a nonnegative integer, $a_n \neq 0$, and $a_n, a_{n-1}, \ldots, a_0$ are real numbers.

Discuss the information for finding zeroes and describing the end behavior of functions that is presented on the worksheet.

Provide this example: Find the zeroes and determine the end behavior of $f(x) = -x^2 + 2x + 3$.

To find the zeroes, set $f(x) = 0$ and factor the expression.

$0 = -x^2 + 2x + 3 = -(x^2 - 2x - 3) = -(x + 1)(x - 3)$ By the zero product property, the zeroes are $x = -1$ and $x = 3$.

To determine the end behavior, note that because the degree of the function is 2, which is even, and the leading coefficient is negative, as $x \to -\infty$, $f(x) \to -\infty$ and as $x \to \infty$, $f(x) \to -\infty$. Using this information, demonstrate how students should sketch the graph.

Go over the directions on the worksheet. Remind your students to complete the statement at the end.

ANSWERS

(1) O   (2) N   (3) S   (4) C   (5) A   (6) T   The end behavior of the "constant" function is always as $x \to -\infty$, $f(x) = k$ and as $x \to \infty$, $f(x) = k$.

5-14: (F-IF.8) REWRITING QUADRATIC EQUATIONS

For this activity, your students will be given three quadratic equations that can be solved by rewriting them and three word problems that can be solved by writing quadratic equations. Students will express the equations in another form. Completing a statement at the end of the worksheet will enable them to check their work.

Review the two ways that quadratic equations can be rewritten, which are detailed on the worksheet. Your students may find it helpful if you review factoring quadratic equations and completing the square. Note that when solving a word problem, students must interpret their answers in terms of the context of the problem.

Go over the directions. Remind students to complete the statement at the end.

ANSWERS

The equations in their rewritten form are provided, followed by the answers to the problems.
(1) $(x - 9)(x + 8) = 0$; G, $x = 9$ and $x = -8$ (2) $y + 10 = (x - 2)^2$; E, $(2, -10)$; $x = 2$
(3) $y - 13 = -(x - 5)^2$; L, $(5, 13)$; $x = 5$ (4) $(x + 5)(x - 4) = 0$; A, $x = 4$
(5) $(x - 8)(x + 9) = 0$; R, $x = 8$ (6) $y - 225 = -(x - 15)^2$; B, $(15, 225)$; $x = 15$.   The vertex, $(15, 225)$, shows that 225 is the largest area. Evariste Galois proved that polynomials with a degree higher than four cannot be solved using "algebra."

5-15: (F-IF.9) COMPARING PROPERTIES OF FUNCTIONS

This activity requires your students to compare the properties of functions. Completing a statement at the end of the worksheet will enable them to check their answers.

Start the activity by reviewing the following properties of functions: intercepts, slope, symmetry, and maximum or minimum values. If necessary, provide examples.

Go over the directions on the worksheet with your students. Seven functions are described either algebraically, graphically, in tables, or by verbal descriptions. You may want to suggest that students express each function graphically, since this makes it easier to compare the properties of the functions. Remind them to complete the statement at the end.

ANSWERS

(1) R, $f(x)$ (2) E, $h(x)$ (3) T, $H(x)$ (4) S, $G(x)$ (5) O, $F(x)$ (6) I, $g(x)$ (7) P, $K(x)$ All functions have "properties."

5-16: (F-BF.1) WRITING FUNCTIONS

For this activity, your students will write functions to model situations. Then they will write and find the sum, difference, product, quotient, or composition of two functions. Completing a statement at the end of the worksheet will enable them to check their work.

Begin by reviewing that functions, like real numbers, may be added, subtracted, multiplied, or divided. Review the notation for showing the sum, difference, product, or quotient of two functions provided on the worksheet. If necessary, provide examples. Also note that functions may be formed by composing one function with another. Discuss the notation for forming the composite function and provide examples, if necessary.

Go over the directions with your students. Your students should write two functions to determine how the two quantities in each problem are related. Students should then use these functions to write another function. Remind them to complete the statement at the end.

ANSWERS

The two functions students are to write for each problem are followed by the function that should be formed, which in turn is followed by the letter of the answer.   (1) $f(x) = 0.1x$; $g(x) = 0.07x$; $(f + g)(x) = 0.17x$, E   (2) $f(x) = 2x + 1$; $g(x) = 2x - 1$; $(f \cdot g)(x) = 4x^2 - 1$, I   (3) $f(x) = 12x$; $g(x) = 2.4x$; $(f - g)(x) = 12x - 2.4x = 9.6x$, D   (4) $g(x) = x - 3$; $f(x) = x^2 - x - 6$; $\left(\dfrac{f}{g}\right)(x) = x + 2$, V   (5) $f(x) = \pi x^2$; $g(x) = 3x$; $(f \circ g)(x) = 9\pi x^2$, B   Some functions may not "be divided."

5-17: (F-BF.2) WRITING ARITHMETIC AND GEOMETRIC SEQUENCES

For this activity, your students will be given a sequence, a part of a sequence, or a description of a sequence, and they will write arithmetic and geometric sequences recursively and with an explicit formula. Answering a question at the end of the worksheet will enable them to verify their work.

Explain that arithmetic and geometric sequences can be written recursively and with an explicit formula. Review the difference between an arithmetic sequence and a geometric sequence and the formulas that are provided on the worksheet.

Offer this example of an arithmetic sequence: $-8, -3, 2, 7, 12, \ldots$. Note that $a_1 = -8$ and $d = 5$. To define this sequence recursively, use the formula $a_n = a_{n-1} + d$ to find $a_n = a_{n-1} + 5$. To define this sequence by using an explicit formula, use the formula $a_n = a_1 + (n-1)d$ to find $a_n = -8 + (n-1)5 = -8 + 5n - 5 = -13 + 5n$. Encourage your students to check this formula by substituting a value for n. For example, $a_4 = -13 + 5(4) = 7$, which is the fourth term in the sequence.

Provide this example of geometric sequence: $-8, -16, -32, -64, -128, \ldots$. Note that $a_1 = -8$ and $r = 2$. To define this sequence recursively, use the formula $a_n = a_{n-1} \cdot r$ to find $a_n = a_{n-1} \cdot 2 = 2a_{n-1}$. To define this sequence by using an explicit formula, use the formula $a_n = a_1 \cdot r^{n-1}$ to find $a_n = -8 \cdot 2^{n-1}$. Encourage your students to check this formula by substituting a value for n. For example, $a_4 = -8 \cdot 2^{4-1} = -8 \cdot 2^3 = -64$, which is the fourth term in the sequence.

Review the directions on the worksheet. Note that students will be working with both arithmetic and geometric sequences. Remind them to answer the question at the end.

ANSWERS

The sequence that is not included in the Answer Bank is shown first, followed by the letter and sequence that is included. (1) $a_n = a_{n-1} - 10$; U, $a_n = 25 - 10n$ (2) $a_n = -2 - 4n$; D, $a_n = a_{n-1} - 4$ (3) $a_n = 10(1.3)^{n-1}$; L, $a_n = 1.3a_{n-1}$ (4) $a_n = 8(0.4)^{n-1}$; C, $a_n = 0.4a_{n-1}$ (5) $a_n = 1.5a_{n-1}$; R, $a_n = 8(1.5)^{n-1}$ (6) $a_n = a_{n-1} + 0.05$; A, $a_n = 0.45 + .05n$ (7) $a_n = -a_{n-1}$; E, $a_n = 2(-1)^{n-1}$ (8) $a_n = 240,000(1.05)^{n-1}$; O, $a_n = 1.05a_{n-1}$ (9) $a_n = a_{n-1} + 0.2$; S, $a_n = 1.3 + 0.2n$ The name of the mathematician is "Edouard Lucas."

5-18: (F-BF.3) TRANSFORMING A FUNCTION

For this activity, your students will identify the effect of k on the graph of $f(x)$ by matching an equation with its graph. Completing two statements at the end of the worksheet will enable students to verify their work. They will need graphing calculators.

Explain that any function can be transformed by writing another function or building on the original function. Review the information on the worksheet that summarizes the effect of k on the graph of $y = f(x)$. Your students may find it helpful if you provide them with a function such as $f(x) = x^3$ for an example. They can build on this function and graph each of the following functions: $f(x) = x^3 + 4$, $f(x) = (x-4)^3 f(x) = -x^3$, $f(x) = (-x)^3$, $f(x) = \frac{1}{4}x^3$, $f(x) = 4x^3$, and $f(x) = (4x)^3$. They can identify the value of k, and examine its effect of the graph of $f(x) = x^3$. Discuss their findings before assigning this activity.

Review the directions, noting that students are to use the function $y = f(x)$ that is graphed on the worksheet and then match each equation with its graph. They are to complete the statements at the end.

(1) O   (2) S   (3) Y   (4) X   (5) I   (6) N   (7) A   (8) G   (9) R   Graphs of even functions such as $f(x) = x^2$ are symmetric with respect to the "y-axis" because $f(x) = f(-x)$.   Graphs of odd functions such as $f(x) = x^3$ are symmetric with respect to the "origin" because $f(-x) = -f(x)$.

5–19: (F-BF.4) FINDING THE INVERSES OF FUNCTIONS

For this activity, your students must match functions with their inverses. Completing a statement at the end of the activity will enable them to verify their answers.

Start the activity by reviewing the horizontal line test with your students. The test states that if no horizontal line intersects the graph of a function more than once, then the inverse of the function is a function. Offer these examples on the board or an overhead projector.

| 1. $f(x) = x^2$ | 2. $f(x) = \pm\sqrt{x}$ | 3. $f(x) = x^3$ | 4. $f(x) = \sqrt[3]{x}$ |

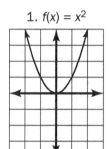 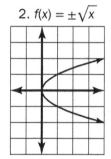 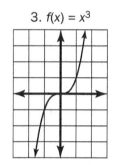 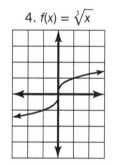

Discuss the graphs and note that the graph of $f(x) = x^2$ does not pass the horizontal line test. If necessary, discuss the process for finding the inverse of a function, and emphasize that students must isolate the value of y before they can find the root of the expression.

Review the directions on the worksheet. Mention that f^{-1} is used to denote the inverse and is read "f inverse." After solving the problems, students are to complete the statement at the end.

(1) N, $f^{-1}(x) = \dfrac{1}{2}x + 2$ (2) S, $f^{-1}(x) = \sqrt[3]{x}$ (3) R, $f^{-1}(x) = \sqrt[5]{x}$ (4) U, $f^{-1}(x) = x$ (5) A, $f^{-1}(x) = \dfrac{1}{2}x - 2$ (6) C, $f^{-1}(x) = \sqrt[3]{2x + 4}$ (7) I, $f^{-1}(x) = x - 7$ (8) T, $f^{-1}(x) = \dfrac{1}{3}x + \dfrac{1}{3}$ (9) L, $f^{-1}(x) = 2x - 2$ (10) F, $f^{-1}(x) = \sqrt[3]{\dfrac{x - 1}{3}}$ (11) O, $f^{-1}(x) = \sqrt[5]{7x - 2}$ (12) E, $f^{-1}(x) = \sqrt[7]{x}$

For each linear function $f(x) = mx + b$ where $m \neq 0$, the inverse "is a linear function."

5-20: (F-LE.1) PROVING LINEAR FUNCTIONS GROW BY EQUAL DIFFERENCES OVER EQUAL INTERVALS

For this activity, your students will complete a table to show that linear functions grow by equal differences over equal intervals. They will also explain how linear functions change over various intervals.

Review that $y = mx + b$ is the general equation of a linear function. Explain that linear functions grow by equal differences over equal intervals.

Discuss the table of values on the worksheet and complete the first row as a class. To find the values of y, students should substitute the values of x into the equation $y = mx + b$. They should interpret the results as the change in y is -6 times m when the change in x is -6. $\frac{\text{Change in } y}{\text{Change in } x} = m$, the slope of the line, which is constant.

Review the directions with your students. Explain that they are to complete rows 2, 3, and 4 in the table. After completing the table they are to write an explanation of how linear functions change in various intervals.

ANSWERS

Rows	Values of x	Values of y	Change in y	Change in x	$\dfrac{\text{Change in } y}{\text{Change in } x}$
1	$x = -10$ $x = -4$	$y = -10m + b$ $y = -4m + b$	$-10m + b - (-4m + b) = -6m$	$-10 - (-4) = -6$	$\dfrac{-6m}{-6} = m$
2	$x = -3$ $x = -1$	$y = -3m + b$ $y = -m + b$	$-2m$	-2	m
3	$x = 0$ $x = 5$	$y = b$ $y = 5m + b$	$-5m$	-5	m
4	$x = x_2$ $x = x_1$	$y = x_2m + b$ $y = x_1m + b$	$(x_2 - x_1)m$	$x_2 - x_1$	m

Explanations may vary. One possible explanation is that linear functions grow by a constant rate, which is the slope of the line.

5-21: (F-LE.1) PROVING EXPONENTIAL FUNCTIONS GROW BY EQUAL FACTORS OVER EQUAL INTERVALS

For this activity, your students will complete a table to show that exponential functions grow by equal factors over equal intervals. After completing the table, they will explain how exponential functions change over various intervals.

Review that $y = ab^x$ is the general equation of an exponential function, where $a \neq 0$, $b > 0$, and $b \neq 1$. a represents the initial value of the function. Your students may find it helpful if you graph two exponential functions, one where $b > 1$ and the other where $0 < b < 1$, as examples.

Explain that students will complete a table to show how exponential functions grow over equal intervals. Refer to the table of values on the worksheet and complete the first row as a class. Note that to find the values of y, students should substitute the values of x into the equation $y = ab^x$. Ask how the change in x and the exponent of the quotient of the values of y compare. (They are the same.)

Review the directions with your students. They are to complete rows 2, 3, and 4. After completing the table they are to write an explanation of how exponential functions change over various intervals.

ANSWERS

Row	Values of x	Values of y	Quotient of the values of y	Change in x
1	$x = 1$ $x = 0$	$y = ab^1 = ab$ $y = ab^0 = a$	$\dfrac{ab}{a} = b^1$	$1 - 0 = 1$
2	$x = 5$ $x = 3$	$y = ab^5$ $y = ab^3$	$\dfrac{ab^5}{ab^3} = b^2$	2
3	$x = 12$ $x = 8$	$y = ab^{12}$ $y = ab^8$	$\dfrac{ab^{12}}{ab^8} = b^4$	4
4	$x = x_2$ $x = x_1$	$y = ab^{x_2}$ $y = ab^{x_1}$	$\dfrac{ab^{x_2}}{ab^{x_1}} = b^{x_2 - x_1}$	$x_2 - x_1$

Explanations may vary. One possible explanation is that exponential functions grow by equal factors because the change in x is always the same as the exponent of the quotient of the values of y.

5–22: (F-LE.2) CONSTRUCTING LINEAR AND EXPONENTIAL FUNCTIONS

For this activity, your students will select a linear or exponential function, given a table of values, a verbal description, or a graph. Answering a question at the end of the worksheet will enable them to check their work.

Review the definitions of linear functions and exponential functions, which are on the worksheet. In all cases, students should try to find the relationship between the x- and y-values. Note that arithmetic sequences may be expressed as a linear function because the difference between successive terms is a constant. Geometric sequences may be expressed as an exponential function because successive terms have the same ratio. If necessary, provide examples of linear functions, exponential functions, arithmetic sequences, and geometric sequences.

Go over the directions with your students. Encourage them to determine whether the data is an arithmetic or geometric sequence as this may help them to write the functions. Remind them to answer the question at the end.

(1) N, $f(x) = -x + 1$ (2) C, $f(x) = 4(0.5)^x$ (3) E, $f(x) = 0.5(2)^x$ (4) T, $f(x) = 2(0.5)^x$ (5) I, $f(x) = 4x + 1$ (6) H, $f(x) = 0.5x - 4$ (7) A, $f(x) = 2^x$ (8) M, $f(x) = (0.5)^x$ (9) O, $f(x) = x$
Leonhard Euler was the first "mathematician to" use $f(x)$ to show a function.

5–23: (F-LE.3) OBSERVING THE BEHAVIOR OF QUANTITIES THAT INCREASE EXPONENTIALLY

For this activity, your students will use graphing calculators to create tables of values of exponential functions and then compare the growth of the exponential functions with the growth of polynomial functions. By completing a statement at the end of the worksheet, students will be able to check their work.

Explain that exponential functions can be expressed as $f(x) = b^x$, $b > 0$ and $b \neq 1$.

Polynomial functions can be expressed as $f(x) = a_n x^n + a_{n-1} x^{n-1} + \ldots + a_1 x + a_0$, $a_n \neq 0$. Note that linear, quadratic, and cubing functions are all polynomial equations and that each of these functions grows at a different rate.

Refer to the table on the worksheet and point out that it includes the values of x, y_1, which is an exponential function, and y_2, which is a cubing function. When $x \geq 6$, the value of the exponential function exceeds the value of the cubing function. Encourage your students to enter each equation in their graphing calculator and generate a table of values. Set up the table so that the values of x are integers and the change in x is 1. They can scroll up or down to the table to observe the values of y_1 and y_2 as x changes.

Go over the directions with your students. They are to find the values of x that will complete the statement.

(1) D, $x > 1$ (2) R, $x > 3$ (3) P, x is any real number.   (4) O, $x \geq -1$ (5) I, $x \geq 3$ (6) G, $x > 16$ (7) Y, $x \geq 4$ (8) L, $x \geq 10$ (9) W, $x \geq 2$ (10) A, $x \geq 7$ Quantities that increase exponentially "grow rapidly."

5–24: (F-LE.4) WRITING AND SOLVING EXPONENTIAL EQUATIONS

For this activity, your students will match logarithmic equations with an equivalent exponential equation or the solution to the exponential equation. Completing a statement at the end of the worksheet will enable them to check their work.

Review the information on the worksheet and present the following three examples, showing equivalent equations and solutions.

	Logarithmic Equation	Exponential Equation	Solution
1	$\log_2 x = 5$	$x = 2^5$	$x = 32$
2	$\ln x = 2$	$x = e^2$	$x \approx 7.39$
3	$\log x = 4$	$x = 10^4$	$x = 10,000$

Go over the directions with your students. Note that students are given a logarithmic equation and must match either the exponential equation or the solution—not both.

ANSWERS

The equations and solutions that are not included in the Answer Bank are provided first, followed by the letter and the equivalent exponential equation or solution. (1) $x = 125$; T, $x = 5^3$ (2) $x = -3$; G, $\frac{1}{27} = 3^x$ (3) $x \approx 148$; H, $x = e^5$ (4) $x = 4$; M, $25 = (\sqrt{5})^x$ (5) $x = e^1$; L, $x \approx 2.72$ (6) $x = 100$; O, $x = 10^2$ (7) $x = 25^{\frac{1}{2}}$; S, $x = 5$ (8) $x = 9$; A, $x = 3^2$ (9) $x = \sqrt{10}$; E, $x = 10^{\frac{1}{2}}$ (10) $x = -1$; R, $2^{-3} = 8^x$ (11) $x = -2$; Y, $\frac{1}{100} = 10^x$ (12) $x \approx 22,026$; F, $x = e^{10}$ (13) $x \approx 2.302$; I, $10 = e^x$ Scottish mathematician John Napier is best known as the inventor of the first "system of logarithms."

5–25: (F-LE.5) INTERPRETING PARAMETERS IN A LINEAR OR EXPONENTIAL FUNCTION

For this activity, your students will be given word problems that can be modeled by linear or exponential functions. They will answer questions that require them to interpret parameters in functions, based on the context of the problems.

Explain that linear and exponential functions, as well as other functions, have inherent values. These values are called parameters. One example of a linear function and a parameter is $f(x) = 4x$, which can be used to find the perimeter of a square where x is the length of a side of the square. Discuss this example by posing questions: for example, "What does the 4 represent? (It represents the number of sides of a square and also the rate of change of the function.) What does $f(x) = 0$ mean? (The length of a side is 0 units, therefore there is no square and no perimeter). If necessary, provide an example of an exponential function and pose similar questions.

Go over the directions on the worksheet. Remind your students that they are to explain their reasoning.

ANSWERS

Explanations may vary. (1) Disagree because $f(x) = 1.15x$ or $f(x) = x + 0.15x$. (2) Disagree because her distance is increasing at a constant rate. A negative slope shows a constant decrease. (3) Never, because the total cost must be a multiple of 10. (4) 2,270 represents the initial value of the function before any increase. (5) No, because using

$f(x) = 2,270(1 + 0.012)^x$, $f(0) = 2,270$, $f(1) \approx 2,297$, $f(2) \approx 2,324$, and $f(3) \approx 2,357$, which correctly models the enrollment. Using $f(x) = 2,270 + 2,270(0.012)^x$, $f(0) = 4,540$, $f(1) \approx 2,297$, and $f(2) \approx 2,270$. $f(x) = (0.012)^x$ is decreasing exponentially. (6) Disagree because Luis was able to substitute values for x correctly, but the base of an exponential function, by definition, can never equal 1.

5–26: (F-TF.1) USING RADIAN AND DEGREE MEASURES

For this activity, your students will express angle measures in radians and degrees. Completing a statement at the end of the worksheet will enable them to verify their answers.

Explain that when the central angle intersects an arc that has the same length as the radius of the circle, the measure of the angle is one radian, which is abbreviated as one rad. Discuss the relationship between radians and degrees using the following reasoning:

- The distance around a circle with radius r is $2\pi r$.

- Dividing $2\pi r$ by r, we find 2π arcs of length r on the circle.

- One rotation around a circle is 360°, which is the same as 2π radians.

- It follows that $360° = 2\pi$ rad, $180° = \pi$ rad and $1° = \frac{\pi}{180}$ rad.

Discuss the information and examples on the worksheet. Make sure that your students understand the terminology and the steps for changing degrees to radians and radians to degrees.

Discuss the directions. Explain that for problems 1 to 5 students are to express degrees as radians and for problems 6 to 10 they are to express radians as degrees. They are to also answer the question at the end.

ANSWERS

(1) E, $\frac{2\pi}{3}$ (2) M, $\frac{\pi}{12}$ (3) L, π (4) U, $\frac{\pi}{4}$ (5) N, $\frac{5\pi}{9}$ (6) T, 30° (7) A, 135° (8) G, 75° (9) S, 150° (10) R, 50° Greek mathematician Eratosthenes used "angle measurement" to compute the circumference of the Earth.

5–27: (F-TF.2) USING THE UNIT CIRCLE

For this activity, your students will answer true/false questions about the trigonometric functions that are defined by using the unit circle. By completing a statement at the end of the worksheet, students will be able to check their work.

Review that the unit circle has a 1-unit radius. An angle θ in standard position has its vertex at the origin, and one radius, the initial side of the angle, is on the positive x-axis. The terminal side of the angle is the radius that rotates in a counterclockwise direction about the origin. Rotations in a counterclockwise rotation are positive; clockwise rotations are negative and are designated by a negative sign. For example, a 330° counterclockwise rotation is the same as a

$-30°$ rotation. Note that the value of x on the unit circle is $\cos \theta$, and the value of y on the unit circle is $\sin \theta$. $\tan \theta = \frac{\sin \theta}{\cos \theta}$

Explain that as the terminal side of θ rotates counterclockwise from Quadrant I through Quadrant IV, the signs of the trigonometric functions vary. These are noted in the first table on the worksheet. The second table shows the values of $\sin \theta$, $\cos \theta$, and $\tan \theta$ of the quadrantal angles.

Explain that to find the value of a trigonometric function, students must draw a reference triangle and a reference angle. Make sure your students know that a reference angle is the angle formed by the terminal side of an angle and the x-axis and that they know how to find the value of the reference angle. The reference triangles students need to use in this worksheet are special right triangles. Note that in a 30°-60°-90° triangle, the hypotenuse is 1, the leg opposite the 30°-angle is $\frac{1}{2}$, and the leg adjacent to the 30°-angle is $\frac{\sqrt{3}}{2}$. The leg opposite the 60°-angle is $\frac{\sqrt{3}}{2}$ and the leg adjacent to the 60°-angle is $\frac{1}{2}$. In a 45°-45°-90° triangle, the hypotenuse is 1, and each leg is $\frac{\sqrt{2}}{2}$.

Provide this example. Find $\cos 135°$. Instruct your students to draw a reference triangle and a reference angle θ'. Because the reference angle is 45° and θ' is in Quadrant II, $\cos 135° = -\frac{\sqrt{2}}{2}$.

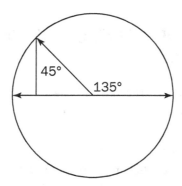

Go over the directions with your students. Remind your students to complete the statement at the end.

ANSWERS

(1) R, true   (2) A, false   (3) O, true   (4) C, false   (5) F, false   (6) U, true   (7) I, false
(8) L, true   (9) T, false   (10) N, true   (11) S, true   The sine and cosine are "circular functions."

5–28: (F-TF.5) MODELING PERIODIC PHENOMENA

For this activity, your students will be given two sets of data. They will make a scatter plot for each set of data and then select functions that model the data. By answering a question at the end of the worksheet, they will be able to verify their work. They will need rulers and graph paper.

Review the following features of the graphs of the sine and cosine functions:

- They both have a period of 2π.

- The graph of $f(x) = \sin\left(x + \frac{\pi}{2}\right)$ coincides with the graph of $f(x) = \cos x$.

- The zeroes of the sine function are $\ldots, -2\pi, -\pi, 0, \pi, 2\pi, \ldots$, and the zeroes of the cosine function are $\ldots, -\frac{3\pi}{2}, -\frac{\pi}{2}, \frac{\pi}{2}, \frac{3\pi}{2}, \ldots$.

Discuss the information on the worksheet. Note how the functions are expressed and also the meanings of A, B, C, D, and t.

Review the directions with your students. To answer the question, they should write the letters of the functions that model the data in the first table in the spaces above the number 1s and then write the letters of the functions that model the data in the second table in the spaces above the number 2s.

ANSWERS

Functions that model the data in table 1: A, M, P, L. Functions that model the data in table 2: I, T, U, D, E. The word is "amplitude."

5–29: (F-TF.8) FINDING THE VALUES OF THE SINE, COSINE, AND TANGENT FUNCTIONS

For this activity, your students will find the value of the sine, cosine, and tangent functions, given a trigonometric function and the quadrant of the angle. By completing a statement at the end, students can check their work.

Explain that the Pythagorean Identity, $\sin^2(\theta) + \cos^2(\theta) = 1$, can be derived from the Pythagorean Theorem, $a^2 + b^2 = c^2$, by drawing θ in standard position in the unit circle. To explain how the Pythagorean Identity can be derived, sketch the figure below. By substituting 1 for c, $\sin(\theta)$ for a, and $\cos(\theta)$ for b in the Pythagorean Theorem, students will find $\sin^2(\theta) + \cos^2(\theta) = 1$.

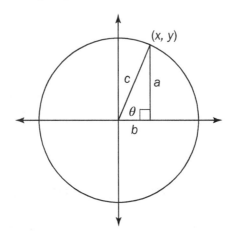

Explain that students can use the Pythagorean identity, $\sin^2(\theta) + \cos^2(\theta) = 1$, to find $\cos(\theta)$ if they are given $\sin(\theta)$ and the quadrant that θ is in. Provide this example: $\sin(\theta) = \frac{1}{5}$ and θ is in Quadrant II. Students should substitute $\sin(\theta) = \frac{1}{5}$ into $\sin^2(\theta) + \cos^2(\theta) = 1$, and solve for $\cos(\theta)$. $\cos^2(\theta) = \frac{24}{25}$, therefore $\cos(\theta) = \pm\sqrt{\frac{24}{25}}$. Since $\cos(\theta)$ is negative in Quadrant II,

$\cos(\theta) = -\sqrt{\frac{24}{25}} = -\frac{2\sqrt{6}}{5}$. To find $\tan(\theta)$, use the ratio $\tan(\theta) = \frac{\sin(\theta)}{\cos(\theta)} = \frac{\frac{1}{5}}{\frac{-2\sqrt{6}}{5}} = -\frac{\sqrt{6}}{12}$. The same procedure can be used to find $\sin(\theta)$ if students are given the value of $\cos(\theta)$ and the quadrant θ is in.

Demonstrate how to find $\sin(\theta)$ and $\cos(\theta)$ when they are given $\tan(\theta)$ and the quadrant θ is in. Provide this example: $\tan(\theta) = \sqrt{3}$, and θ is in Quadrant I. Students must use this ratio:

$$\tan(\theta) = \sqrt{3} = \frac{\sin(\theta)}{\cos(\theta)}$$

$$\sqrt{3}\cos(\theta) = \sin(\theta)$$

$$3\cos^2(\theta) = \sin^2(\theta)$$

$$3\cos^2(\theta) = 1 - \cos^2(\theta)$$

$$3\cos^2(\theta) + \cos^2(\theta) = 1$$

$$4\cos^2(\theta) = 1$$

$$\cos(\theta) = \pm\frac{1}{2}$$

$$\cos(\theta) = \frac{1}{2} \text{ because } \theta \text{ is in Quadrant I.}$$

Substitute $\cos(\theta) = \frac{1}{2}$ into $\sin^2(\theta) + \cos^2(\theta) = 1$ to find $\sin(\theta) = \frac{\sqrt{3}}{2}$.

Discuss the directions on the worksheet with your students, noting that there are five statements about trigonometric functions and the quadrant θ is in. For each statement, students are to select two other related trigonometric functions of the angles from the Answer Bank. They are to then answer the question at the end.

ANSWERS

(1) O, $\frac{\sqrt{7}}{4}$ (2) E, $-\frac{\sqrt{7}}{3}$ (3) H, $-\frac{2\sqrt{2}}{3}$ (4) G, $\frac{\sqrt{2}}{4}$ (5) N, $\frac{\sqrt{7}}{3}$ (6) Y, $-\frac{\sqrt{2}}{3}$ (7) A, $\frac{3}{5}$

(8) T, $\frac{4}{5}$ (9) P, $-\frac{\sqrt{5}}{3}$ (10) R, $-\frac{2\sqrt{5}}{5}$ James Garfield wrote a proof of the "Pythagorean" Theorem.

Reproducibles for Section 5 follow.

Name _____ Date _____ Period _____

5-1: IDENTIFYING FUNCTIONS

A relation is any set of ordered pairs. A function is a special type of relation in which each value of x is paired with exactly one value of y. The graph of a function is the set of ordered pairs. A table can be used to organize ordered pairs to determine if a set of points is a function.

Directions: Complete each table. When you have finished, list the problem numbers of the sets of points that are *not* functions.

1. $y = 3x + 2$

x	y
-2	
-1	
0	
1	
2	

2. $y = -x$

x	y
-2	
-1	
0	
1	
2	

3. $y = 2x^2$

x	y
-2	
-1	
0	
1	
2	

4. $y = |x|$

x	y
-2	
-1	
0	
1	
2	

5. $x = 3y^2$

x	y
	-2
	-1
	0
	1
	2

6. $y = x^3$

x	y
-2	
-1	
0	
1	
2	

7. $x = |y|$

x	y
	-2
	-1
	0
	1
	2

8. $y = \frac{1}{2}x$

x	y
-2	
-1	
0	
1	
2	

9. $y = 3$

x	y
-2	
-1	
0	
1	
2	

10. $x = 5$

x	y
	-2
	-1
	0
	1
	2

Which tables contain sets of points that do not represent functions? Why?

Name _____   Date _____   Period _____

5–2: COMPARING FUNCTIONS

Functions can be described verbally or represented algebraically, graphically, or numerically in tables. Examples of the same function expressed in the four different ways are shown below.

Verbally: The length of a rectangle is 3 more than twice the width, where *x* is the width of a rectangle.

Algebraically: $y = 2x + 3$

Graphically:

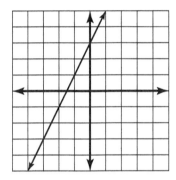

Numerically in a Table:

x	y
1	5
0.5	4
2	7

Two important properties of linear functions are the rate of change and the *y*-intercept. The rate of change is the ratio of the vertical change in *y* to the corresponding horizontal change in *x*. It is often referred to as "rise over run." The *y*-intercept is the *y*-coordinate of a point where the graph intersects the *y*-axis. In each example above, the rate of change is 2 and the *y*-intercept is 3.

Directions: Compare each pair of functions. Determine which function of each pair has the greater rate of change. Complete the statement at the end by writing the letter of each answer in the space above its problem number.

(Continued)

1. P. $y = -3x + 2$

L.

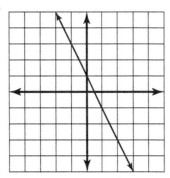

2. O. The cost of a service call for an electrician is $95 plus $75 per hour for labor.

G.

x	y
0	80
2	100
4	120

3. S. $y = 4x - 3$

B.

x	y
3	2
4	3
5	4

4. M. The cost of a pizza is $12.50 plus a $2 delivery charge per pie.

P.

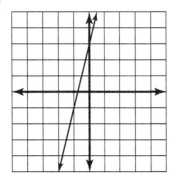

(Continued)

5. T. A person's maximum heart rate is determined by subtracting his age from 220.

E.

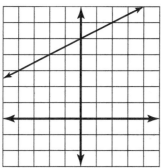

Complete the following statement by writing the letter of each answer in the blank above its problem number.

Another word for the rate of change is _____.

$\overline{3}$ $\overline{1}$ $\overline{2}$ $\overline{4}$ $\overline{5}$

5-3: DETERMINING WHETHER DATA LIES ON A LINE

Data may or may not be presented on a graph as a straight line, especially in real-life situations.

Directions: Graph each set of data on a separate graph to find which set of data results in a line. Write an equation that represents each line. Use the equation $y = mx + b$.

1. On a car trip to Florida, Ms. Wilson checked and recorded the mileage on the odometer every hour. She was then able to record her travel time and distance. The following data describe her trip. The first number in each pair of numbers represents the time she traveled in hours, and the second number represents the distance she traveled in miles.

   (1, 50), (2, 100), (3, 150), (4, 200), (5, 250), (6, 300), (7, 350), (8, 400)

2. The cost of renting a cottage by a lake for the summer is $12,000. A family, including grandparents, aunts, uncles, and cousins, decided that they would like to rent the cottage, but not everyone is able to make a firm commitment. The following data describe the cost per family, depending on the number of families that may rent and assuming that every family that rents pays an equal share of the costs.

   (1, $12,000), (2, $6,000), (3, $4,000), (4, $3,000), (5, $2,400),
   (6, $2,000), (8, $1,500), (10, $1,200), (12, $1,000)

3. According to sources on nutrition, the amount of calories that an average, somewhat active male needs changes as he ages. For example, a five-year-old boy needs 1,500 calories per day, a 10-year-old boy needs 2,000 calories, and so on. The following data describe the amount of calories an average, somewhat active male would require at various ages throughout his life.

   (5, 1,500), (10, 2,000), (15, 2,600), (20, 2,700), (25, 2,700), (30, 2,700),
   (35, 2,500), (40, 2,500), (45, 2,500), (50, 2,500), (55, 2,300), (60, 2,300),
   (65, 2,300), (70, 2,300)

4. Sara works 8 hours per week at a part-time job. The following data describe her cumulative hourly earnings each week.

   (1, $8.25), (2, $16.50), (3, $24.75), (4, $33.00), (5, $41.25), (6, $49.50),
   (7, $57.75), (8, $66.00)

Name_____ Date_____ Period_____

5-4: FINDING THE SLOPE AND Y-INTERCEPT OF A LINE

To find the slope, or rate of change, do either of the following:

- If you are given two points, use the formula $m = \frac{y_2 - y_1}{x_2 - x_1}$, where m stands for the slope and (x_1, y_1) and (x_2, y_2) are two points on the line.

- If you are given an equation in slope-intercept form, use the equation $y = mx + b$, where m stands for the slope.

To find the y-intercept, or initial value, do either of the following:

- If you are given a table, find the value of y when $x = 0$.

- If you are given an equation, use the equation $y = mx + b$ where b represents the y-intercept.

To write a function rule for a linear function, determine the slope and y-intercept. Then write the rule in the form of $y = mx + b$.

Directions: Each line below is described by two points, an equation, table, graph, or a verbal description. Follow the directions for each part. Then find your answers in the Answer Bank and complete the statements at the end by writing the letter of each answer in the space above its problem number. Some answers will not be used.

Part One: Find the slope.

1. $y = 2x + 4$

2.

x	y
−1	1
0	−1
1	−3

3. $y = 6x - 1$

4.

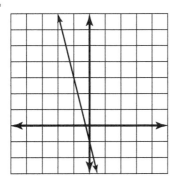

(Continued)

Part Two: Find the *y*-intercept.

5. $y = 4x + 3$

6.

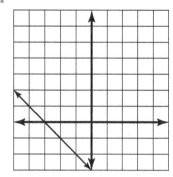

7.

x	y
−1	4
0	−1
2	−6

Part Three: Write a function to model each relationship.

8. A cell phone company charges $100 for 10 gigabytes of data per month. They charge $12 for every gigabyte after the first 10. Write a function rule to show the monthly data bill where *y* represents the total charge and *x* represents the amount of data over 10 gigabytes.

9.

x	y
0	20
1	21
2	22

10.

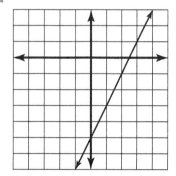

(*Continued*)

H. −1	G. 2	E. 6	U. −4	D. $y = x + 20$	S. $y = 20x + 10$
W. 1	N. 3	R. −2	T. −3	O. $y = 2x − 5$	I. $y = 12x + 100$

William _____ first used the symbol for parallel.

$\overline{10}$ $\overline{4}$ $\overline{1}$ $\overline{7}$ $\overline{6}$ $\overline{2}$ $\overline{3}$ $\overline{9}$

Pierre _____ first used the symbol for perpendicular.

$\overline{7}$ $\overline{3}$ $\overline{2}$ $\overline{8}$ $\overline{1}$ $\overline{10}$ $\overline{5}$ $\overline{3}$

5–5: ANALYZING AND GRAPHING FUNCTIONS

Graphs can be used to show a relationship between two quantities. Being able to interpret graphs and create graphs are important skills.

Directions, Part One: Write a description of the following graphs.

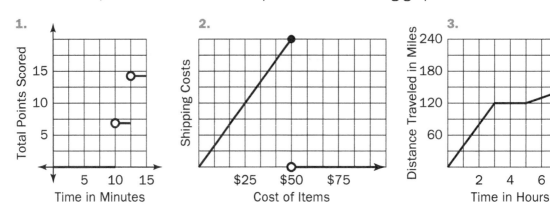

Directions, Part Two: Sketch graphs that show the relationship between the quantities described below. You may wish to create a table of values to help you draw your graphs.

4. When Sarah begins her morning run, she warms up for 5 minutes by running at a rate of 5 miles per hour. She then increases her speed to 7 miles per hour for 55 minutes. She ends her run with a 5 minute cool-down by walking at a rate of 3 miles per hour.

5. Before exercising, Sarah's heart rate is constant. When she runs, her heart rate increases. Use the information in problem 4 to show the relationship between her heart rate and her running rate.

Name _____ Date _____ Period _____

5–6: UNDERSTANDING FUNCTIONS

A function is a relation in which each element of the domain is paired with exactly one element of the range.

Directions: Determine if each statement is *true* or *false*. Write the letter of each correct answer in the space above its statement number at the end.

1. $f(x) = x^2$ is a function because every element in the domain is assigned to exactly one element in the range. (I. True   G. False)

2. $f(x) = x^2$ is not a function because the number 4 in the range is paired with both −2 and 2 in the domain. (A. True   P. False)

3. If $f(x) = x^2$ and the input is 2, then $f(2)$ is the output of the function. (S. True   M. False)

4. If $f(x) = x^2$, then the graph is the same as the graph of $y = x^2$. (R. True   N. False)

5. All linear equations in the form of $y = mx + b$ are functions because every real number in the domain is assigned exactly one real number in the range. (R. True   C. False)

6. The graph of $y = 3$ is the graph of $f(x) = 3$ where x is a real number. (O. True   A. False)

7. The graph of $x = 3$ is a function. (F. True   E. False)

8. If $f(1) = 1$ and $f(-1) = -1$, then f is a function. (W. True   U. False)

Your work is _____.

$$\overline{3} \quad \overline{8} \quad \overline{2} \quad \overline{7} \quad \overline{5} \quad \overline{1} \quad \overline{6} \quad \overline{4}$$

Name _____ Date _____ Period _____

5-7: FINDING THE VALUES OF FUNCTIONS

A function is a set of points and a rule that pairs each value of x with exactly one value of y. Functions can be described in two ways:

- $f : x \to 3x - 4$, which means that the function f pairs x with $3x - 4$. If $x = 3$, then 3 is paired with 5. This is written as $f(3) = 5$.

- $h(x) = -5x + 2$, which means that the function h pairs x with $-5x + 2$. If $x = 4$, then 4 is paired with -18. This is written as $h(4) = -18$.

A function cannot be evaluated if the denominator is zero. Such functions are undefined, and the value is $\varnothing$.

Directions: Find the value of each function, if possible. Then find each value in the Answer Bank. Some answers will not be used. Complete the statement at the end by writing the letter of each answer in the space above its problem number. You will need to divide the letters into words.

$$f : x \to 3x - 4 \qquad P : x \to x^2 \qquad h(x) = -5x + 2$$
$$F(x) = \frac{10}{x} \qquad H(x) = \frac{x+2}{x^2-4} \qquad g(x) = \sqrt{x}$$

1. $P\left(\frac{1}{5}\right) =$ _____   2. $H(0) =$ _____   3. $g(36) =$ _____

4. $P(0) =$ _____   5. $h\left(-\frac{1}{10}\right) =$ _____   6. $F\left(-\frac{1}{2}\right) =$ _____

7. $f\left(\frac{1}{3}\right) =$ _____   8. $f(-1) =$ _____   9. $F\left(\frac{1}{2}\right) =$ _____

10. $f(1) =$ _____   11. $P\left(\frac{1}{2}\right) =$ _____   12. $h(0) =$ _____

13. $F(0) =$ _____   14. $f(-3) =$ _____   15. $F(10) =$ _____

Answer Bank

T. $\frac{1}{4}$	N. 2	R. 20	H. $\frac{1}{3}$	I. $\varnothing$	C. 6	O. 4	B. $-\frac{1}{2}$	F. -3
G. -13	S. -7	U. $\frac{1}{25}$	M. -2	E. 0	L. -20	A. $2\frac{1}{2}$	Y. -1	D. 1

In mathematics, a function _____
what operations must be performed.

$\overline{13}$ $\overline{8}$ $\overline{15}$ $\overline{4}$ $\overline{7}$ $\overline{13}$ $\overline{12}$ $\overline{4}$ $\overline{15}$ $\overline{2}$ $\overline{10}$ $\overline{5}$

$\overline{9}$ $\overline{1}$ $\overline{6}$ $\overline{4}$ $\overline{13}$ $\overline{12}$ $\overline{15}$ $\overline{13}$ $\overline{3}$ $\overline{5}$ $\overline{11}$ $\overline{13}$ $\overline{12}$ $\overline{14}$

Copyright © 2016 by Judith A. Muschla, Gary Robert Muschla, and Erin Muschla-Berry.

Name _____ Date _____ Period _____

5–8: DEFINING SEQUENCES RECURSIVELY

A sequence is a set of numbers whose domain is the set of positive integers or a subset of the positive integers that consists of 1, 2, 3, ... , n. Some sequences are functions that may be defined recursively, which means that they can be defined by the first term or first few terms, and then the other terms are defined using preceding terms.

For example, the multiples of five, 5, 10, 15, 20, ... , n represent a function. This function can be defined recursively as $f(1) = 5$, $f(n) = f(n - 1) + 5$ for $n > 1$. Using this definition, we can express the sequence as $f(1) = 5$, $f(2) = f(1) + 5 = 5 + 5 = 10$, $f(3) = f(2) + 5 = 10 + 5 = 15$, ... , $f(n) = f(n - 1) + 5$ for $n > 1$.

Directions: Find the specified term in each sequence and match your answers with the answers in the Answer Bank. One answer will not be used. Then answer the question at the end by writing the letter of each answer in the space above its problem number.

1. $f(1) = 12$, $f(n) = 0.5f(n - 1)$. Find $f(3)$.

2. $f(1) = 2$, $f(n) = 2f(n - 1)$. Find $f(4)$.

3. $f(1) = 100$, $f(n) = 0.4f(n - 1)$. Find $f(4)$.

4. $f(1) = 36$, $f(2) = 18$, $f(n) = f(n - 1) + f(n - 2)$. Find $f(5)$.

5. $f(1) = 12$, $f(2) = 7$, $f(n) = f(n - 1) - f(n - 2)$. Find $f(6)$.

6. $f(1) = 0.5$, $f(n) = f(n - 1) + 0.5$. Find $f(5)$.

7. $f(1) = -1$, $f(2) = 3$, $f(n) = f(n - 1) - f(n - 2)$. Find $f(4)$.

8. $f(1) = 2$, $f(2) = 3$, $f(n) = (n - 1) + f(n - 2)$. Find $f(5)$.

Answer Bank

| L. 16 | R. 5 | U. 13 | H. 9 | N. 1 | I. 2.5 | G. 3 | T. 126 | A. 6.4 |

The sequence defined recursively as $f(1) = 1$, $f(n) = f(n - 1) + n$ is known as a certain type of number. What type of number is this? _____

$\overline{4}$ $\overline{5}$ $\overline{6}$ $\overline{3}$ $\overline{7}$ $\overline{1}$ $\overline{8}$ $\overline{2}$ $\overline{3}$ $\overline{5}$

Name _____ Date _____ Period _____

5–9: IDENTIFYING KEY FEATURES OF GRAPHS

The graphs of functions can be described with key features, such as intercepts, intervals where the function is increasing, decreasing, positive, or negative, relative maximums and relative minimums, symmetry, and end behavior.

- The x-intercept is the value of x when $f(x) = 0$.

- The y-intercept is the value of $f(x)$ when $x = 0$.

- A function is increasing in an interval if $f(x)$ increases as x increases.

- A function is decreasing in an interval if $f(x)$ decreases as x increases.

- A function is positive in the interval where the graph of the function is above the x-axis.

- A function is negative in the interval where the graph of the function is below the x-axis.

- A relative maximum is a "hill" on the graph. The function is increasing to the left of the relative maximum and is decreasing to the right of the relative maximum.

- A relative minimum is a "valley" on the graph. The function is decreasing to the left of the relative minimum and is increasing to the right of the relative minimum.

- An axis of symmetry is a line where one side of the graph is a mirror image of the other side.

- The end behavior of the graph describes the values of $f(x)$ as x becomes very large and the values of $f(x)$ as x becomes very small.

Directions: Graph each function. Then select the key features from the Answer Bank that apply to each graph. Some features apply to more than one graph. Write the letters of the key features in the spaces above the function's number to complete a statement. You may have to unscramble the letters, and you will need to divide the letters into words.

(Continued)

Copyright © 2016 by Judith A. Muschla, Gary Robert Muschla, and Erin Muschla-Berry.

1. $f(x) = x^3 + 3x^2 - 4$

2. $f(x) = x^4 - 2x^3 - 11x^2 + 12x + 37$

3. $f(x) = -x - 4$

4. $f(x) = x^2 - 2x + 2$

Answer Bank

C. Decreasing in $(-2, 0)$

E. Positive in $(-\infty, \infty)$

N. The x-intercept is 1.

P. $y \to -\infty$ as $x \to \infty$

H. Increasing in $(1, \infty)$

G. $x = 0.5$ is the axis of symmetry.

D. $x = 1$ is the axis of symmetry.

B. There are two relative minimums.

A. The y-intercept is -4.

R. The relative maximum is $(0.5, 40.0625)$.

Every function _____.

$\overline{1}$ $\quad$ $\overline{1}$ $\quad$ $\overline{1}$ $\quad$ $\overline{2}$ $\quad$ $\overline{2}$ $\quad$ $\overline{2}$ $\quad$ $\overline{2}$ $\quad$ $\overline{3}$ $\quad$ $\overline{3}$ $\quad$ $\overline{4}$ $\quad$ $\overline{4}$ $\quad$ $\overline{4}$

5-10 RELATING THE DOMAIN OF A FUNCTION TO ITS GRAPH OR DESCRIPTION

You can find the domain of a function if you are given a graph or if you are given a verbal description of the quantities it describes.

To find the domain of a function by looking at a graph, consider the *x*-axis and determine what values are graphed. Then express these values using interval notation that is summarized below.

- An interval is closed if both endpoints are included. For example, [−4, 5] is a closed interval that includes −4, 5 and all real numbers between them.

- An interval is open if none of the endpoints are included. For example (−4, 5) is an open interval that includes all real numbers between −4 and 5.

- An interval is half open if only one endpoint is included. For example [−4, 5) is a half-open interval that includes −4 and all real number between −4 and 5. It does not include 5. (−4, 5] is a half-open interval that includes 5 and all real numbers between −4 and 5. It does not include −4.

- An interval that continues indefinitely is expressed as (−∞, ∞).

To find the domain of a function, given a description of the quantities it describes, determine the values of *x* for which the description makes sense.

Directions: Find the domain of each function. Match your answers with the answers in the Answer Bank. Some answers will be used more than once, and some will not be used. Complete the statement at the end by writing the letter of each answer in the space above its problem number. You will need to divide the letters into words.

1.
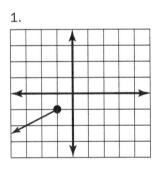

2.
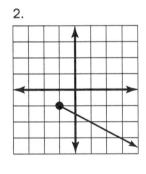

3.
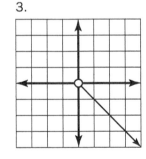

4.
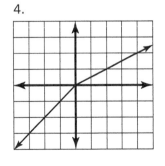

5.
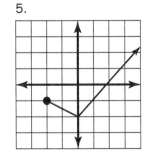

6.
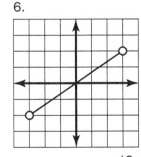

(Continued)

7. The square root of a positive number

8. The multiples of 2

9. The cube root of a number

Answer Bank

M. [−2, ∞)	F. [−1, ∞)	P. (−3, 3)
A. [∞, −1)	T. (−∞, −1]	E. The positive integers
R. (−∞, ∞)	O. (0, ∞)	S. The negative integers

Function is taken from the Latin term "functio" which means _____.

$\overline{1}$ $\overline{7}$ $\overline{6}$ $\overline{8}$ $\overline{4}$ $\overline{2}$ $\overline{3}$ $\overline{9}$ $\overline{5}$

5-11: FINDING THE AVERAGE RATE OF CHANGE OVER SPECIFIED INTERVALS

Use the formula $m = \frac{y_2 - y_1}{x_2 - x_1}$ to find the average rate of change of a function in a given interval. If a function is linear, the average rate of change is the slope of the line that is the graph of the function. If the function is nonlinear, the average rate of change is the slope of the line containing the points whose values of x are the endpoints of the interval. Unlike a linear function, however, the average rate of change of a nonlinear function may change in different intervals.

Directions: Find the average rate of change of each function over the specified interval and match your answers with the answers in the Answer Bank. One answer will not be used. Write the letter of each answer in the space above its problem number to complete the statement. You will need to divide the letters into words.

1. Interval: [0, 2]

x	y
0	6
2	8
4	10

2. Interval: [−1, 1]

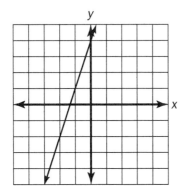

3. Interval: [0, 2]

x	y
0	0
1	1
2	4

(Continued)

Copyright © 2016 by Judith A. Muschla, Gary Robert Muschla, and Erin Muschla-Berry.

4. Interval: [−2, 1]

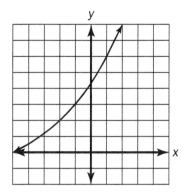

5. Interval: [1, 3]

x	y
−1	5
1	−3
3	−9

6. Interval: [−2, 0]

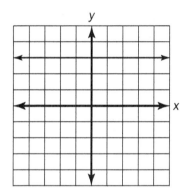

7. Interval: [−5, −1]

x	y
−5	10
−3	1
−1	5

(Continued)

8. Interval: [−1, 1]

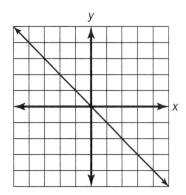

9. Interval: [4, 8]

x	y
2	7
4	15
8	21

Answer Bank

| L. 0 | S. $\frac{3}{2}$ | N. 2 | C. −1 | T. 3 | A. −3 | I. −2 | E. $\frac{4}{3}$ | P. $-\frac{5}{4}$ | O. 1 |

The graphs of linear functions have a _____.

$\overline{8}$ $\quad$ $\overline{1}$ $\quad$ $\overline{3}$ $\quad$ $\overline{9}$ $\quad$ $\overline{2}$ $\quad$ $\overline{5}$ $\quad$ $\overline{3}$ $\quad$ $\overline{2}$ $\quad$ $\overline{9}$ $\quad$ $\overline{6}$ $\quad$ $\overline{1}$ $\quad$ $\overline{7}$ $\quad$ $\overline{4}$

194

Name _____ Date _____ Period _____

5-12: GRAPHING LINEAR AND QUADRATIC FUNCTIONS

The graph of a linear function is a line, and the graph of a quadratic function is a parabola.

To graph a linear function, follow these steps:

- Find the y-intercept by finding $f(0)$.

- Find the x-intercept by letting $f(x) = 0$ and solving for x.

- Draw a straight line through these two points.

To graph a quadratic function follow these steps:

- Find the y- and x-intercepts.

- Find the vertex by writing the equation as $y = ax^2 + bx + c$. The x-coordinate of the vertex is $\frac{-b}{2a}$. The y-coordinate is $f\left(\frac{-b}{2a}\right)$.

- Determine if the parabola opens upward or downward by looking at the value of a. If $a > 0$, the parabola opens upward, and the vertex is the minimum value. If $a < 0$, the parabola opens downward, and the vertex is the maximum value.

- Make a table of values, including the intercepts and maximum and minimum values.

- Use these values to draw the parabola.

Directions: Graph each function and then find which graphs match each description. Some descriptions may apply to more than one graph. Write the letter of each graph after its description, and then complete the statement at the end by writing the letters of your answers. You may need to switch the order of the letters, and you will need to break the letters into words.

Y. $f(x) = 4x + 3$ S. $f(x) = x^2 + 3$ A. $f(x) = x^2 - 5x + 4$ I. $f(x) = -x^2 - 5$
E. $f(x) = x - 3$ N. $f(x) = -x - 6$ W. $f(x) = x^2 + 2x + 7$ L. $f(x) = x^2 - 4x + 4$

1. The y-intercept is 4. _____

2. The minimum value is $(-1, 6)$.
_____

3. The x-intercepts are 1 and 4. _____

4. The y-intercept is 3. _____

5. The minimum value is $(2.5, -2.25)$.

6. The minimum value is $(2, 0)$.
_____

7. The maximum value is $(0, -5)$. _____

8. The y-intercept is -6. _____

9. The x-intercept is 3. _____

The graph of a linear function is _____.

Name _____ Date _____ Period _____

5–13: GRAPHING POLYNOMIAL FUNCTIONS

Before you can sketch the graph of a polynomial function, you must find the zeroes and then determine the end behavior of the graph of the function. The zeroes are the points where $f(x) = 0$. Graphically, they are the points where the graph intersects the x-axis. The end behavior of the function refers to the behavior of the graph as the values of x get very small (approach $-\infty$) and as the values of x become very large (approach ∞).

To find the zeroes, set $f(x) = 0$, factor the expression, and then solve for x. The number of zeroes of the function is always less than or equal to the degree of the function.

To determine the end behavior, identify the degree of the function and the leading coefficient of the function.

- If the degree of the polynomial is odd and the leading coefficient is positive, then as $x \to -\infty$, $f(x) \to -\infty$, and as $x \to \infty$, $f(x) \to \infty$.

- If the degree of the polynomial is odd and the leading coefficient is negative, then as $x \to -\infty$, $f(x) \to \infty$, and as $x \to \infty$, $f(x) \to -\infty$.

- If the degree of the polynomial is even and the leading coefficient is positive, then as $x \to -\infty$, $f(x) \to \infty$, and as $x \to \infty$, $f(x) \to \infty$.

- If the degree of the polynomial is even and the leading coefficient is negative, then as $x \to -\infty$, $f(x) \to -\infty$, and as $x \to \infty$, $f(x) \to -\infty$.

Directions: Match each polynomial equation with its zeroes and end behavior. Find the zeroes and end behavior in the Answer Box. Some answers will not be used. Sketch the graph. Then complete the statement at the end by writing the letter of each answer in the space above its problem number.

Copyright © 2016 by Judith A. Muschla, Gary Robert Muschla, and Erin Muschla-Berry.

(Continued)

1. $f(x) = -x^2 + x + 12$ 2. $f(x) = x^2 - 2x - 3$ 3. $f(x) = x^3 - x^2 - x + 1$

4. $f(x) = x^3 + 2x^2 - 3x$ 5. $f(x) = x^4 - 5x^2 + 4$ 6. $f(x) = -x^3 + x^2 + 9x - 9$

Answer Box

S. $x = -1$ and $x = 1$; as $x \to -\infty$, $f(x) \to -\infty$, and as $x \to \infty$, $f(x) \to \infty$.

R. $x = -1$ and $x = 3$; as $x \to -\infty$, $f(x) \to -\infty$, and as $x \to \infty$, $f(x) \to -\infty$.

O. $x = -3$ and $x = 4$; as $x \to -\infty$, $f(x) \to -\infty$, and as $x \to \infty$, $f(x) \to -\infty$.

E. $x = -1$ and $x = 1$; as $x \to -\infty$, $f(x) \to -\infty$, and as $x \to \infty$, $f(x) \to -\infty$.

A. $x = -2$, $x = -1$, $x = 1$, and $x = 2$; as $x \to -\infty$, $f(x) \to \infty$, and as $x \to \infty$,
   $f(x) \to \infty$.

T. $x = -3$, $x = 1$, and $x = 3$; as $x \to -\infty$, $f(x) \to \infty$, and as $x \to \infty$, $f(x) \to -\infty$.

C. $x = -3$, $x = 0$, and $x = 1$; as $x \to -\infty$, $f(x) \to -\infty$, and as $x \to \infty$, $f(x) \to \infty$.

N. $x = -1$ and $x = 3$; as $x \to -\infty$, $f(x) \to \infty$, and as $x \to \infty$, $f(x) \to \infty$.

The end behavior of the _____ function is always as $x \to -\infty$, $f(x) = k$
and as $x \to \infty$, $f(x) = k$.

$\overline{4}$ $\overline{1}$ $\overline{2}$ $\overline{3}$ $\overline{6}$ $\overline{5}$ $\overline{2}$ $\overline{6}$

Name _____ Date _____ Period _____

5-14: REWRITING QUADRATIC EQUATIONS

Quadratic equations can be expressed in different ways, depending on whether you need to know the zeroes, vertex, or symmetry of the graph.

If you need to know the zeroes, write the equation in factored form. For example, $x^2 - 13x + 36 = 0$ can be expressed as $(x - 9)(x - 4) = 0$. The zeroes are 9 and 4.

If you need to know the vertex and the axis of symmetry of the graph, express the equation as $y - k = a(x - h)^2$. The vertex is (h, k), and the axis of symmetry is the vertical line $x = h$. If $a > 0$, the graph opens upward, and the vertex is the minimum value. If $a < 0$, the graph opens downward, and the vertex is the maximum value. For example, $y = x^2 + 6x - 15$ can be rewritten by completing the square as $y + 24 = (x + 3)^2$. The vertex, $(-3, -24)$, is the minimum value. The axis of symmetry is $x = -3$.

Directions: Solve each problem and match each answer with an answer in the Answer Bank. Not all answers will be used. Then complete the statement at the end by writing the letter of each answer in the space above its problem number. You will need to reverse the order of the letters.

1. Find the zeroes of $y = x^2 - x - 72$.

2. Find the vertex and axis of symmetry of $y = x^2 - 4x - 6$.

3. Find the vertex and axis of symmetry of $y = -x^2 + 10x - 12$.

4. The length of a rectangle is 3 less than x. The width of the rectangle is 4 more than x. The area of the rectangle is 8 square units. Find the value of x.

5. The sum of a positive number, x, and its square is 72. Find the number.

6. Raymundo has 60 yards of fencing to enclose a rectangular garden. Write an equation to find the value of x that results in the largest area he can enclose. Let x equal the length of the garden and $30 - x$ equal the width. Then solve for x.

Answer Bank

H. $(-15, 225)$; $x = -15$	R. $x = 8$	E. $(2, -10)$; $x = 2$
G. $x = 9$ and $x = -8$	S. $x = -4$	A. $x = 4$
L. $(5, 13)$; $x = 5$	P. $x = -9$ and $x = -8$	B. $(15, 225)$; $x = 15$

Evariste Galois proved that polynomials with a degree higher than four cannot be solved using _____.

$\overline{4}$ $\qquad$ $\overline{5}$ $\qquad$ $\overline{6}$ $\qquad$ $\overline{2}$ $\qquad$ $\overline{1}$ $\qquad$ $\overline{3}$ $\qquad$ $\overline{4}$

Name_____ Date_____ Period_____

5-15: COMPARING PROPERTIES OF FUNCTIONS

Functions may be described in four different ways: algebraically, graphically, in tables, or by verbal descriptions. To compare the properties of functions, describe each function in the same way.

Directions: Seven functions are described below.

1. $f(x)$ is one less than a number, x, squared.

2. $g(x) = (x - 1)^2$

3. $G(x)$ is one more than a number, x, squared.

4. $F(x) = x^3$

5.

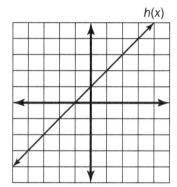

6.

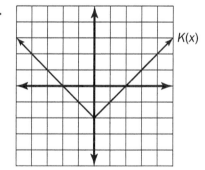

7.

x	−2	0	2	3
$H(x)$	−3	3	9	12

Refer to the functions above and answer the following questions. Choose your answers from the two functions that follow each question. Complete the statement at the end by writing the letter of each answer in the space above its question number.

1. Which of the following two functions has the smaller minimum value? (R. $f(x)$ A. $g(x)$)

(Continued)

2. Which of the following two functions has the larger *y*-intercept? (E. $h(x)$ M. $f(x)$)

3. Which of the following two functions has the larger rate of change? (U. $h(x)$ T. $H(x)$)

4. Which of the following two functions has the larger minimum value? (N. $g(x)$ S. $G(x)$)

5. Which of the following two functions is symmetric to the origin? (O. $F(x)$ E. $H(x)$)

6. Which of the following two functions is symmetric to $x = 1$? (T. $K(x)$ I. $g(x)$)

7. Which of the following two functions has the smaller minimum value? (D. $f(x)$ P. $K(x)$)

All functions have _____.

$$\overline{7} \qquad \overline{1} \qquad \overline{5} \qquad \overline{7} \qquad \overline{2} \qquad \overline{1} \qquad \overline{3} \qquad \overline{6} \qquad \overline{2} \qquad \overline{4}$$

Copyright © 2016 by Judith A. Muschla, Gary Robert Muschla, and Erin Muschla-Berry.

5–16: WRITING FUNCTIONS

Functions can be added, subtracted, multiplied, and divided to form other functions. The sum, difference, product, and quotient are defined below:

- $(f + g)(x) = f(x) + g(x)$

- $(f - g)(x) = f(x) - g(x)$

- $(f \cdot g)(x) = f(x) \cdot g(x)$

- $\left(\dfrac{f}{g}\right)(x) = \dfrac{f(x)}{g(x)}, g(x) \neq 0$

Functions may also be formed by the composition of one function with another. $(f \circ g)(x) = f(g(x))$

Directions: Write $f(x)$ and $g(x)$ to model the situations described in each problem. Then combine the functions to write a sum, difference, product, quotient, or composition of the two functions. Select the proper notation from the answers in the Answer Bank and complete the statement at the end by writing the letter of each answer in the space above its problem number. One answer will not be used. You will need to divide the letters into words.

1. An online company charges 10% of the total purchase price, x, for shipping. (The total purchase price does not include sales tax.) Write $f(x)$ to represent the shipping cost. The same company charges a 7% sales tax on the total purchase for in-state customers who buy their products. There is no sales tax on the shipping cost. Write $g(x)$ to represent the sales tax. Use these two functions to create another function to show the total cost of the order, including shipping and sales tax.

2. Write $f(x)$ to show that the length of a rectangle is one more than twice a number, x. Write $g(x)$ to show that the width of the rectangle is one less than twice x. Use these two functions to create another function to model the area of the rectangle.

3. Mikal is starting a part-time job. He earns $12 per hour. Write $f(x)$ to show his gross earnings. Use x to represent the number of hours Mikal works. 20% of his gross earnings are deducted. Write $g(x)$ to show the amount that is deducted. Use these two functions to create another function to model his take-home pay.

4. Write $g(x)$ to show the length of a rectangle that is three less than a number, x. Write $f(x)$ to show that the area of this rectangle is six less than the difference of x squared and x. Use these two functions to create another function to model the width of the rectangle.

(Continued)

5. Write $f(x)$ to show the area of a circle with radius x. Write $g(x)$ to show that the radius of a circle is tripled. Use these two functions to create another function that shows the area of a circle when the radius is tripled.

Answer Bank

I. $(f \cdot g)(x)$	V. $\left(\dfrac{f}{g}\right)(x)$	A. $(g \circ f)(x)$	D. $(f - g)(x)$	B. $(f \circ g)(x)$	E. $(f + g)(x)$

Some functions may not _____.

$\overline{5}$ $\quad$ $\overline{1}$ $\quad$ $\overline{3}$ $\quad$ $\overline{2}$ $\quad$ $\overline{4}$ $\quad$ $\overline{2}$ $\quad$ $\overline{3}$ $\quad$ $\overline{1}$ $\quad$ $\overline{3}$

5-17: WRITING ARITHMETIC AND GEOMETRIC SEQUENCES

Arithmetic and geometric sequences can be written recursively or with an explicit formula.

In an arithmetic sequence, each term is found by adding a constant to each preceding term. The constant is called the common difference. To define this sequence recursively, use the formula $a_n = a_{n-1} + d$. To define it by using an explicit formula, use the formula $a_n = a_1 + (n - 1)d$. In both formulas, a_1 is the initial term, a_n is the nth term, and d is the common difference.

In a geometric sequence, each term is found by multiplying each preceding term by a constant. This constant is called the common ratio. To define this sequence recursively, use the formula $a_n = a_{n-1} \cdot r$. To define it by using an explicit formula, use the formula $a_n = a_1 \cdot r^{n-1}$. In both formulas, a_1 is the initial term, a_n is the nth term, and r is the common ratio.

Directions: Write each sequence recursively and by using an explicit formula. One way of writing each sequence is included in the Answer Bank. Match one of your answers for each sequence with an answer in the Answer Bank. Not all of the answers will be used. Then answer the question by writing the letter of each answer in the space above its sequence number.

1. 15, 5, −5, −15, −25, ...
2. −6, −10, −14, −18, −22, ...
3. 10, 13, 16.9, 21.97, 28.561, ...
4. 8, 3.2, 1.28, 0.512, ...
5. 8, 12, 18, 27, 40.5, ...
6. 0.5, 0.55, 0.6, 0.65, 0.7, ...
7. 2, −2, 2, −2, 2, ...

8. A house purchased for $240,000 appreciates at a rate of 5% per year.

9. Olivia began training by running 1.5 miles on the first day, and she increases the length of the run by 0.2 miles per day.

Answer Bank

R. $a_n = 8(1.5)^{n-1}$	N. $a_n = 1 + 6n$	A. $a_n = 0.45 + .05n$
I. $a_n = -2 + 4n$	C. $a_n = 0.4a_{n-1}$	T. $a_n = 0.5_{n-1} + 0.5$
L. $a_n = 1.3a_{n-1}$	U. $a_n = 25 - 10n$	O. $a_n = 1.05a_{n-1}$
E. $a_n = 2(-1)^{n-1}$	S. $a_n = 1.3 + 0.2n$	D. $a_n = a_{n-1} - 4$

The numbers 1, 3, 4, 7, 11, 18, ... are part of a sequence named after a French mathematician. Who was he?

$\overline{7}$　$\overline{2}$　$\overline{8}$　$\overline{1}$　$\overline{6}$　$\overline{5}$　$\overline{2}$　　$\overline{3}$　$\overline{1}$　$\overline{4}$　$\overline{6}$　$\overline{9}$

5–18: TRANSFORMING A FUNCTION

A function may be transformed by building another function. Following are some functions that can be built on $y = f(x)$.

- $y = f(x) + k$: If k is positive, the graph of $y = f(x)$ is shifted up. If k is negative, the graph of $y = f(x)$ is shifted down.

- $y = f(x - k)$: If k is positive, the graph of $y = f(x)$ is shifted to the right. If k is negative, the graph of $y = f(x)$ is shifted to the left.

- $y = -f(x)$: The graph of $y = f(x)$ is reflected in the x-axis.

- $y = f(-x)$: The graph of $y = f(x)$ is reflected in the y-axis.

- $y = kf(x)$: If $0 < k < 1$, the graph of $y = f(x)$ is vertically compressed. If $k > 1$, the graph of $y = f(x)$ is vertically stretched.

- $y = f(kx)$: If $0 < k < 1$, the graph of $y = f(x)$ is horizontally stretched. If $k > 1$, the graph of $y = f(x)$ is horizontally compressed.

Directions: Consider the graph of the function $y = f(x)$.

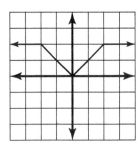

Match each equation with its graph. Then complete the statements by writing the letter of each graph in the space above its matching equation's number. One of the terms will require a hyphen, and you will need to divide the letters into words. (The first term completes the first statement, and the second term completes the second statement.)

1. $y = f(x) - 1$ 2. $y = 0.5f(x)$ 3. $y = -f(x)$

4. $y = f(-x)$ 5. $y = f(x - 0.5)$ 6. $y = f(x + 1)$

7. $y = f(x - 1)$ 8. $y = 1.5f(x)$ 9. $y = f(1.5x)$

(Continued)

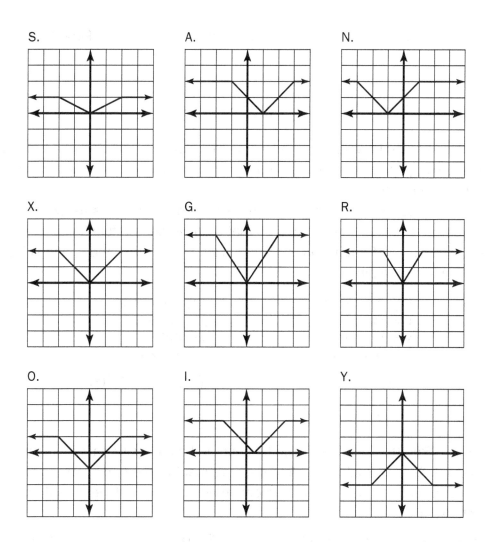

S.

A.

N.

X.

G.

R.

O.

I.

Y.

Graphs of even functions such as $f(x) = x^2$ are symmetric with respect to the
_____ because $f(x) = f(-x)$. Graphs of odd functions such as $f(x) = x^3$ are symmetric with respect to the _____ because $f(-x) = -f(x)$.

$\overline{3}$ $\overline{7}$ $\overline{4}$ $\overline{5}$ $\overline{2}$ $\overline{1}$ $\overline{9}$ $\overline{5}$ $\overline{8}$ $\overline{5}$ $\overline{6}$

5-19: FINDING THE INVERSES OF FUNCTIONS

Every function has an inverse, but the inverse may not be a function. If a horizontal line intersects a graph of the function more than once, then the inverse of the function is not a function.

Functions whose inverses are not functions have even numbers as exponents. It is then necessary to restrict the domain, so that the inverse is a function.

To find the inverse of a function, replace $f(x)$ with y, switch x and y, and solve for y. Following are two examples.

$$f(x) = 7x - 10$$
$$y = 7x - 10$$
$$x = 7y - 10$$
$$x + 10 = 7y$$
$$\frac{x+10}{7} = y$$
$$\frac{x}{7} + \frac{10}{7} = y = f^{-1}(x)$$

$$f(x) = 4x^3 + 2$$
$$y = 4x^3 + 2$$
$$x = 4y^3 + 2$$
$$x - 2 = 4y^3$$
$$\sqrt[3]{\frac{x-2}{4}} = y = f^{-1}(x)$$

Directions: Find the inverse of each function and match your answers with the answers in the Answer Bank. Complete the statement at the end by writing the letter of each answer in the space above its problem number. You will need to divide the letters into words.

1. $f(x) = 2x - 4$
2. $f(x) = x^3$
3. $f(x) = x^5$
4. $f(x) = x$
5. $f(x) = 2x + 4$
6. $f(x) = \frac{1}{2}x^3 - 2$
7. $f(x) = x + 7$
8. $f(x) = 3x - 1$
9. $f(x) = \frac{1}{2}x + 1$
10. $f(x) = 3x^3 + 1$
11. $f(x) = \frac{x^5 + 2}{7}$
12. $f(x) = x^7$

Answer Bank

O. $f^{-1}(x) = \sqrt[5]{7x - 2}$ S. $f^{-1}(x) = \sqrt[3]{x}$ I. $f^{-1}(x) = x - 7$

A. $f^{-1}(x) = \frac{1}{2}x - 2$ L. $f^{-1}(x) = 2x - 2$ N. $f^{-1}(x) = \frac{1}{2}x + 2$

E. $f^{-1}(x) = \sqrt[7]{x}$ R. $f^{-1}(x) = \sqrt[5]{x}$ F. $f^{-1}(x) = \sqrt[3]{\frac{x-1}{3}}$

T. $f^{-1}(x) = \frac{1}{3}x + \frac{1}{3}$ C. $f^{-1}(x) = \sqrt[3]{2x + 4}$ U. $f^{-1}(x) = x$

For each linear function $f(x) = mx + b$ where $m \neq 0$, the inverse _____.

$\overline{\quad}$ $\overline{\quad}$ $\overline{\quad}$ $\overline{\quad}$ $\overline{\quad}$ $\overline{\quad}$ $\overline{\quad\;}$ $\overline{\quad}$ $\overline{\quad}$
  7   2   5   9   7   1   12   5   3

$\overline{\quad\;}$ $\overline{\quad}$ $\overline{\quad}$ $\overline{\quad}$ $\overline{\quad}$ $\overline{\quad}$ $\overline{\quad\;}$ $\overline{\quad}$
  10   4   1   6   8   7   11   1

Name _____ Date _____ Period _____

5–20: PROVING LINEAR FUNCTIONS GROW BY EQUAL DIFFERENCES OVER EQUAL INTERVALS

Linear functions can be written as $y = mx + b$. The graph of a linear function is a line whose slope is m and whose y-intercept is b.

Directions: Complete the chart. Then explain how linear functions change in various intervals.

Row	Values of x	Values of y	Change in y	Change in x	$\dfrac{\text{Change in } y}{\text{Change in } x}$
1	$x = -10$ $x = -4$				
2	$x = -3$ $x = -1$				
3	$x = 0$ $x = 5$				
4	$x = x_2$ $x = x_1$				

Name _____ Date _____ Period _____

5–21: PROVING EXPONENTIAL FUNCTIONS GROW BY EQUAL FACTORS OVER EQUAL INTERVALS

Exponential functions can be written as $y = ab^x$, where a and b are each greater than 0. a represents the initial value of the function.

Directions: Complete the chart. Then explain how exponential functions change in various intervals.

Row	Values of x	Values of y	Quotient of the Values of y	Change in x
1	$x = 1$ $x = 0$			
2	$x = 5$ $x = 3$			
3	$x = 12$ $x = 8$			
4	$x = x_2$ $x = x_1$			

Name _____ Date _____ Period _____

5-22: CONSTRUCTING LINEAR AND EXPONENTIAL FUNCTIONS

A linear function is a function of the form $f(x) = mx + b$, where m is the slope of the line and b is the y-intercept. An exponential function is a function of the form $f(x) = ab^x$, where a is the initial value of the function. When $b > 0$, the function models exponential growth, and when $0 < b < 1$, $b \neq 0$, the function models exponential decay.

Directions: Find the linear or exponential function that models the data. Match your functions with the functions in the Answer Bank. Some answers will not be used. Then answer the question by writing the letter of each function in the space above its problem number. You will need to divide the letters into words.

1.

x	y
−3	4
0	1
1	0

2.

x	y
−3	32
−2	16
−1	8

3.

x	y
4	8
5	16
6	32

4. The initial term is 1. Each successive term is 0.5 of the preceding term.

5. The initial term is 5. Each successive term is 4 more than the preceding term.

6. The initial term is −3.5. Each successive term is 0.5 more than the preceding term.

(Continued)

209

7.

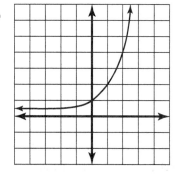

8.

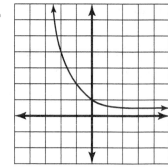

9.

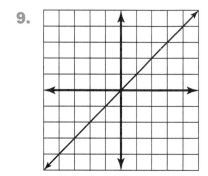

Answer Bank

I. $f(x) = 4x + 1$	U. $f(x) = -x + 1$	H. $f(x) = 0.5x - 4$	N. $f(x) = -x + 1$
C. $f(x) = 4(0.5)^x$	A. $f(x) = 2^x$	T. $f(x) = 2(0.5)^x$	M. $f(x) = (0.5)^x$
S. $f(x) = -x$	O. $f(x) = x$	W. $f(x) = 4x - 1$	E. $f(x) = 0.5(2)^x$

Leonhard Euler was the first _____ use $f(x)$ to show a function.

$\overline{8}$ $\overline{7}$ $\overline{4}$ $\overline{6}$ $\overline{3}$ $\overline{8}$ $\overline{7}$ $\overline{4}$ $\overline{5}$ $\overline{2}$ $\overline{5}$ $\overline{7}$ $\overline{1}$ $\overline{4}$ $\overline{9}$

Name_____ Date_____ Period_____

5-23: OBSERVING THE BEHAVIOR OF QUANTITIES THAT INCREASE EXPONENTIALLY

Tables and graphs can be used to compare the growth of different functions. The table below compares the growth of y_1, an exponential function, with y_2, a cubing function. According to the table, when $x \geq 6$, the value of the exponential function exceeds the value of the cubing function. These values can be verified by graphing each equation.

x	$y_1 = 3^x$	$y_2 = 3x^3$
0	1	0
1	3	3
2	9	24
3	27	81
4	81	192
5	243	375
6	729	648
7	2,187	1,029

Directions: Use your graphing calculator to create a table of values for the functions below. Set up the table so that the values of x are integers and the change in x is 1. Find the values of x that will make each statement true. Find your answers in the Answer Bank and then write the letter of each answer in the space above its problem number to complete the statement. You will need to divide the letters into words.

1. $y_1 = 2^x$ always exceeds $y_2 = 2$ when _____.

2. $y_1 = 2^x$ always exceeds $y_2 = x + 5$ when _____.

3. $y_1 = 2^x$ always exceeds $y_2 = x - 4$ when _____.

4. $y_1 = 2^x + 9$ always exceeds $y_2 = x^2 - 3x + 1$ when _____.

5. $y_1 = 3^x - 1$ always exceeds $y_2 = x^2 + 12$ when _____.

6. $y_1 = 2^x$ always exceeds $y_2 = x^4$ when _____.

7. $y_1 = 2^x - 3$ always exceeds $y_2 = 2x + 1$ when _____.

8. $y_1 = 2^x$ always exceeds $y_2 = x^3 - 5$ when _____.

9. $y_1 = 10^x$ always exceeds $y_2 = 2x + 10$ when _____.

10. $y_1 = 4^x$ always exceeds $y_2 = 5x^4$ when _____.

(Continued)

Y. $x \geq 4$ W. $x \geq 2$ R. $x > 3$ I. $x \geq 3$ P. x is any real number.

O. $x \geq -1$ G. $x > 16$ A. $x \geq 7$ L. $x \geq 10$ D. $x > 1$

Quantities that increase exponentially _____.

$\overline{6}$ $\overline{2}$ $\overline{4}$ $\overline{9}$ $\overline{2}$ $\overline{10}$ $\overline{3}$ $\overline{5}$ $\overline{1}$ $\overline{8}$ $\overline{7}$

Name_____ Date_____ Period_____

5-24: WRITING AND SOLVING EXPONENTIAL EQUATIONS

Following are types of logarithmic functions:

- $f(x) = \log_b x$ is a logarithmic function. The logarithmic equation $y = \log_b x$ is equivalent to the exponential equation $x = b^y$ whose base is b, $b > 0$, $b \neq 1$.

- $f(x) = \ln x$ is the natural logarithmic function. The logarithmic equation $y = \ln x$ is equivalent to the exponential equation $x = e^y$ whose base is e.

- $f(x) = \log x$ is the common logarithmic function. The logarithmic equation $y = \log x$ is equivalent to the exponential equation $x = 10^y$ whose base is 10.

Directions: Write an equivalent exponential equation for each logarithmic equation. Then find the solution. For each problem, match the exponential equation or the solution with an answer in the Answer Bank. Complete the statement at the end by writing the letter of each answer in the space above its problem number. You will need to divide the letters into words.

1. $\log_5 x = 3$

2. $\log_3 \frac{1}{27} = x$

3. $\ln x = 5$

4. $\log_{\sqrt{5}} 25 = x$

5. $\ln x = 1$

6. $\log x = 2$

7. $\log_{25} x = \frac{1}{2}$

8. $\log_3 x = 2$

9. $\log x = \frac{1}{2}$

10. $\log_2 8^x = -3$

11. $\log \frac{1}{100} = x$

12. $\ln x = 10$

13. $\ln 10 = x$

Answer Bank

A. $x = 3^2$	M. $25 = \left(\sqrt{5}\right)^x$	Y. $\frac{1}{100} = 10^x$	S. $x = 5$	T. $x = 5^3$
I. $10 = e^x$	E. $x = 10^{\frac{1}{2}}$	O. $x = 10^2$	R. $2^{-3} = 8^x$	G. $\frac{1}{27} = 3^x$
L. $x \approx 2.72$	F. $x = e^{10}$	H. $x = e^5$		

Scottish mathematician John Napier is best known as the inventor of the first

_____ .

$\overline{7}$ $\overline{11}$ $\overline{7}$ $\overline{1}$ $\overline{9}$ $\overline{4}$ $\overline{6}$ $\overline{12}$ $\overline{5}$ $\overline{6}$ $\overline{2}$ $\overline{8}$ $\overline{10}$ $\overline{13}$ $\overline{1}$ $\overline{3}$ $\overline{4}$ $\overline{7}$

Name _____ Date _____ Period _____

5-25: INTERPRETING PARAMETERS IN A LINEAR OR EXPONENTIAL FUNCTION

Parameters are values that are built into a function. These values may have various meanings, depending on the context of the problem.

Directions: Answer each question.

1. Attendance at a high school play on Friday was 15% more than the attendance on Thursday. This can be modeled by $f(x) = 0.15x$, where x is the number of people who attended on Thursday. Do you agree? Explain your answer.

2. Sally found that the distance she power-walked can be modeled by $f(x) = \frac{2}{3}x$, where x is the time in seconds and $f(x)$ is the distance she walked in feet. Because $\frac{2}{3}$ is less than 1, her distance is declining. Do you agree? Explain your answer.

3. The price of an adult ticket at a matinee is $10. This can be modeled by $f(x) = 10x$, where x is the number of adult tickets that are purchased and $f(x)$ is the total cost of adult tickets. When will $f(x) = \$35.00$? Explain your answer.

4. The average increase in a school's enrollment has been 1.2% per year for the past 10 years. This is modeled by $f(x) = 2{,}270(1 + 0.012)^x$, where x is the number of years. What does the 2,270 represent?

5. In problem 4, can $f(x) = 2{,}270(1 + 0.012)^x$ also be expressed as $f(x) = 2{,}270 + 2{,}270(0.012)^x$ by using the Distributive Property? Explain your answer.

6. Luis feels that an exponential function may not grow at all. He noted that $f(x) = 1^x$ will always equal one. Do you agree? Explain your answer.

Name _____ Date _____ Period _____

5-26: USING RADIAN AND DEGREE MEASURES

Angles may be expressed in degrees and radians. A degree is the measure of a central angle subtended by $\frac{1}{360}$ of the circumference of the circle. A radian is the measure of a central angle that intersects an arc that has the same length as the radius of the circle. The abbreviation for radian is rad.

To change degrees to radians, multiply the number of degrees by $\frac{\pi}{180}$. Example: Express 90° in radians. $90 \cdot \frac{\pi}{180} = \frac{\pi}{2}$

To change radians to degrees, multiply the number of radians by $\frac{180}{\pi}$. Example: Express $\frac{\pi}{3}$ in degrees. $\frac{\pi}{3} \cdot \frac{180}{\pi} = 60°$

Directions: For problems 1 to 5 express the degrees as radians. For problems 6 to 10 express the radians as degrees. Find each answer in the Answer Bank, and then answer the question by writing the letter of each answer in the space above its problem number. Some answers will not be used. You will need to divide the letters into words.

1. 120° 2. 15° 3. 180° 4. 45° 5. 100°

6. $\frac{\pi}{6}$ 7. $\frac{3\pi}{4}$ 8. $\frac{5\pi}{12}$ 9. $\frac{5\pi}{6}$ 10. $\frac{5\pi}{18}$

Answer Bank

N. $\frac{5\pi}{9}$	H. $\frac{\pi}{5}$	U. $\frac{\pi}{4}$	M. $\frac{\pi}{12}$	L. π	E. $\frac{2\pi}{3}$
R. 50°	T. 30°	W. 70°	G. 75°	S. 150°	A. 135°

Greek mathematician Eratosthenes used this to compute the circumference of the earth. What did he use?

$\overline{\quad}$ $\overline{\quad}$ $\overline{\quad}$ $\overline{\quad}$ $\overline{\quad}$ $\overline{\quad}$ $\overline{\quad}$ $\overline{\quad}$ $\overline{\quad}$ $\overline{\quad}$ $\overline{\quad}$ $\overline{\quad}$ $\overline{\quad}$ $\overline{\quad}$ $\overline{\quad}$ $\overline{\quad}$
7   5   8   3   1   2   1   7   9   4   10   1   2   1   5   6

Name_____ Date_____ Period_____

5-27: USING THE UNIT CIRCLE

When the terminal side of an angle θ in standard position in the unit circle rotates counterclockwise, the signs of the trigonometric functions vary. They are summarized in the following table.

Quadrant I	Quadrant II	Quadrant III	Quadrant IV
$\sin \theta$ is positive.	$\sin \theta$ is positive.	$\sin \theta$ is negative.	$\sin \theta$ is negative.
$\cos \theta$ is positive.	$\cos \theta$ is negative.	$\cos \theta$ is negative.	$\cos \theta$ is positive.
$\tan \theta$ is positive.	$\tan \theta$ is negative.	$\tan \theta$ is positive.	$\tan \theta$ is negative.

When the terminal side of an angle θ in standard position lies on the x-axis, θ is called a quadrantal angle. The values of x, y, r, and the trigonometric functions of quadrantal angles are shown in the following table.

$\theta = 0°$ or 0 rad	$\theta = 90°$ or $\frac{\pi}{2}$ rad	$\theta = 180°$ or π rad	$\theta = 270°$ or $\frac{3\pi}{2}$ rad
$y = 0, x = 1,$ $r = 1$ $\sin \theta = 0,$ $\cos \theta = 1,$ $\tan \theta = 0$	$y = 1, x = 0, r = 1$ $\sin \theta = 1,$ $\cos \theta = 0,$ $\tan \theta$ is undefined.	$y = 0, x = -1,$ $r = 1$ $\sin \theta = 0,$ $\cos \theta = -1,$ $\tan \theta = 0$	$y = -1, x = 0,$ $r = 1$ $\sin \theta = -1,$ $\cos \theta = 0,$ $\tan \theta$ is undefined.

Directions: Determine whether each statement is true or false. Complete the statement at the end by writing the letter of each answer in the space above its statement number.

1. $\sin 90° = 1$. (R. True   H. False)

2. $\cos \frac{3\pi}{4}$ is positive. (E. True   A. False)

3. $\cos 30° = \cos -30°$. (O. True   M. False)

4. $\sin 30° = \sin -30°$. (B. True   C. False)

5. $\sin -270° = -1$. (K. True   F. False)

6. $\tan \pi = \tan -\pi$. (U. True   P. False)

7. $\cos 210° = \cos -30°$. (Q. True   I. False)

8. $\tan 45° = \tan 225°$. (L. True   D. False)

(Continued)

216

9. $\sin -\frac{\pi}{2} = \sin \frac{\pi}{2}$. (G. True   T. False)

10. $\sin 150° = \sin 30°$ (N. True   J. False)

11. $\sin \frac{11\pi}{6} = -0.5$ (S. True   Y. False)

The sine and cosine are _____.

$\overline{\frac{4}{5}}$ $\qquad$ $\overline{\frac{7}{6}}$ $\qquad$ $\overline{\frac{1}{10}}$ $\qquad$ $\overline{\frac{4}{4}}$ $\qquad$ $\overline{\frac{6}{9}}$ $\qquad$ $\overline{\frac{8}{7}}$ $\qquad$ $\overline{\frac{2}{3}}$ $\qquad$ $\overline{\frac{1}{10}}$ $\qquad$ $\overline{\frac{1}{11}}$

Name_____ Date_____ Period_____

5–28: MODELING PERIODIC PHENOMENA

Some periodic phenomena such as temperature and rainfall can be modeled by the following sine and cosine functions: $f(x) = A\sin(B(t - C) + D)$ or $f(x) = A\cos(B(t - C) + D)$.

- A, the amplitude, is the difference between the highest and lowest points divided by 2.

- B is equal to 2π divided by the period. The period is 12 months.

- C is the horizontal shift.

- D, the midline, is the sum of the highest and lowest points divided by 2.

- t is the time in months.

Directions: Sketch a scatter plot of the data shown in each table, letting 0 represent January. Find the functions that model the data in table 1 and the functions that model the data in table 2. Answer the question by writing the letters of the functions in the spaces above their table number. Some functions will not be used. You may have to rearrange the letters to form the word.

Table 1: Monthly High Temperature in Anchorage, Alaska (in Degrees Fahrenheit)

Jan.	Feb.	Mar.	Apr.	May	June	July	Aug.	Sept.	Oct.	Nov.	Dec.
21.7°	26.1°	32.7°	43.6°	55.1°	62.3°	65.3°	63.3°	55.1°	40.6°	28.0°	22.8°

Table 2: Monthly High Temperature in Miami, Florida (in Degrees Fahrenheit)

Jan.	Feb.	Mar.	Apr.	May	June	July	Aug.	Sept.	Oct.	Nov.	Dec.
75.6°	77.0°	79.7°	82.7°	85.8°	88.1°	89.5°	89.8°	88.3°	84.9°	80.6°	76.8°

(Continued)

N. $f(x) = 7.1 \sin\left(\frac{\pi}{6}x + \frac{\pi}{2}\right) + 82.7$

E. $f(x) = 7.1 \sin\left(\frac{\pi}{6}x + \frac{3\pi}{2}\right) + 82.7$

I. $f(x) = 7.1 \cos\left(\frac{\pi}{6}x + 3\pi\right) + 82.7$

M. $f(x) = 21.8 \sin\left(\frac{\pi}{6}x - \frac{\pi}{2}\right) + 43.5$

P. $f(x) = 21.8 \cos\left(\frac{\pi}{6}x + \pi\right) + 43.5$

R. $f(x) = -21.8 \sin\left(\frac{\pi}{6}x + \pi\right) + 43.5$

D. $f(x) = -7.1 \sin\left(\frac{\pi}{6}x - \frac{3\pi}{2}\right) + 82.7$

O. $f(x) = 7.1 \cos\left(\frac{\pi}{6}x - \frac{3\pi}{2}\right) + 82.7$

T. $f(x) = 7.1 \cos\left(\frac{\pi}{6}x + \pi\right) + 82.7$

L. $f(x) = -21.8 \cos\left(\frac{\pi}{6}x\right) + 43.5$

A. $f(x) = 21.8 \sin\left(\frac{\pi}{6}x + \frac{3\pi}{2}\right) + 43.5$

U. $f(x) = 7.1 \cos\left(\frac{\pi}{6}x - \pi\right) + 82.7$

This word is associated with the graphs of the sine and cosine functions. What is it?

$\overline{1}$　　$\overline{1}$　　$\overline{1}$　　$\overline{1}$　　$\overline{2}$　　$\overline{2}$　　$\overline{2}$　　$\overline{2}$　　$\overline{2}$

Name _____ Date _____ Period _____

5-29: FINDING THE VALUES OF THE SINE, COSINE, AND TANGENT FUNCTIONS

The Pythagorean Identity, $\sin^2(\theta) + \cos^2(\theta) = 1$, can be used to find $\sin(\theta)$ if you know $\cos(\theta)$, or this identity can be used to find $\cos(\theta)$ if you know $\sin(\theta)$. Another useful identity is $\tan(\theta) = \frac{\sin(\theta)}{\cos(\theta)}$, where $\cos(\theta) \neq 0$. This, along with the Pythagorean Identity, is used when you know $\tan(\theta)$ and can be used to find $\sin(\theta)$ and $\cos(\theta)$.

Directions: Following are five statements about a trigonometric function and the quadrant θ is in. Find the values of the other trigonometric functions in the Answer Bank. Answer the question by writing the letter of each answer in the space above its problem number. You will need to divide the letters to form a name.

$\cos(\theta) = -\frac{3}{4}$; θ is in Quadrant II.   1. $\sin(\theta) = $ _____   2. $\tan(\theta) = $ _____

$\sin(\theta) = -\frac{1}{3}$; θ is in Quadrant III.   3. $\cos(\theta) = $ _____   4. $\tan(\theta) = $ _____

$\tan(\theta) = -\frac{\sqrt{14}}{7}$; θ is in Quadrant IV.   5. $\cos(\theta) = $ _____   6. $\sin(\theta) = $ _____

$\tan(\theta) = \frac{3}{4}$; θ is in Quadrant I.   7. $\sin(\theta) = $ _____   8. $\cos(\theta) = $ _____

$\sin(\theta) = \frac{2}{3}$; θ is in Quadrant II.   9. $\cos(\theta) = $ _____   10. $\tan(\theta) = $ _____

Answer Bank

H. $-\frac{2\sqrt{2}}{3}$	T. $\frac{4}{5}$	G. $\frac{\sqrt{2}}{4}$	P. $-\frac{\sqrt{5}}{3}$	Y. $-\frac{\sqrt{2}}{3}$
R. $-\frac{2\sqrt{5}}{5}$	E. $-\frac{\sqrt{7}}{3}$	O. $\frac{\sqrt{7}}{4}$	A. $\frac{3}{5}$	N. $\frac{\sqrt{7}}{3}$

American President James Garfield wrote a proof of this theorem. What theorem was it?

$\overline{}$ $\overline{}$ $\overline{}$ $\overline{}$ $\overline{}$ $\overline{}$ $\overline{}$ $\overline{}$ $\overline{}$ $\overline{}$ $\overline{}$
9   6   8   3   7   4   1   10   2   7   5

Statistics and Probability

Teaching Notes for the Activities of Section 6

6-1: (6.SP.1) IDENTIFYING STATISTICAL QUESTIONS

For this activity, your students are to decide whether questions are statistical questions. Correct answers will enable students to complete a statement at the end of the worksheet and verify their work.

Explain that statistics is the mathematics of collecting, organizing, and interpreting numerical data. Any conclusions drawn from a data set are dependent upon the accuracy of the data. In collecting data, care must be taken so that accurate information is obtained.

Explain that understanding the difference between types of questions—especially statistical and non-statistical questions—can help researchers collect useful data. Discuss the difference between statistical and non-statistical questions that is provided on the worksheet. Emphasize that a statistical question expects various answers and that a non-statistical question typically expects one answer.

Go over the directions on the worksheet. Remind your students that only the letters of the statistical questions are to be used in completing the statement at the end.

ANSWERS

(1) A   (2) E   (3) U   (4) A   (5) C   (6) T   (7) R   (8) A   (9) A   (10) T   (11) C   (12) D
Conclusions should always be based on "accurate data."

6-2: (6.SP.2) DESCRIBING DATA DISTRIBUTIONS

For this activity, your students will describe the data collected from a statistical question by its center, spread, and shape. They will need rulers to complete the activity.

Review that a statistical question is a question that anticipates a variety of answers. For example, asking students how many hours they sleep during a typical school night is a statistical question because different students will provide different responses. However, asking Amy how many hours she sleeps during a typical school night is not a statistical question because only one answer is anticipated.

Explain that there are several ways to describe the data collected from a statistical question. You can use measures of center—the mean, median, and mode—the spread of the data—for example, the range—and the shape of the data—for example, a dot plot. Each provides a description that can be useful to interpreting the data. If necessary, review the following terms and provide examples.

- The mean is the average of the values in a set of data.

- The median is the middle value when the numbers are arranged in ascending or descending order. For an even number of values, the two middle values should be added and divided by 2 to find the median.

- The mode is the value that occurs most often in a set of data. If no value repeats, there is no mode. If different values repeat the same number of times, there is more than one mode.

- The range is the difference between the largest value and the smallest value in a set of data.

Also review dot plots and provide examples, if necessary. A dot plot, which is also frequently referred to as a line plot, displays the frequency of data over a number line. Examples of dot plots are likely to be in your math text and can be found on numerous online sites.

Go over the directions on the worksheet with your students. Suggest that to find the median and mode, students list the times in order from least to most. You might also suggest that students use intervals of 5 minutes for the numbers on their number lines.

ANSWERS

The mean = 19, the median = 20, the mode = 20, and the range = 40. Answers to the question may vary. The dot plot makes it easy to see that most students in the class spend between 15 minutes and 25 minutes on math homework each night, with more students spending 20 minutes than any other time.

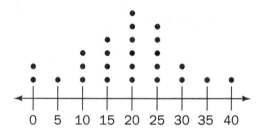

6-3: (6.SP.3) FINDING THE MEAN, MEDIAN, MODE, AND RANGE

For this activity, your students will be given two sets of data. They are to find the mean, median, mode, and range for each. Completing a statement at the end of the worksheet will enable your students to check their answers.

Review that the mean, median, and mode are measures of central tendency. The range is a measure of variability. If necessary, review the terms, which were discussed in the teacher's notes for Activity 6-2.

Go over the directions on the worksheet. Note that the sets of data are labeled A and B, while the problem numbers are labeled 1 through 8. Students should complete the statement at the end.

(1) A, 21   (2) U, 20   (3) H, 13   (4) M, 26   (5) T, 22   (6) S, 17   (7) R, 16   (8) E, 40
"Three measures" of central tendency are the mean, median, and mode.

6-4: (6.SP.4) USING DOT PLOTS TO DISPLAY DATA

This activity requires your students to construct dot plots showing the heights of students in a class. Your students will need rulers to complete this activity.

Explain that a dot plot, which is also called a line plot, displays the frequency of data over a number line. Because dot plots provide a visual representation of data, relationships of the values of the data can be more easily seen than when the values are contained in a table or list.

Discuss the steps for constructing a dot plot that are provided on the worksheet. If your students are unfamiliar with dot plots, provide some examples, which are likely to be found in your math text, or can easily be found online.

Go over the directions on the worksheet with your students. They are to construct two dot plots—one showing the heights of the boys and the other showing the heights of the girls. Suggest that students use the numbers 55 through 63 for their number lines and place the numbers at $\frac{1}{2}$ -inch intervals along the line. Remind them to answer the questions at the end.

The dot plots are shown below. The dot plot on the left shows the heights of the boys, and the dot plot on the right shows the heights of the girls.

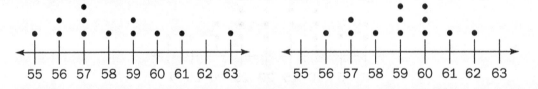

Answers may vary.   (1) The visual presentation of the data clearly shows the distribution of the data.   (2) Most of the girls are slightly taller than most of the boys in this class.

6-5: (6.SP.4) CONSTRUCTING A BOX PLOT

In this activity, your students will be given six sets of data and six box plots. They are to match each set of data with its box plot. Completing a statement at the end of the worksheet will enable them to verify their work. They will need rulers.

Begin the activity by reviewing the steps for finding the quartiles of a set of data. If necessary, explain that quartiles are three numbers that separate data into four parts. Use the following example:

Mike has a spinner divided into eight congruent sectors. Each sector is numbered from 1 to 8. He spun the spinner 12 times with the following results: 1, 1, 4, 7, 8, 2, 4, 5, 2, 3, 2, 7. When he arranged the data in ascending order, 1, 1, 2, 2, 2, 3, 4, 4, 5, 7, 7, 8, he found that median Q_2 is 3.5, which is the average of the two middle numbers, 3 and 4. Q_2 divides the data into the lower part, 1, 1, 2, 2, 2, 3, and the upper part, 4, 4, 5, 7, 7, 8. Q_1 is 2, the median of the lower part, and Q_3 is 6, the median of the upper part.

Discuss the steps for making box plots provided on the worksheet. Use the example above and construct a box plot to highlight the steps.

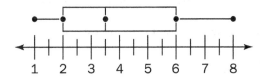

Review the directions on the worksheet, noting that students should construct a box plot for each set of data in order to match the data to the correct box plot. They are to complete the statement at the end.

ANSWERS

(1) E   (2) T   (3) Y   (4) L   (5) N   (6) A   You should always construct graphs accurately and "neatly."

6-6: (6.SP.5) SUMMARIZING AND DESCRIBING DATA

For this activity, your students will summarize and describe data by using measures of center, the interquartile range, and a box plot. They are to answer questions about the distribution of the data. They will need rulers to complete the activity.

Explain that summarizing and describing data can help to make data understandable. Any relationships and patterns become more apparent.

Review measures of center—mean, median, and mode—the interquartile range, outliers, and box plots.

- The mean is the average of the values in a set of data.

- The median is the middle value when the numbers are arranged in ascending or descending order. If there is an even number of values, add the two middle values and divide by 2 to find the median.

- The mode is the value that occurs most often in a set of data. There is no mode if no value occurs more than once. There will be more than one mode if different values repeat the same number of times.

- The interquartile range (IQR) is the spread of the middle 50% of the data. Because it focuses on the middle 50% of the data, it is less affected by outliers. The IQR can be found by following the steps below:

  - Find the median of the entire set of data, which is the second quartile, Q_2, and divide the data into the upper half and lower half.

  - Find the median of the lower half of the data set. This median is the first quartile, Q_1.

  - Find the median of the upper half of the data set. This median is the third quartile, Q_3.

  - Subtract: $IQR = Q_3 - Q_1$.

- An outlier is a value that is unusually small or large compared to the rest of the data.

- A box plot is a data display that divides data into four parts. A box represents half of the data with whiskers that extend to the smallest and largest data. If necessary, review the steps for constructing a box plot (see Activity 6–5).

Go over the directions on the worksheet with your students. Also go over the background of the data and the questions, making sure your students understand what they are to do.

ANSWERS

Answers may vary. (1) 15 responses were obtained.   (2) The data was collected randomly from 15 sixth grade students at various times and places.   (3) No, students were asked to round the screen time to the nearest half-hour. This could affect the accuracy of the data. (4) The mean is 5, the median is 4.5, and the mode is 4. These values indicate that most of the values are close to the center.   (5) 9.5 hours is an outlier. It is 4.5 hours more than the mean, 5 hours more than the median, and 5.5 hours more than the mode.   (6) Since $Q_1 = 4$ and $Q_3 = 6$, the interquartile range is 2, indicating the middle 50% of the values of the data are close together.   (7) Screen time increases rather consistently from 3 hours with nearly half of the students spending between 4 and 5 hours with media screens. (8) The box plot visually confirms that the values are concentrated toward the middle of the distribution.

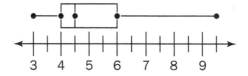

6-7: (7.SP.1) DRAWING INFERENCES FROM SAMPLES

For this activity, your students will be given information about a survey on after-school clubs that was conducted by middle school students of their classmates. Your students are to consider the survey's design, interpret the results, and draw inferences.

Explain that statistics are useful for gaining information about a population. Ideally, every member of the population should be examined, but this is usually impossible because most populations are simply too large. Instead, a sample of the population can be examined, but samples are useful only if they are truly representative of the population. The best samples are random because random samples tend to produce representative samples that support accurate inferences.

Go over the directions on the worksheet. Your students may find it helpful if you read and discuss the background on the survey together. Students should consider the background information as well as the survey's results when answering the questions.

ANSWERS

(1) Four eighth grade students conducted the survey. Sixth, seventh, and eighth grade students took part in the survey. Eighth graders had the most representation with 50 students taking part in the survey. The data reflects the opinions of eighth graders more than the opinions of seventh or sixth graders. (2) Students were randomly surveyed and asked to select five clubs out of 10 that they might be interested in joining. This was a reasonably effective method. It might be improved by reworking the question from giving a choice of five to a choice of three. This might focus the results. (3) The survey favors the opinions of eighth graders because they make up half of the sample. A more representative sample would have surveyed about the same number of students in each grade. (4) Random samples help to ensure that results are representative of the overall population. (5) In general, the question that was asked provided helpful, if not, precise data. (6) The three most popular choices were dance club (75), fitness club (69), and computer club (65). The three least popular choices were chess club (31), reading club (34), and hobby club (36).

6-8: (7.SP.2) DRAWING INFERENCES ABOUT A POPULATION USING RANDOM SAMPLES

For this activity, your students will draw inferences from data from a random sample and run simulations of the sample to determine variations in the results. To complete the simulations, your students will need a deck of standard playing cards; however, technology can also be used to run the simulations.

Explain that inferences from random samples can provide general information about the population from which the sample was drawn. But because samples are usually limited to a small part of the population, there is likely to be variability in the results of other similar samples of the same population. Researchers can study the variability of samples through simulations.

Discuss the sample that is provided on the worksheet. Explain that students are to take the random sample of 20 seventh grade students from the population of seventh graders of Morning

Glory Middle School to estimate the proportion of seventh graders who prefer reading fiction to nonfiction. Ask your students: What is the sample proportion preferring fiction? (55%) Ask your students if this sample proportion is accurate in terms of the population. Students should realize that because inferences drawn from the data of a sample only provide estimates in relation to the population, they should expect variability in the results of numerous similar-sized samples. Running multiple samples of the same size or running simulations can help researchers weigh estimates or predictions about the sample.

Go over the directions on the worksheet. Explain that students are to generate simulated samples to find variations in the results and then answer the questions. Although there are many ways you can run simulations, for this activity standard decks of cards work well. You may prefer to have students work in groups. A group of six students, for example, with three decks of cards, can speed the rate of the simulations. To use the cards to generate simulations, provide the following guidelines:

- Make a population of 40 cards with 22 red cards (representing the sample proportion of students preferring fiction, 55%) and 18 black cards (representing the proportion of students preferring nonfiction, 45%).

- Have students shuffle the 40 cards, place them face down, randomly draw 20 cards, and record the number of red cards.

- After placing the red cards back into the population, they should repeat the process.

- After conducting as many simulations as possible, perhaps up to 200, students should interpret their results.

ANSWERS

Answers may vary; possible answers follow.   (1) More students (55%) prefer fiction; 45% prefer nonfiction.   (2) If students were to conduct about 200 simulations, they would find that some of the results were several percentage points higher or lower than the original sample proportion.   (3) Most students should find that the results of their simulations compare favorably with the original sample.

6-9: (7.SP.3) COMPARING TWO DATA SETS

For this activity, your students will be given data for the monthly average high temperatures of New York City and the monthly average high temperatures of Los Angeles. They will construct dot plots of these data sets on the same graph, interpret the data sets, and then complete a paragraph that compares aspects of the data. They will need rulers, graph paper, and colored pencils.

Because students will need to use the median and range to analyze the data, review these terms, providing examples as necessary. Also, if necessary, review dot plots and how students can select a scale for their dot plots.

Go over the directions on the worksheet with your students. Remind them to construct both dot plots on the same graph and to use a different colored pencil for each one. Students will need to compare the two data sets to complete the paragraph.

(1) 84° F   (2) 75.25° F   (3) 13.25° F   (4) 16° F   (5) 46° F   (6) Higher   (7) Less

6-10: (7.SP.4) DRAWING INFERENCES ABOUT POPULATIONS

For this activity, your students will use measures of center—the mean, median, and mode—and a measure of variability—the range—to compare two sets of data. They are to answer questions about the sets of data.

Explain that measures of center and measures of variability can show the similarities and differences between sets of data. Comparing data can help you to interpret and understand the data, which in turn can help you to draw inferences about the data. If necessary, review the terms "mean," "median," "mode," and "range," and how students can find each for a set of data.

- The mean is the average of the values in a set of data.

- The median is the middle value when the numbers are arranged in ascending or descending order. For an even number of values, the two middle values should be added and divided by 2 to find the median.

- The mode is the value that occurs most often in a set of data. If no value repeats, there is no mode. If different values repeat the same number of times, there is more than one mode.

- The range is the difference between the largest and smallest values in a set of data.

Go over the directions on the worksheet with your students. Suggest that to find the median, students should list the heights for each set of data from smallest to largest. Listing the data in this way can also make it easier to find the mode.

Student explanations will vary.   (1) 71.5; 68   (2) 72; 68.5   (3) 67, 74; 69   (4) 11; 11
(5) Overall, the members of the boys' basketball team are taller than the members of the girls' basketball team, which is what a person would expect since high school boys tend to be taller than high school girls.

6-11: (7.SP.5) UNDERSTANDING THE PROBABILITY OF EVENTS

For this activity, your students will be given situations that describe possible events. Based on the information they are given, they are to determine whether an event is likely, neither likely nor unlikely, or unlikely to occur. Completing a statement at the end of the worksheet will enable your students to check their answers.

Explain that the probability of a chance event occurring is expressed by a number between 0 and 1. A probability of 0 means that an event will not occur, while a probability of 1 means that an event will occur. The numbers between 0 and 1 can be expressed as fractions with a number close to 0 indicating an unlikely event, a number close to $\frac{1}{2}$ indicating an event that is neither likely nor unlikely, and a number close to 1 indicating a likely event.

Go over the directions on the worksheet with your students. Caution them to read the description of each situation carefully as they decide the likelihood of the event occurring. Note that students should think of probability in terms of fractions. Remind them to complete the statement at the end.

ANSWERS

(1) H, likely   (2) T, unlikely   (3) S, likely   (4) I, neither likely nor unlikely   (5) V, neither likely nor unlikely   (6) N, neither likely nor unlikely   (7) A, unlikely   (8) G, unlikely   (9) E, likely (10) P, neither likely nor unlikely   Probability is the branch of mathematics that addresses the chances of "events happening."

6-12: (7.SP.6) PROBABILITIES AND PREDICTIONS

For this activity, your students will be given a probability model that they will use to predict the frequencies of specific events. They will also answer a question about their predictions.

Discuss that although a given event may have a specific probability of occurring, the event may or may not occur at the expected frequency. For example, when tossing a coin, the probability of the coin landing head up is $\frac{1}{2}$. Likewise, the probability of the coin landing tail up is $\frac{1}{2}$. Given these probabilities, a coin tossed 100 times would be expected to land 50 times head up and 50 times tail up. In reality though, this is unlikely to happen because of randomness. However, as the number of tosses increases, the frequency of the events is likely to approach the probability.

Discuss the directions on the worksheet with your students. Note that although the spinner has eight equal-sized sectors, only four numbers are represented. When answering the questions, students should make their predictions based on probability. Remind them to explain their answer for the last question.

ANSWERS

(1) 200   (2) 300   (3) 100   (4) 400   (5) 500   (6) 800   (7) 0   (8) 600   (9) The predictions should be relatively close to the actual number of times the arrow lands on a number or combination of numbers because of the large amount of trials. But it is unlikely that the numbers would match the predictions exactly.

6-13: (7.SP.7) USING PROBABILITY MODELS TO FIND PROBABILITIES OF EVENTS

For this activity, your students will interpret data in a table to find probabilities of events. Completing a statement at the end of the worksheet will enable them to check their work.

Present the following table that shows the number of students in gym classes during periods 6, 7, and 8, which are the only times gym classes are held.

	Period 7	Period 8	Period 9
Sixth Grade	70	20	10
Seventh Grade	8	75	12
Eighth Grade	21	19	65

Point out that 300 students take gym classes in this school, which can be found by adding the number of students in each gym class. Provide the following examples:

- The probability of randomly selecting a student who is in sixth grade and who is in the seventh period gym class can be written as P(sixth grader in gym period 7). P(sixth grader in gym period 7) $= \frac{70}{300} = \frac{7}{30}$.

- The probability of randomly selecting a student who is in the ninth period gym class can be written as P(student in gym period 9). P(student in gym period 9) $= \frac{10+12+65}{300} = \frac{87}{300}$. Provide more examples, if necessary.

Discuss the probability model on the worksheet. Note that the headings for the columns indicate the number of books and the numbers in the rows indicate the number of students by grade. Remind your students that probabilities expressed as fractions should be simplified.

Go over the directions. After finding the probabilities for problems 1 to 11, students are to answer the question for number 12. They are also to complete the statement at the end.

ANSWERS

(1) E, $\frac{1}{60}$ (2) A, $\frac{3}{50}$ (3) I, $\frac{7}{150}$ (4) B, $\frac{7}{75}$ (5) P, $\frac{26}{75}$ (6) L, $\frac{11}{150}$ (7) N, $\frac{3}{25}$ (8) S, $\frac{4}{25}$

(9) T, $\frac{43}{300}$ (10) Y, $\frac{8}{15}$ (11) D, $\frac{47}{300}$ (12) Explanations may vary. One correct response is that it is probable that students may take fewer books home on Friday. "Data displayed in a table" can be used to find probabilities.

6-14: (7.SP.8) UNDERSTANDING THE PROBABILITY OF COMPOUND EVENTS

For this activity, your students will create a sample space and use the outcomes to determine the probability of compound events. Completing a statement at the end of the worksheet will enable them to check their work.

Explain that a compound event consists of at least two simple events. The probability of a compound event can be determined by finding the fraction of outcomes in the sample space for which the compound event occurs. For example, if you have a fair coin (head and tail) and a spinner (green and red) of equal sectors, and you flipped the coin and spun the spinner, the possible outcomes could be listed as (H, G), (H, R), (T, G), (T, R). These four outcomes are the sample space. Some examples of probability when flipping the coin and spinning the spinner include: the probability of the outcomes with a head and a red sector is $\frac{1}{4}$; the probability of the outcomes with a tail is $\frac{1}{2}$; and the probability of the outcomes with a green sector is $\frac{1}{2}$.

Go over the directions on the worksheet with your students. Students should simplify all fractions. Remind them to complete the statement at the end.

ANSWERS

The sample space follows the probabilities and statement.   (1) H, $\frac{1}{18}$ (2) S, 0   (3) A, $\frac{1}{36}$
(4) M, $\frac{1}{4}$ (5) I, $\frac{1}{2}$ (6) E, $\frac{4}{9}$ (7) T, $\frac{1}{12}$ Compound events are two or more simple events happening "at the same time."

(1, 7)	(2, 7)	(3, 7)	(4, 7)	(5, 7)	(6, 7)
(1, 8)	(2, 8)	(3, 8)	(4, 8)	(5, 8)	(6, 8)
(1, 9)	(2, 9)	(3, 9)	(4, 9)	(5, 9)	(6, 9)
(1, 10)	(2, 10)	(3, 10)	(4, 10)	(5, 10)	(6, 10)
(1, 11)	(2, 11)	(3, 11)	(4, 11)	(5, 11)	(6, 11)
(1, 12)	(2, 12)	(3, 12)	(4, 12)	(5, 12)	(6, 12)

6-15: (7.SP.8) FINDING PROBABILITIES OF COMPOUND EVENTS USING TABLES, LISTS, AND TREE DIAGRAMS

For this activity, your students will create organized lists or tree diagrams from data provided in a table. They will use this information to find probabilities of compound events. Unscrambling the letters of correct answers will enable them to check their answers.

Review that a sample space is the set of all possible outcomes in a given situation. Present the following example.

Two spinners can be used to generate a sample space and determine the probability of compound events. The first event is spinning the first spinner, and the second event is spinning the second spinner.

Spinner 1	Spinner 2
The spinner is divided into 4 equal-sized sectors. Each sector is labeled 1, 2, 3, or 4.	The spinner is divided into 4 equal-sized sectors. Each sector is labeled A, B, C, or D.

Demonstrate how to create an organized list and tree diagram to show the 16 possible outcomes when spinning the first spinner and then spinning the second spinner. Following is an example of one organized list: 1A, 1B, 1C, 1D, 2A, 2B, 2C, 2D, 3A, 3B, 3C, 3D, 4A, 4B, 4C, 4D.

Provide examples such as $P(1) = \frac{1}{4}$ because 4 of the 16 outcomes contain a 1; $P(4 \text{ and } D) = \frac{1}{16}$ because 1 of the 16 outcomes has both 4 and D; $P(2 \text{ or } 3) = \frac{1}{2}$ because 8 of the 16 outcomes have either a 2 or 3. Make sure your students understand the probability notation and what elements in the sample space they should consider.

Go over the information and directions on the worksheet. Note that there are two parts to the assignment. Before students begin part two, correct the sample spaces they listed.

ANSWERS

Part One: Following is an organized list.

(A, 1, H)	(A, 1, T)	(B, 1, H)	(B, 1, T)	(C, 1, H)	(C, 1, T)	(D, 1, H)	(D, 1, T)
(A, 2, H)	(A, 2, T)	(B, 2, H)	(B, 2, T)	(C, 2, H)	(C, 2, T)	(D, 2, H)	(D, 2, T)
(A, 3, H)	(A, 3, T)	(B, 3, H)	(B, 3, T)	(C, 3, H)	(C, 3, T)	(D, 3, H)	(D, 3, T)
(A, 4, H)	(A, 4, T)	(B, 4, H)	(B, 4, T)	(C, 4, H)	(C, 4, T)	(D, 4, H)	(D, 4, T)
(A, 5, H)	(A, 5, T)	(B, 5, H)	(B, 5, T)	(C, 5, H)	(C, 5, T)	(D, 5, H)	(D, 5, T)
(A, 6, H)	(A, 6, T)	(B, 6, H)	(B, 6, T)	(C, 6, H)	(C, 6, T)	(D, 6, H)	(D, 6, T)

Part Two

(1) E, $\frac{1}{48}$ (2) E, $\frac{1}{48}$ (3) C, 1 (4) L, $\frac{3}{4}$ (5) S, $\frac{1}{12}$ (6) M, $\frac{1}{3}$ (7) A, $\frac{1}{8}$ (8) S, $\frac{1}{12}$

(9) P, $\frac{1}{4}$ (10) A, $\frac{1}{8}$ (11) P, $\frac{1}{4}$ The letters "ecapselpmas" can be reversed and written as "sample space."

6-16: (8.SP.1) CONSTRUCTING AND INTERPRETING SCATTER PLOTS

For this activity, your students will be given the number of hours of sleep per night and the grade point average (GPA) for 24 college students. Your students will construct a scatter plot and describe any patterns they find in the data. They will need either a graphing calculator or a ruler and graph paper to complete this activity.

Review that scatter plots are often used to find relationships between quantities. Unlike a function, one value of x may be paired with more than one value of y. The points on a scatter plot should not be connected.

Discuss the information and table on the worksheet. Suggest that students plot the number of hours slept on the x-axis and the GPAs on the y-axis. After they have constructed their scatter plots, they should note where the points are clustered (or graphed), identify any outliers (numbers that are significantly different from other numbers), and whether the data are related. If the data resembles a line with a positive slope, there is a positive linear correlation.

Go over the directions. Remind your students to identify any clusters, outliers, and relationships.

ANSWERS

Explanations may vary; possible explanations follow.   (1) About half of the data is between 5.5 and 7.25 hours of sleep.   (2) The person who slept 10.5 hours and had a GPA of 3.0 is an outlier.   (3) There is a positive correlation between the number of hours slept and GPA.

6-17: (8.SP.2) FITTING LINES TO DATA

For this activity, your students are to draw scatter plots and determine which equations best fit the data. Students will need either a graphing calculator or a ruler and graph paper to complete the activity.

Explain that students can draw scatter plots to model real-world data; however, the points of the scatter plot may not always lie in a line. If the points resemble a line with a positive slope, there is a positive linear correlation, and the line of best fit will have a positive slope. If the points resemble a line with a negative slope, there is a negative linear correlation, and the line of best fit will have a negative slope. If the points do not resemble a line, there is relatively no linear correlation.

Review the information and table on the student worksheet. Note that the numbers in the first column, 1 to 12, refer to the dances, four for each of the last three years. Also note that the total revenue is the sum of the money collected from the admission and raffles sales.

Go over the directions with your students. Emphasize that they must make four different scatter plots. Suggest that for each one they plot the number of students who paid on the x-axis. After they have drawn each scatter plot, they must select the equation of the line of best fit that best models the data. Suggest that they graph the line they selected on each scatter plot to help them decide how well the line "fits" the data.

ANSWERS

(1) $y = 7.6x - 140$ (2) Relatively no linear correlation   (3) $y = 8.5x + 114$
(4) $y = 13x - 287$

6-18: (8.SP.3) USING EQUATIONS OF LINEAR MODELS

For this activity, your students will be given equations that they will use to solve problems. They will also identify slopes and y-intercepts.

Explain that linear equations are of the form $y = mx + b$. m stands for the slope and b stands for the y-intercept, which is the value of y when x is equal to 0.

Provide this example: Monthly membership at a local gym is $50 plus $3.50 for each aerobics class a member takes. This can be modeled by the equation $y = 3.50x + 50$, where x is the number of aerobics classes a member takes. The graph of this equation is a line that has a slope of 3.5 and intersects the y-axis at 50. The y-intercept, 50, represents the cost without extra classes. It is also called the initial value of the function associated with the equation. $3.50 represents the cost per aerobics class, or the rate of change of the monthly cost. If $x = 5$, meaning that 5 aerobics classes were taken during a month, $y = 3.50 \times 5 + 50 = \$67.50$.

Go over the directions on the worksheet with your students. They are to use the equations to solve the problems and answer the questions.

ANSWERS

Problem 1: (1) The charge per hour (2) 75 (3) $375 (4) 2.5 hours   Problem 2: (1) The number of points deducted for each incorrect answer (2) The score if no answers were incorrect (3) 70 (4) 2   Problem 3: (1) 0.75 (2) 9.99 (3) 12.24 (4) 4   Problem 4: (1) The slope is 0.8; each dollar increase in x results in a 0.8 increase in y. (2) 0 (3) $64 (4) $100

6-19: (8.SP.4) CONSTRUCTING AND INTERPRETING TWO-WAY TABLES

For this activity, your students will complete a two-way table and answer questions that require them to interpret the values in the table. Completing a statement at the end of the worksheet will enable them to check their work.

Explain that data may be displayed in a two-way table. Provide this example: There are 30 students in Mr. Lin's eighth grade math class. 13 of the students are girls. Of the 30 students in the class, 9 are in the math league. 5 of the students in the math league are girls.

Present the following partial table and ask your students to complete it, based on the information above.

	Boys	Girls	Totals
In math league			
Not in math league			
Totals			

The completed table follows.

	Boys	Girls	Totals
In math league	4	5	9
Not in math league	13	8	21
Totals	17	13	30

Help your students interpret the table by posing questions, such as the following: How many boys are in Mr. Lin's math class? (17) Are most of the students in math league boys? (No, 4 out of 9 are boys.) Are most of the students who are not in the math league boys? (Yes, 13 out of 21 are boys.)

Go over the directions on the worksheet with your students. Students must complete the table before answering the questions. Note that the letters in the spaces in the table are used for identification. Remind your students to complete the statement at the end.

ANSWERS

	Eighth Grade Student	Not an Eighth Grade Student	Totals
Will attend trip	(a) 90	(b) 51	(c) 141
Will not attend trip	(d) 60	(e) 169	(f) 229
Totals	(g) 150	(h) 220	(i) 370

(1) T, true   (2) R, false   (3) E, true   (4) B, false   (5) D, false   (6) I, false   (7) V, cannot be determined   (8) A, true   "Bivariate data" is used in this activity.

6-20: (S-ID.1) REPRESENTING DATA WITH PLOTS ON THE REAL NUMBER LINE

This activity requires your students to use a dot plot and box plot to display a data set. They are then to compare the two plots and answer questions about them. Your students will need rulers to complete the activity.

If necessary, review dot plots and box plots and how students can construct them. Examples of these data displays are likely to be in your math text or can be easily found online by searching for the display by name.

- A dot plot, also sometimes referred to as a line plot, represents the values of a set of data by dots being placed over a number line.

- A box plot, also referred to as a box-and-whisker plot, shows the values of a data set divided into four parts called quartiles.

Go over the directions on the worksheet with your students. They are to represent the set of data with a dot plot and a box plot and then answer the question.

ANSWERS

(1) Both the dot plot and the box plot show that most of the students scored from 80 to 90.
(2) The score of 60 is an outlier. (3) Answers will vary. (4) Answers will vary. (5) One possible data display is a histogram. Answers will vary.

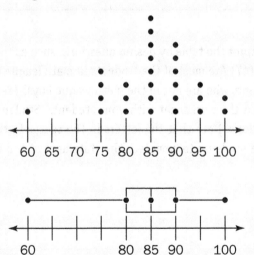

6-21: (S-ID.2) COMPARING TWO DATA SETS

For this activity, your students will compare two data sets: the cost of pre-owned cars and the cost of pre-owned SUVs. After interpreting the data, they will complete a paragraph that describes the data sets.

Explain that the graphs of data sets may have various shapes, depending on whether the data are evenly distributed.

- If the data are evenly distributed, the graph is bell-shaped and symmetric, and the mean, median, and mode have the same value. The mean best describes the measure of center, and the standard deviation best describes the spread.

- If the data are not evenly distributed, the graph is not bell-shaped and not symmetric, and the mean, median, and mode vary. The median best describes the measure of center, and the interquartile range (IQR) best describes the spread.

Review the information on the worksheet. There are two data sets, and students must determine how to describe the data of each set. Suggest that they find the mean, median, and mode of each data set to see if the data are evenly distributed. Then they must decide if they should use the mean or median to compare the center and the standard deviation or IQR to compare the spread of the data sets.

Go over the directions. Students are to use their descriptions of the data to complete the paragraphs.

ANSWERS

The answers are rounded to the nearest dollar. (1) $10,351 (2) $7,795 (3) $4,995 and $16,995 (4) Median (5) IQR (6) $9,000 (7) $21,124 (8) $18,895 (9) $16,955 (10) Median (11) IQR (12) $7,000

6-22: (S-ID.3) INTERPRETING DIFFERENCES IN SHAPE, CENTER, AND SPREAD OF DATA DISTRIBUTIONS

For this activity, your students will be given 4 data sets and 10 statements about the data. They are to correct the incorrect statements.

Review that all data can be graphed by sketching a frequency graph or a box and whisker plot.

- The frequency graph is a visual representation that shows whether the data are symmetric or skewed. Another way to determine whether the data are symmetric or skewed is by following these guidelines:

  - If the mean equals the median, the data are symmetric.

  - If the mean is greater than the median, the data are skewed right.

  - If the mean is less than the median, the data are skewed left.

- The box and whisker plot is particularly useful in determining the IQR (Interquartile Range). Using this information, students can mathematically identify any outliers by following these formulas:

  - If a value is less than $Q_1 - 1.5IQR$, the value is an outlier.

  - If a value is greater than $Q_3 + 1.5IQR$, the value is an outlier.

Mention that students may look at either graph to determine if there are any outliers, values that are way above or way below the other values in the data set.

Discuss the information and directions on the worksheet. Emphasize that students must correct false statements.

ANSWERS

(1) Correct   (2) Incorrect; it has two outliers, 50 and 100.   (3) Incorrect; the data in section 4 also have no outliers.   (4) Incorrect; the data are shewed left.   (5) Correct
(6) Correct   (7) Incorrect; 40 is not an outlier.   (8) Correct   (9) Incorrect; the data in section 3 have two modes.   (10) Correct

6–23: (S-ID.4) RECOGNIZING CHARACTERISTICS OF NORMAL DISTRIBUTIONS

For this activity, your students will decide whether statements describing normal distributions are true or false. Completing a statement at the end of the worksheet will enable students to verify their answers.

To complete this activity successfully, your students should have a general understanding of normal distributions and related terminology, including mean, median, and mode, standard deviation, lines of symmetry, relative frequency, and histograms. If necessary, review these terms.

Explain that data sets that are normally distributed have similar characteristics. They are also referred to as normal curves.

Discuss the two distributions on the worksheet. Ask your students which one is a normal distribution. Of course, students should recognize that the first distribution is normal. Note that the data is in the shape of a bell curve.

Go over the directions. Caution your students to read the statements carefully. They are to also complete the statement at the end.

ANSWERS

(1) A, true   (2) R, false   (3) I, false   (4) U, true   (5) E, true   (6) C, false   (7) P, true
(8) L, false   (9) M, true   Given the mean and standard deviation, the "empirical rule" provides an estimate of the spread of data in a normal distribution.

6–24: (S-ID.5) SUMMARIZING CATEGORICAL DATA IN TWO-WAY FREQUENCY TABLES

For this activity, your students will be given a frequency table. Using this table, they will construct a relative frequency table and interpret relative frequencies.

Review that a two-way frequency table consists of rows and columns that show the frequency of responses. The entries in the total row and total columns frequencies are called marginal frequencies. The entries in the body of the table are called joint frequencies.

Discuss the frequency table on the worksheet, noting that there are a total of 75 students, 35 boys and 40 girls. Ask your students questions, such as the following: How many boys will consider rescuing a pet? (25) How many girls will consider rescuing a pet? (32) How many students in all would not consider rescuing a pet? (18)

Explain that the data in a two-way frequency table can be used to construct a relative frequency table. In a relative frequency table, the number of responses is expressed as a fraction of the total number of responses.

Go over the directions on the worksheet. Note that students are to complete the relative frequency table, using the data in the frequency table. The first entry is done for them. They are also to use the information in the table to evaluate the effectiveness of the presentation.

ANSWERS

The completed relative frequency table is shown below. Answers may vary for the question. A possible answer is that after the presentation 76% of the students who attended the presentation would consider rescuing a pet; however, we do not know the percentage of students who would have considered rescuing a pet before the presentation, making it difficult to determine the effectiveness of the presentation.

	Will Consider Rescuing a Pet	Will Not Consider Rescuing a Pet	Totals
Boys	$\frac{25}{75} = 0.3\overline{3}$	$\frac{10}{75} = 0.1\overline{3}$	$\frac{35}{75} = 0.4\overline{6}$
Girls	$\frac{32}{75} = 0.42\overline{6}$	$\frac{8}{75} = 0.10\overline{6}$	$\frac{40}{75} = 0.5\overline{3}$
Totals	$\frac{57}{75} = 0.76$	$\frac{18}{75} = 0.24$	$\frac{75}{75} = 1$

6–25: (S-ID.6) FINDING THE EQUATION OF THE LINE OF BEST FIT

This activity requires your students to make a scatter plot by plotting sets of data, draw the line of best fit, and find the equation of the line they have drawn. They will need a ruler and enough graph paper to draw three graphs.

Review that a scatter plot represents data by points in a coordinate plane, but the points are not connected. Note that for this activity, all of the points are in the first quadrant. Also review that a line of best fit, which is sometimes referred to as a trend line, is a line that best represents the data on a scatter plot. A line of best fit may pass through all of the points, some of the points, or none of the points.

Provide this example to your students: On a car trip to Florida, Ms. Wilson checked and recorded the mileage on the odometer every hour. She was then able to record her travel time and distance. The data below describe her trip.

$$(1, 55), \ (2, 100), \ (3, 150), \ (4, 180), \ (5, 240), \ (6, 300), \ (7, 350), \ (8, 400)$$

The first number in each pair of numbers represents the time in hours, and the second number represents the miles. For example, (4, 180) means that after traveling four hours, she traveled a total of 180 miles. Your students may find it helpful if you list the points on the board and have them plot the points on graph paper. Instruct your students to use rulers to draw a line of best fit. Next, ask them to select any two points on the line they have drawn to find the equation of the line. Answers may vary, depending upon how accurately they have drawn their lines. One answer is $y = 50x$.

Go over the directions on the worksheet. Note that all sets of data will determine a line. Encourage your students to be accurate in plotting points, drawing lines, and writing the equations. Note that the third problem also requires students to analyze the data and find the exact equation of the line.

ANSWERS

Answers may vary; possible answers include the following.   (1) $y = 2x$ (2) $y = \frac{1}{4}x + 40$

(3) $y = -\frac{9}{10}x + 88$ Complementary angles: $y = -x + 90$

6–26: (S-ID.6) USING LINEAR AND QUADRATIC MODELS

For this activity, your students will be given six data sets. They will determine how two quantities in each set are related by finding the equation of the line that relates the quantities. Students will need graphing calculators.

Discuss that to find the line of best fit students should use their graphing calculator to enter the data in a list, set the viewing window, and make a scatter plot. If the points resemble a straight line, they should find the linear regression. If the points in the scatter plot resemble part of a parabola, they should find the quadratic regression.

Go over the directions on the worksheet. Note that the relationships will either be linear or quadratic.

ANSWERS

(1) $y = x^2 + x$; the area of rectangle B   (2) $y = 18x^2 + 10x$; the surface area of the rectangular prism   (3) $y = 4x$; one side of rectangle A   (4) $y = 4x^2 + 4x$; the area of rectangle C   (5) $y = x + 1$; one side of rectangle B or one side of rectangle C   (6) $y = 4x^2$; the area of rectangle A

6-27: (S-ID.7) INTERPRETING THE SLOPE AND Y-INTERCEPT OF A LINEAR MODEL

For this activity, your students will be given three situations. They will answer questions based on each situation; these questions require knowledge of slopes and y-intercepts. Completing a statement at the end of the worksheet will enable students to check their work.

Review that linear equations are of the form $y = mx + b$. m stands for the slope, and b stands for the y-intercept, which is the value of y when x is equal to 0.

Provide the following example. Keisha recently bought a pre-owned car that had 14,000 miles on its odometer. According to the manufacturer, the car averages 30 miles per gallon of gasoline. The distance displayed on the odometer can be modeled by $y = 30x + 14,000$. The slope of the line is 30, which means that for every gallon of gas the car uses, the mileage on the odometer increases by 30 miles. The y-intercept, which is 14,000, means that she has not yet driven her car. Note that x, the number of gallons, is the independent variable, and y, the mileage on the odometer, is the dependent variable because the number of miles she travels depends on the amount of gasoline she uses.

Go over the directions on the worksheet with your students. Note that the situations are labeled A to C. Remind students to complete the statement at the end.

ANSWERS

(1) O, 25   (2) I, 15   (3) R, l_1 (4) L, O   (5) N, −1   (6) A, 8   (7) M, 6   (8) D, x   (9) E, y
"A linear model" can be written as $y = mx + b$.

6-28: (S-ID.8) COMPUTING AND INTERPRETING THE CORRELATION COEFFICIENT

For this activity, your students will be provided with tables that show two quantities. They will compute correlation coefficients for the quantities of the tables and then identity the table that has the strongest correlation. Completing a statement at the end of the worksheet will enable them to check their work. Students will need graphing calculators.

Discuss the information about the correlation coefficient that is provided on the worksheet. The correlation coefficient of a linear fit can be found by using a graphing calculator and following these steps:

1. Enter the data for x and y in a list.

2. Set the viewing window.

3. Make a scatter plot.

4. Find the linear regression of $ax + b$, and the value of r will be displayed.

Go over the directions. Students should complete the statement at the end and answer the final question.

(1) C, 0.141   (2) U, −0.878   (3) E, −0.672   (4) O, 0.608   (5) Y, 0.980   (6) R, 0.962
(7) S, 0.968   Your knowledge in this activity positively correlates to "your score." Table 5
shows the strongest correlation.

6-29: (S-ID.9) DISTINGUISHING BETWEEN CORRELATION AND CAUSATION

For this activity, your students are to determine whether statements are examples of correlation or causation. Completing a statement at the end of the worksheet will enable them to verify their answers.

Explain that distinguishing between correlation and causation is important to statistical investigations. However, it can be tricky to identify which is which.

Discuss the definitions of correlation and causation that are on the worksheet. To help your students understand the difference, suggest that they ask themselves questions such as the following:

- Did a specific action or event cause another action or event to happen? If the answer is yes, this is an example of causation.

- Is an action or event connected to another action or event in some way, but one did not necessarily cause the other to happen? If the answer is yes, this is an example of correlation.

Emphasize that in instances of causation, one action or event must clearly cause another. The second would not occur without the first. To help make sure that your students understand the difference, ask volunteers to offer some examples.

Go over the directions on the worksheet with your students. Remind them to complete the final statement.

(1) T   (2) S   (3) E   (4) N   (5) E   (6) U   (7) O   (8) A   (9) O   (10) L   (11) D   (12) Q
Correlation "does not equal" causation.

6-30: (S-IC.1) UNDERSTANDING THE TERMINOLOGY OF STATISTICAL EXPERIMENTS

For this activity, your students are to complete statements that have missing statistical terms. Completing a statement at the end of the worksheet will enable them to check their answers.

Explain that random processes underlie statistical experiments. Evaluating these processes can help researchers design effective experiments with which they can gather accurate data and from which they can make valid inferences. A poorly designed or controlled experiment will yield poor data that will likely lead to invalid inferences. Understanding the terminology associated with statistical experiments is essential if students are to understand the processes.

Go over the directions on the worksheet with your students. They are to complete each statement and then write the designated letter of each answer in the space above its statement number at the end.

ANSWERS

(1) T, data   (2) T, population   (3) I, randomization   (4) A, parameter   (5) S, sample
(6) S, inferences   (7) I, experiments   (8) S, sample   (9) T, population   (10) C, inferences
"Statistics" is an important branch of mathematics.

6–31: (S-IC.2) EVALUATING PROBABILITY MODELS THROUGH SIMULATIONS

For this activity, your students will be given three problems. For each problem, they will be given a probability model and the results of a small sample that do not support the model. Students are to evaluate the probability models by running simulations. They will need calculators that can run simulations.

Explain that randomness can affect the results of statistical experiments. Suppose a spinner has only two equal-sized sectors, 0 and 1. The probability of spinning the arrow and it landing on 0 is 0.5, and the probability of the arrow landing on 1 is 0.5. According to the model, 10 spins should result in 5 zeroes and 5 ones. However, because of randomness, ten spins might produce other results, for example 3 zeroes and 7 ones, or 6 zeroes and 4 ones, or various other combinations. This is particularly true for small samples, but this does not mean that the model is invalid.

Explain that probability models can be evaluated by running simulations. If necessary, review how your students can run simulations on their calculators. The more simulations they run, the closer their results should come to the probability model.

Go over the directions on the worksheet with your students. Suggest that they run between 100 and 200 or more simulations for each problem. They are to answer the questions and write a summary of their results for each problem.

ANSWERS

Answers may vary. For each problem, students should find that with the more simulations they run, their results will become more consistent with the probability model. The results of the small samples of Raphael and his classmates, Callie, and Jamie can be attributed to randomness (unless, for example, a coin or die was weighted or the surface of some of the sectors of the spinner were slightly raised to impede the arrow's movement passing over them). Discuss your students' methods for evaluation of the models, including the number of simulations they ran and how they ran their simulations. Compare their results.

6-32: (S-IC.3) RECOGNIZING SURVEYS, EXPERIMENTS, AND OBSERVATIONAL STUDIES

In this activity, your students must decide whether a statement describes a survey, an experiment, or an observational study. Answering a question at the end of the worksheet will enable them to check their answers.

Explain that three common research methods are surveys, experiments, and observational studies.

- In a survey, researchers collect data from a population. There are a variety of ways they may collect the data, for example, with a questionnaire or an interview, perhaps in a face-to-face meeting, by telephone, e-mail, or regular mail.

- In an experiment, researchers manipulate a sample population in some way. For example, the researcher may introduce a variable and record the variable's effects.

- In an observational study, researchers observe a population without interfering in the population's habits or routines. The researcher maintains as little contact with the population as possible and the members of the population often are not aware that they are being studied.

Your students might find it helpful if you ask them to suggest examples of surveys, experiments, and observational studies. Discuss the differences between the methods.

Go over the directions on the worksheet. Remind your students to answer the question at the end.

ANSWERS

(1) T   (2) M   (3) A   (4) D   (5) I   (6) Z   (7) N   (8) R   (9) O   The answer to the question is "randomization."

6-33: (S-IC.4) USING SIMULATIONS WITH RANDOM SAMPLING

For this activity, your students will run simulations to develop a margin of error for random sampling. They will need graphing calculators to complete the activity.

Explain that simulations can help researchers to determine how much variation there might be among sample proportions for random samples. This can be particularly helpful in the case of small samples.

Review the following terms and provide examples, if necessary:

- Sample proportion is the frequency of data divided by the total sample size.

- Population mean is the average of all values of the entire population of a data set.

- Sample mean is the average of the values of the sample data set.

- Standard deviation is a measure of how spread out data is about the mean in a set of data.

- Margin of error is the maximum expected difference between the true population parameter and a sample estimate of that parameter.

Explain that students will need to use their graphing calculators to run simulations of data for this activity. If necessary, review how they may run simulations on their calculators.

Explain that to find the margin of error through the use of their simulations, students should first find the mean and standard deviation of the distributions of the sample proportions. They should choose a 95% confidence interval when determining the margin of error.

Go over the directions on the worksheet with your students. Answer any questions they may have about the scenario that presents the data they are to use in their simulations.

ANSWERS

(1) 0.45   (2) Descriptions may vary, but most should find that the plot is roughly mound-shaped and symmetric.   (3) Answers may vary but should be close to 0.5. (4) Answers may vary but should be about 0.08.   (5) Answers may vary but should be close to 0.16.   (6) Answers may vary but should be between about 0.29 and 0.61.

6–34: (S-IC.5) COMPARING TWO TREATMENTS USING SIMULATIONS

In this activity, your students are to determine if the results of an initial trial of a new weight-loss supplement are valid. After re-randomizing the results and running simulations, students will answer questions about the data. Calculators are needed for this activity.

Explain that when developing new substances or procedures, researchers will initially often do small, limited trials to study the effects of a treatment. Small trials are far less costly than large ones. However, the results of small trials may not be valid due to randomization. To ensure that the data obtained from the trial is in fact valid, the data can be re-randomized, and simulations can be performed to verify the validity of the data.

If necessary, explain that re-randomizations and simulations can be done by combining the data, randomly splitting the data into different groups (essentially mixing the data up), and calculating the difference between the sample means. If the original difference of the means is not reproduced after many simulations, it is likely that the initial data are valid. Of course, the more re-randomizations and simulations that are performed, the greater the likelihood that the answer to whether the initial data was valid will be found.

Go over the directions on the worksheet with your students. They might find it helpful if you read and discuss the trial and data as a class.

ANSWERS

(1) −7.61; 1.7; 9.31   (2) Combine the initial data, separate the data randomly into two groups of 10, run simulations, and find the absolute value of the difference of the means. (3) The number of simulations will vary. Conclusions may vary, but most should confirm the validity of the initial data. Student certainty regarding the conclusions will vary.

6-35: (S-IC.6) EVALUATING DATA IN REPORTS

This activity requires your students to evaluate a report based on data of the effectiveness of a special traffic program. After analyzing the data in the report, students are to offer a recommendation whether the program should be continued.

Explain that every day, inferences, conclusions, and decisions are based on the evaluation of data contained in reports. While in some cases the data may be thorough and clear-cut, making evaluation relatively straightforward, in other cases the data may be lacking or ambiguous, making evaluation more difficult. Whatever the case, effective evaluation is founded on careful analysis and interpretation of the data.

Go over the directions on the worksheet with your students. They might find it helpful if you read the background information and review the data as a class. After evaluating the data, students are to answer the questions, justifying their answers.

ANSWERS

(1) Answers will vary.   (2) Answers will vary.   (3) The types and numbers of traffic violations might have been helpful, especially those that were not speed related. This might help to clarify exactly how many traffic violations were a result of speeding, which is the purpose of the special traffic program. Also, a breakdown by roads and streets of the costs and revenues obtained from violations might be helpful in case a modified program is considered. (4) Answers will vary. Students might suggest that the program be modified and limited to the highways and roads where the highest numbers of speeding incidents occur.

6-36: (S-CP.1) DESCRIBING EVENTS AS SUBSETS OF A SAMPLE SPACE

This activity requires your students to identify events that are subsets of a sample space. Completing a statement at the end of the worksheet will enable them to check their work.

Discuss the information on the worksheet, making sure that your students understand the probability model. You may want to ask questions such as the following: Which event generates a fraction that is equivalent to $0.1\overline{6}$? Students should realize that the answer is (1, 6), which means spinning a 1 on the first spinner and spinning a 2 on the second spinner. Which event generates a fraction that is equivalent to a repeating decimal and the second number is 7? Students should find (3, 7).

Go over the directions. Note that some answers consist of two fractions. Remind your students to complete the statement at the end.

ANSWERS

(1) C, (1, 8)   (2) N, (4, 6)   (3) O, (4, 8)   (4) S, (3, 7)   (5) A, (1, 6) and (1, 7) (6) E, (4, 5) and (4, 6)   (7) R, (2, 8)   (8) I, (1, 6)   (9) F, (4, 6) and (4, 7)   The mathematical theory of probability "arose in France" in the seventeenth century.

6-37: (S-CP.2) IDENTIFYING INDEPENDENT EVENTS

For this activity, your students will be given sets of events, and they must identify whether the events are independent. Completing a statement at the end of the worksheet will enable them to check their work.

Discuss the information on the worksheet and emphasize that independent events have no effect on each other. Caution your students to not merely assume that events that happen at about the same time under similar circumstances depend on each other in some way. In such cases, they should ask themselves how exactly the events affect each other. If the events have no effect on each other, they are independent.

Explain that the probability of independent events occurring together can be represented by the equation $P(A \text{ and } B) = P(A) \cdot P(B)$. Offer the following example:

One standard die is tossed two times. The first toss results in a 1, and the second toss results in a 4. These events are independent because the results of the first toss in no way affect the results of the second. The probability of tossing a 1 and then tossing a 4 can be found as follows: $P(A \text{ and } B) = P(A) \cdot P(B) = \frac{1}{6} \cdot \frac{1}{6} = \frac{1}{36}$.

Go over the directions on the worksheet. Suggest that if students are unsure whether events are independent, they consider that the probability of the events occurring together is the product of their probabilities. Remind them to complete the statement at the end.

ANSWERS

(1) W, yes   (2) E, no   (3) L, yes   (4) O, yes   (5) E, no   (6) D, no   (7) K, yes   (8) G, yes
(9) N, no   Your score on this assignment depends on your "knowledge" of events.

6-38: (S-CP.3) INTERPRETING CONDITIONAL PROBABILITY

For this activity, your students will be given three scenarios for which they will find the probabilities of events occurring. Completing a statement at the end of the worksheet will enable them to check their work. Students will also identify independent events.

Discuss the information on the worksheet, making sure that students understand the probability notation. Provide the following example:

There are 10 algebra books and 8 reference books in the classroom library. Event A is randomly selecting an algebra book, and Event R is randomly selecting a reference book. The probabilities can be written as the following: $P(A) = \frac{10}{18} = \frac{5}{9}$, $P(R) = \frac{8}{18} = \frac{4}{9}$, $P(A|R) = \frac{10}{17}$, and $P(R|A) = \frac{8}{17}$.

Explain that to determine if the events are independent, students should compare $P(A|R)$ with $P(A)$ and compare $P(R|A)$ with $P(R)$. Because $P(A|R) \neq P(A)$, the events are dependent. Students could also state that $P(R|A) \neq P(R)$.

Go over the directions. Note that the scenarios are labeled A, B, and C and that the problem numbers are labeled 1 to 12. After completing the problems, students should complete the statement and answer the final question at the end.

(1) P, $\frac{3}{7}$ (2) A, $\frac{4}{7}$ (3) U, $\frac{9}{20}$ (4) O, $\frac{3}{5}$ (5) E, $\frac{1}{3}$ (6) B, $\frac{1}{2}$ (7) E, $\frac{1}{3}$ (8) B, $\frac{1}{2}$ (9) I, $\frac{4}{11}$

(10) R, $\frac{7}{11}$ (11) L, $\frac{8}{21}$ (12) Q, $\frac{2}{3}$ A probability space where each simple event has an

equal probability is called an "equiprobable" space. Events 3 and H are independent
because $P(3|H) = P(3)$ and $P(H|3) = P(H)$.

6-39: (S-CP.4) UNDERSTANDING TWO-WAY FREQUENCY TABLES

For this activity, your students will use data to construct a two-way frequency table and find
probabilities based on the data. Completing a statement at the end of the worksheet will enable
them to check their work.

Explain that not only can two-way tables be used to organize data, they can be used to find
conditional probabilities as well. Review that conditional probability is the probability of an event
based on the occurrence of a previous event. $P(A|B)$ is the probability of Event A occurring given
that Event B has occurred.

Provide the following example: Mr. Wright's first period math class has 30 students. Of these 30
students, 15 watch reality singing competitions and reality dancing competitions. One student
watches dancing competitions only, 9 watch singing competitions only, and 5 watch neither. These
results are summarized in the table below. Sketch the table on the board, have your students help
you to fill in the data, and then discuss the table. Pose questions, such as the following: What is
the probability of randomly selecting a student who watches singing and dancing competitions?
$\frac{15}{30} = \frac{1}{2}$ What is the probability of selecting a student who does not watch singing competitions
given that a student who watches dancing competitions has been selected? $\frac{1}{16}$

	Watch Singing Competitions	Do Not Watch Singing Competitions	Totals
Watch Dancing Competitions	15	1	16
Do Not Watch Dancing Competitions	9	5	14
Totals	24	6	30

Go over the background information and directions on the worksheet with your students.
Remind them to complete the statement at the end.

The answers to the questions are followed by the table.   (1) A, $\frac{11}{60}$ (2) D, $\frac{4}{9}$ (3) N, $\frac{6}{13}$

(4) V, $\frac{2}{13}$ (5) P, $\frac{3}{8}$ (6) T, $\frac{11}{25}$ (7) E, $\frac{7}{13}$ (8) R, $\frac{9}{26}$ (9) I, $\frac{1}{7}$ Dependent events "are
never independent."

	Social Media	E-Mail	Playing Video Games	Research and Writing Reports	Watching Videos	Totals
Boys	8	11	15	20	6	60
Girls	12	14	9	25	10	70
Totals	20	25	24	45	16	130

6-40: (S-CP.5) EXPLORING CONCEPTS OF CONDITIONAL PROBABILITY

For this activity, your students will be given two everyday scenarios. They will explain how conditional probability and independence relate to these situations.

Explain that probability may be applied to everyday situations. Discuss the probability equations for independent and dependent events that are presented on the worksheet.

Go over the directions with your students. In each case, students must identify the two events and show how conditional probability may be used to determine if the events are independent.

ANSWERS

(1) Event A is getting an "A" on the test. Event S is studying more than 2 hours. $P(A) = \frac{5}{6}$ and $P(A|S) = \frac{10}{11}$. The events are not independent because $P(A|S) \neq P(A)$. (2) Event W is the team wins. Event A is Kelvin attends the game. $P(A) = \frac{1}{2}$, $P(A|W) = \frac{1}{2}$, $P(W) = \frac{1}{2}$, $P(W|A) = \frac{1}{2}$. The events are independent because $P(A|W) = P(A)$ and $P(W|A) = P(W)$.

6-41: (S-CP.6) FINDING CONDITIONAL PROBABILITIES AS A FRACTION OF OUTCOMES

For this activity, your students will find the conditional probability of Event A given Event B by using a table to determine the fraction of B's outcomes that belong to A. Completing a statement at the end of the worksheet will enable students to check their answers.

Discuss the table on the worksheet, noting that there are three types of bagels, one in each row and four types of toppings, one in each column. The totals of each are shown in the last row and the last column. There are 78 bagels in all.

Point out that events based on the table are also noted on the worksheet. Each event is represented by the first letter of the type of bagel or its topping.

Provide this example: Event S is randomly selecting a bagel that has sesame seeds. Event B is randomly selecting a bran bagel. $P(S|B)$, which means the probability of randomly selecting a bagel that has sesame seeds, given that a bran bagel has been selected, can be found by using the table. Row 1 shows that there are 25 bran muffins. Of these 25 bran muffins, 5 have sesame seeds. $P(S|B) = \frac{5}{25} = \frac{1}{5}$

Go over the directions with your students. They should find the conditional probabilities by using the table, and looking at the fraction of outcomes of the first item selected that belongs to the second event. Remind your students to complete the statement at the end.

(1) Z, $\frac{11}{23}$ (2) K, $\frac{6}{13}$ (3) E, $\frac{9}{16}$ (4) B, $\frac{1}{4}$ (5) O, $\frac{5}{13}$ (6) A, $\frac{4}{13}$ (7) S, $\frac{3}{13}$ (8) N, $\frac{3}{14}$

(9) R, $\frac{7}{39}$ (10) D, $\frac{2}{5}$ "A baker's dozen" equals 13. (Note: The term "baker's dozen" stems from the Middle Ages when unsavory bakers began selling goods that weighed a little less than what their customers were paying for. To prevent dishonest bakers from cheating people, laws with severe penalties were instituted. To stay on the right side of the law, and avoid punishment, bakers began including an extra item with the typical order of a dozen rolls or cakes, ensuring that they would not be accused of breaking the law.)

6–42: (S-CP.7) APPLYING THE ADDITION RULE

For this activity, your students will apply the Addition Rule to find the probability of two events. Answering a question at the end of the worksheet will enable them to check their answers.

Explain the Addition Rule that is presented on the worksheet. Note that in probability the word "or" means *union* and the word "and" means *intersection*. The Addition Rule may also be expressed as $P(A \cup B) = P(A) + P(B) - P(A \cap B)$.

Present this example: One fair six-sided die is tossed. Find the probability of rolling a 5 or an odd number. The probability of rolling a 5 can be written as $P(5)$, and the probability of rolling an odd number can be written as $P(\text{odd})$. $P(5) = \frac{1}{6}$, and $P(\text{odd}) = \frac{3}{6} = \frac{1}{2}$. $P(5 \text{ and odd}) = \frac{1}{6}$ because only one outcome, 5, is both 5 and odd. The Addition Rule can be applied to find $P(5 \text{ or odd})$. $P(5 \text{ or odd}) = P(5) + P(\text{odd}) - P(5 \text{ and odd}) = \frac{1}{6} + \frac{3}{6} - \frac{1}{6} = \frac{3}{6} = \frac{1}{2}$

Next ask your students to find the probability of rolling a 4 or an odd number. $P(4) = \frac{1}{6}$, $P(\text{odd}) = \frac{1}{2}$, $P(4 \text{ and odd}) = 0$, meaning that rolling a 4 and an odd number is impossible. The Addition Rule applies as follows: $P(4 \text{ or odd}) = P(4) + P(\text{odd}) - P(4 \text{ and odd}) = \frac{1}{6} + \frac{1}{2} - 0 = \frac{4}{6} = \frac{2}{3}$ or simply $P(4 \text{ or odd}) = P(4) + P(\text{odd}) = \frac{1}{6} + \frac{1}{2} = \frac{4}{6} = \frac{2}{3}$.

Discuss the probability model on the worksheet. If necessary, review the notation: for example, $P(\text{prime or composite number})$ means the probability of randomly selecting a prime or a composite number from the numbers in the hat. Encourage your students to write the possible outcomes and refer to them as they find the probabilities. If necessary, review terms such as prime, composite, and multiples.

Go over the directions. Remind your students to answer the question at the end.

(1) B, $\frac{9}{10}$ (2) R, $\frac{1}{2}$ (3) E, $\frac{3}{5}$ (4) G, $\frac{4}{5}$ (5) O, $\frac{7}{10}$ (6) O, $\frac{7}{10}$ (7) L, $\frac{2}{5}$ (8) E, $\frac{3}{5}$

(9) E, $\frac{3}{5}$ (10) O, $\frac{7}{10}$ (11) G, $\frac{4}{5}$ The mathematician was "George Boole."

Reproducibles for Section 6 follow.

Name_____ Date_____ Period_____

6–1: IDENTIFYING STATISTICAL QUESTIONS

The answers to a statistical question are expected to vary. For example: "What kinds of pets do the students in sixth grade have?" There are likely to be many answers to this question.

A non-statistical question has one answer. For example: "What kind of pet does Anna have?" There is only one answer to this question.

Directions: Identify whether each question is a statistical question or a non-statistical question. Write the letter of each answer in the space above its question number to complete the statement at the end. You will need to divide the letters into words.

1. What is Carmella's favorite dessert? (E. Statistical   A. Non-Statistical)

2. How many students are in Sam's math class? (I. Statistical   E. Non-Statistical)

3. How many minutes do the students in sixth grade spend on math homework each night? (U. Statistical   O. Non-Statistical)

4. What are the favorite student lunches in Harris Middle School? (A. Statistical   N. Non-Statistical)

5. How many hours of sleep does the average middle school student get each night? (C. Statistical   R. Non-Statistical)

6. How tall is DeShawn's older brother? (L. Statistical   T. Non-Statistical)

7. Which languages do the sixth grade students in Ashley's school speak? (R. Statistical   A. Non-Statistical)

8. What are the favorite colors of students in Evan's class? (A. Statistical   I. Non-Statistical)

9. How many minutes does the typical worker commute to work in Martinsville? (A. Statistical   O. Non-Statistical)

10. How many days does February have this year? (E. Statistical   T. Non-Statistical)

11. What is Callie's favorite sport? (H. Statistical   C. Non-Statistical)

12. What are the ages of the students in the high school band? (D. Statistical   M. Non-Statistical)

Conclusions should always be based on _____.

$\overline{9}$ $\overline{5}$ $\overline{11}$ $\overline{3}$ $\overline{7}$ $\overline{1}$ $\overline{6}$ $\overline{2}$ $\overline{12}$ $\overline{8}$ $\overline{10}$ $\overline{4}$

Name _____ Date _____ Period _____

6-2: DESCRIBING DATA DISTRIBUTIONS

Understanding the different ways data can be described can help you interpret data more accurately.

Directions: The set of data below has been collected to answer a statistical question. Find the mean, median, mode, and range. Then construct a dot plot to display the data. Finally, answer the question at the end.

Mrs. Fielder asked the students in her first period math class the following statistical question: How much time do you usually spend on math homework each night?

Following are her students' answers (rounded to the nearest 5 minutes): 0, 0, 5, 10, 10, 10, 15, 15, 15, 15, 20, 20, 20, 20, 20, 20, 25, 25, 25, 25, 25, 30, 30, 35, 40.

Mean = _____   Median = _____   Mode = _____   Range = _____

How are the mean, median, mode, and range related to the dot plot?

Name _____ Date _____ Period _____

6–3: FINDING THE MEAN, MEDIAN, MODE, AND RANGE

The mean, median, mode, and range may be used to describe a set of data.

    Directions: Find the mean, median, mode, and range of each set of data. Then find each answer in the Answer Bank. Complete the statement at the end by writing the letter of each answer in the space above its problem number. Some answers will not be used. You will need to divide the letters into words.

A. The fat content (rounded to the nearest gram) in food served by a local fast-food restaurant is shown below.

Hamburger	19
Double hamburger	36
Cheeseburger	23
Fish sandwich	13
Hot dog	33
Fried chicken	21
French fries	13
Taco	10

1. Mean _____ 2. Median _____ 3. Mode _____ 4. Range _____

B. Several towns in the same area vary greatly in elevation. Because of the varying elevations, their snowfall totals can be quite different. Following are their snowfall totals (rounded to the nearest inch) for last year.

Ralston	35
Millersville	17
Mountainside	47
Rock River	16
Cedar Town	22
Thompson Valley	7
Jonah's Creek	22
Fredericks	16
Maple Hill	16

5. Mean _____ 6. Median _____ 7. Mode _____ 8. Range _____

(Continued)

253

Answer Bank

| U. 20 | R. 16 | N. 34 | T. 22 | W. 25 |
| H. 13 | E. 40 | M. 26 | S. 17 | A. 21 |

_____ of central tendency are the mean, median, and mode.

$\overline{5}$ $\overline{3}$ $\overline{7}$ $\overline{8}$ $\overline{8}$ $\overline{4}$ $\overline{8}$ $\overline{1}$ $\overline{6}$ $\overline{2}$ $\overline{7}$ $\overline{8}$ $\overline{6}$

Name_____ Date_____ Period_____

6-4: USING DOT PLOTS TO DISPLAY DATA

A dot plot shows the frequency of data over a number line. Dot plots provide a visual display of data.

To make a dot plot, do the following:

- Draw a number line and label the numbers. The numbers should represent the values of your data.

- Place a dot (or similar mark) for each value above its matching number on the number line.

Directions: Construct two dot plots to display the data of the heights of the students in Mr. Martin's class. Then answer the questions.

Heights of boys (rounded to the nearest inch): 55, 59, 56, 60, 57, 57, 58, 59, 56, 61, 57, 63

Heights of girls (rounded to the nearest inch): 56, 57, 60, 59, 59, 57, 62, 59, 60, 58, 60, 61

1. How do the dot plots help you to interpret the data?

2. What conclusions can you draw from the dot plots?

6–5: CONSTRUCTING A BOX PLOT

A box plot, also known as a box-and-whisker plot, is a data display that divides data into four parts. A box represents half of the data with "whiskers" that extend to the smallest and largest data points. Follow the steps below to construct a box plot:

1. Arrange the data in ascending order.

2. Find the median of the set of data, Q_2. If there is an odd number of data, the median is the middle number. If there is an even number of data, find the median by dividing the two middle numbers by 2. The median divides the data into two parts, an upper part and a lower part.

3. Find Q_1, the median of the lower part.

4. Find Q_3, the median of the upper part.

5. Find the smallest and largest data points.

6. Draw a number line that includes the smallest and largest data points. Choose an appropriate scale.

7. Show the smallest data value, Q_1, Q_2, Q_3, and the largest data value as points above the number line.

8. Draw a rectangular box around Q_1 and Q_3 to show the second and third quartiles.

9. Draw a vertical line through the box at Q_2.

10. Draw a whisker from Q_1 to the smallest data point and draw a whisker from Q_3 to the largest data point.

Directions: Six sets of data and six box plots are shown below. Match each set of data with its box plot. Then complete the statement.

1. 12, 1, 2, 12, 12, 8, 10, 5, 3, 7, 5, 12   2. 10, 7, 12, 2, 1, 4, 11, 8, 11, 9, 4, 4

3. 4, 12, 9, 7, 7, 12, 3, 10, 5, 1, 5, 5   4. 3, 6, 6, 1, 2, 9, 4, 6, 11, 3, 7, 12

5. 1, 10, 4, 9, 11, 12, 7, 2, 9, 7, 4, 10   6. 2, 7, 9, 10, 6, 12, 5, 9, 6, 3, 12, 1

(Continued)

Copyright © 2016 by Judith A. Muschla, Gary Robert Muschla, and Erin Muschla-Berry.

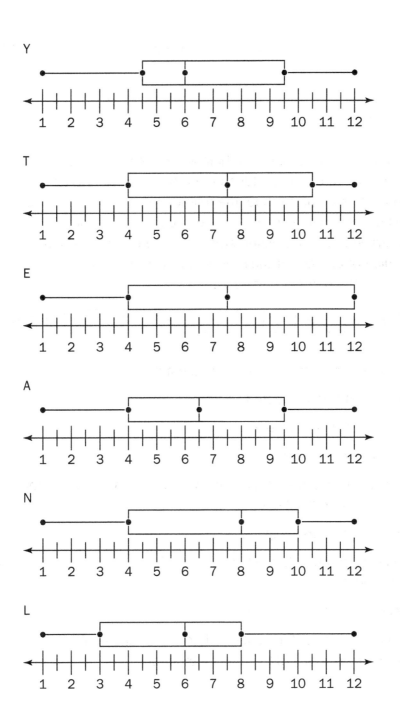

Y

T

E

A

N

L

You should always construct graphs accurately and _____.

$\overline{5}$ $\overline{1}$ $\overline{6}$ $\overline{2}$ $\overline{4}$ $\overline{3}$

6-6: SUMMARIZING AND DESCRIBING DATA

Summarizing and describing data can help you to draw accurate conclusions.

Suresh and Gina were working together on a project for statistics. They asked random sixth graders in their school the following question: How much time do you usually spend using a media screen—TV, computer, smartphone, tablet, and so on—on an average day? They asked students before school, during lunch, and after school. They did not ask any of their friends. Following are the students' responses in hours (rounded to the nearest half-hour):

4	5	6.5	3.5	3	4	4.5	6	9.5	6	3.5	4	5	6.5	4

Directions: Use the data to answer the questions.

1. How much data was collected?

2. How was the data collected?

3. Was the data exact? Explain.

4. What are the mean, median, and mode of the data? Describe these measures of center to the overall set of data.

5. Are there any outliers? Explain.

6. What is the interquartile range of the data? Based on the interquartile range, describe the data.

7. Describe any patterns you see with the data.

8. Construct a box plot of the data. Relate the mean, median, mode, and interquartile range to the shape of the data distribution.

Name_____ Date_____ Period_____

6-7: DRAWING INFERENCES FROM SAMPLES

Statistics can be used to collect data about a population. A sample of the population can be used to obtain the data.

Directions: Study the survey taken of the students of Harper Township's two middle schools. Then answer the questions.

Harper Township has two middle schools with a total student population of 1,524. (Both middle schools contain sixth, seventh, and eighth grades.) Because of budget cuts, the school board is considering reducing the number of after-school clubs at the two schools from ten clubs to five. Many students are understandably upset. Four eighth grade students, two in each middle school, decided to survey students in the sixth, seventh, and eighth grades to find out which clubs should be offered.

The students conducting the survey tried to design it to be as accurate as possible. Realizing that it would very difficult to survey every student in both middle schools, they decided to survey a random sample. They designed a sample question: "Of the following 10 clubs, which 5 might you be interested in joining?" They then proceeded to ask 50 students in each of the middle schools for a total of 100 students. They asked students during free time, such as before and after school and during lunch. Because all of the students conducting the survey were eighth graders, most of the students surveyed were also eighth graders. It turned out that 50 eighth graders, 30 seventh graders, and 20 sixth graders were surveyed. Following are the results.

Student Club Preferences	
Cooking Club	48
Fitness Club	69
Chess Club	31
History Club	46
Science Club	54
Math Club	42
Computer Club	65
Reading Club	34
Dance Club	75
Hobby Club	36

1. Who conducted the survey? Who took part in the survey? Which grade had the most representation? Do you think this might have affected the data? Explain.

(Continued)

2. How was the survey conducted? Was this an effective way to conduct the survey? How might it have been improved?

3. Do you feel that the survey fairly represents the opinions of the students in sixth, seventh, and eighth grade? Explain.

4. Why is random sampling necessary when gathering statistical data?

5. Do you think the question asked in the survey provided accurate results? Explain.

6. Based on the survey, which three clubs were the most popular choices? Which three were the least popular?

Name _____ Date _____ Period _____

6–8: DRAWING INFERENCES ABOUT A POPULATION USING RANDOM SAMPLES

Inferences about a population can be drawn from random samples. But because samples are only a part of the population being studied, different samples will give slightly different results. To understand these variations in results, researchers can conduct more samples of the same size or run simulations of the sample.

Directions: Use the data from the random sample below to generate multiple simulations of the same-size sample to find variations in the results, and help you to make predictions about the overall population. Then answer the questions.

Twenty random seventh grade students at Morning Glory Middle School were asked if they preferred to read fiction or nonfiction. The results of the survey are shown below.

	Fiction	Nonfiction
Students	11	9

1. What inferences can you draw from the data obtained from the original sample?

2. Describe the variations you found in the results of your simulations.

3. How do the results of the simulations compare to the results of the original sample?

Name _____ Date _____ Period _____

6-9: COMPARING TWO DATA SETS

The monthly average high temperatures of New York City and the monthly average high temperatures of Los Angeles are shown in the following chart.

	New York City	Los Angeles
January	38° F	68° F
February	42° F	69° F
March	50° F	70° F
April	61° F	73° F
May	71° F	75° F
June	79° F	78° F
July	84° F	83° F
August	83° F	84° F
September	75° F	83° F
October	64° F	79° F
November	54° F	73° F
December	43° F	68° F

Directions: Use the data in the table to construct two dot plots on the same sheet of graph paper. Use a different colored pencil for each dot plot. Then interpret the data and complete the paragraph.

Although the highest average monthly temperature, 1. _____° F, is the same for both New York City and Los Angeles, throughout the year Los Angeles is warmer than New York City. The mean of the average monthly high temperatures in Los Angeles is 2. _____° F, which is 3. _____° F higher than the mean of the average monthly high temperatures in New York City. The range of the average monthly high temperatures in Los Angeles is 4. _____° F, compared with the range of the average monthly high temperatures in New York City, which is 5. _____° F. The temperatures for Los Angeles were positioned 6. _____ on the graph and the values are 7. _____ spread out than those of New York City.

Name _____ Date _____ Period _____

6-10: DRAWING INFERENCES ABOUT POPULATIONS

Measures of center and measures of variability can be used to compare populations.

Directions: The heights of the members of the Free Valley High School boys' basketball team and the members of the Free Valley High School girls' basketball team are shown below. Use the data to answer the questions.

Heights of the members of the boys' basketball team (rounded to the nearest inch): 70, 67, 68, 74, 73, 74, 66, 67, 71, 77, 75, 76.

Heights of the members of the girls' basketball team (rounded to the nearest inch): 64, 68, 67, 74, 70, 69, 63, 65, 68, 70, 69, 69.

1. What is the mean of the heights of the boys? What is the mean of the heights of the girls?

2. What is the median of the heights of the boys? What is the median of the heights of the girls?

3. What is the mode, or modes, of the heights of the boys? What is the mode, or modes, of the heights of the girls?

4. What is the range of the heights of the boys? What is the range of the heights of the girls?

5. How would you describe the heights of the boys compared to the heights of the girls?

6–11: UNDERSTANDING THE PROBABILITY OF EVENTS

Understanding the probability of events occurring can help you to predict events. This in turn can help you make decisions.

Directions: Read each situation and decide whether the event is likely, neither likely nor unlikely, or unlikely to happen. Then complete the statement at the end by writing the letter of each answer in the space above its situation number. You will need to divide the letters into words.

1. Three-fourths of the seventh graders in Oakley Middle School plan to go on the class trip. What is the likelihood of a randomly selected seventh grader going on the class trip? (H. Likely   E. Neither likely nor unlikely   S. Unlikely)

2. There are 52 cards in a standard deck of cards. After shuffling the cards and keeping them face down, Joe picked a card. What is the likelihood of Joe picking a card with the number 7 on it? (R. Likely   N. Neither likely nor unlikely   T. Unlikely)

3. The weather forecast says that the probability of rain tomorrow is 90%. What is the likelihood of rain tomorrow? (S. Likely   M. Neither likely nor unlikely   O. Unlikely)

4. In Lincoln Middle School, 5 out of 10 students buy pizza for lunch every Friday. What is the likelihood of a randomly selected student buying pizza for lunch this Friday? (U. Likely   I. Neither likely nor unlikely   E. Unlikely)

5. Cassie has made arrangements to adopt a puppy from a local shelter. Cassie's puppy was one of a litter of six—three males and three females. All of the puppies except one from this litter have already been adopted. What is the likelihood that the puppy Cassie is adopting is a male? (H. Likely   V. Neither likely nor unlikely   R. Unlikely)

6. In math class, Tamara's teacher gave her students spinners with ten equal-sized sectors, numbered 0 to 9. What is the likelihood of Tamara spinning the spinner and having it land on any of the numbers from 0 to 4? (S. Likely   N. Neither likely nor unlikely   I. Unlikely)

7. A poll taken at Anissa's school found that $\frac{1}{5}$ of the students enjoy reading science fiction stories. Anissa was one of the students who took part in the poll. What is the likelihood that Anissa enjoys reading science fiction? (E. Likely   W. Neither likely nor unlikely   A. Unlikely)

(Continued)

8. A local restaurant is running a promotion. With every dinner purchased, diners receive a scratch-off card for a free appetizer, a free salad, a free beverage, or a free dessert with the next purchase of a dinner. The chances of winning any one of the four prizes are equal. What is the likelihood that when Charles purchases a dinner, he will receive a card for a free dessert? (S. Likely   N. Neither likely nor unlikely   G. Unlikely)

9. The Cardinals won 8 of their last 10 baseball games this season against opponents who have won at least 50% of their games. The Cardinals' next game is against the Ravens, who have won 5 of their last 10 games. What is the likelihood of the Cardinals beating the Ravens? (E. Likely   T. Neither likely nor unlikely   S. Unlikely)

10. Claire and Jamaal are running for seventh grade class president. In a recent poll of the school's seventh graders, 46% said they intended to vote for Claire, and 42% said they intended to vote for Jamaal. 12% were undecided at the time of the poll. What is the likelihood that Claire will win the election? (H. Likely   P. Neither likely nor unlikely   T. Unlikely)

Probability is the branch of mathematics that addresses the chances of

_____ .

$\overline{9}$ $\overline{5}$ $\overline{9}$ $\overline{6}$ $\overline{2}$ $\overline{3}$ $\overline{1}$ $\overline{7}$ $\overline{10}$ $\overline{10}$ $\overline{9}$ $\overline{6}$ $\overline{4}$ $\overline{6}$ $\overline{8}$

6–12: PROBABILITIES AND PREDICTIONS

In mathematics, probability is a number expressing the likelihood of a specific event occurring. Probability ranges from 0 to 1, with 0 meaning that an event will never happen, and 1 meaning that an event is certain to happen.

A spinner is divided into eight equal-sized sectors, as shown below.

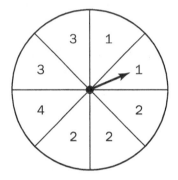

Directions: Assume that the spinner is spun 800 times. Answer the questions.

1. How many times would you predict that the arrow of the spinner lands on 1?

2. How many times would you predict that the arrow of the spinner lands on 2?

3. How many times would you predict that the arrow of the spinner lands on 4?

4. How many times would you predict that the arrow of the spinner lands on 1 or 3?

5. How many times would you predict that the arrow of the spinner lands on 1 or 2?

6. How many times would you predict that the arrow of the spinner lands on a number less than 5?

7. How many times would you predict that the arrow of the spinner lands on a number greater than 4?

8. How many times would you predict that the arrow of the spinner lands on a number greater than 1?

9. For problem numbers 1 to 8, you made predictions of the number of times the arrow would land on a number or combination of numbers. If you were to actually spin this spinner, how accurate do you feel your predictions would be? Explain your answer.

Name _____ Date _____ Period _____

6-13: USING PROBABILITY MODELS TO FIND PROBABILITIES OF EVENTS

The nurse at Hollander Middle School is concerned that students who carry too many books in their backpacks may suffer back injuries. On Friday morning, with the principal's approval, she asked teachers to ask the students in their first period class how many books the students took home on Thursday night. The results were tabulated in the following table.

	None	One	Two	Three	Four or More
Sixth Grade	18	15	30	32	5
Seventh Grade	10	12	25	34	14
Eighth Grade	6	16	28	38	17

Directions: Use the data in the table to find the probabilities for problems 1–11. Then answer the question in problem 12. Find your answers for problems 1 to 11 in the Answer Bank. One answer will not be used. Write the letter of each answer in the space above its problem number to complete the statement at the end. You will need to break the letters into words.

1. *P*(sixth grader who took home 4 or more books)

2. *P*(sixth grader who took home no books)

3. *P*(seventh grader who took home 4 or more books)

4. *P*(eighth grader who took home 2 books)

5. *P*(student who took home 3 books)

6. *P*(eighth grader who took home less than 2 books)

7. *P*(student who took home 4 or more books)

8. *P*(seventh grader who took home 3 or more books)

9. *P*(student who took home 1 book)

10. *P*(student who took home 2 books or less)

11. *P*(seventh grader who took home 2 books or less)

12. Do you think the same results would be obtained if students were polled on a different day? Why or why not?

(Continued)

N. $\frac{3}{25}$	Y. $\frac{8}{15}$	D. $\frac{47}{300}$	I. $\frac{7}{150}$	T. $\frac{43}{300}$	A. $\frac{3}{50}$
C. $\frac{1}{5}$	S. $\frac{4}{25}$	P. $\frac{26}{75}$	B. $\frac{7}{75}$	E. $\frac{1}{60}$	L. $\frac{11}{150}$

_____ can be used to find probabilities.

$\overline{11}$ $\overline{2}$ $\overline{9}$ $\overline{2}$ $\overline{11}$ $\overline{3}$ $\overline{8}$ $\overline{5}$ $\overline{6}$ $\overline{2}$ $\overline{10}$ $\overline{1}$ $\overline{11}$

$\overline{3}$ $\overline{7}$ $\overline{2}$ $\overline{9}$ $\overline{2}$ $\overline{4}$ $\overline{6}$ $\overline{1}$

Name _____ Date _____ Period _____

6–14: UNDERSTANDING THE PROBABILITY OF COMPOUND EVENTS

A compound event is made up of two or more simple events. To find the probability of a compound event, you must find the fraction of outcomes in the sample space for which the compound event occurs.

Directions: A pair of special six-sided fair dice are numbered 1 to 6 and 7 to 12. List the possible outcomes in the sample space and answer the questions. Match each answer with an answer in the Answer Bank. Some answers will not be used. Complete the statement at the end by writing the letter of each answer in the space above its problem number. You will need to divide the letters into words.

1. What is the probability of rolling two numbers whose sum 9?

2. What is the probability of rolling two numbers whose product is 6?

3. What is the probability of rolling two even numbers whose sum is greater than 16?

4. What is the probability of rolling two odd numbers?

5. What is the probability of rolling an odd and an even number?

6. What is the probability of rolling a prime and a composite number?

7. What is the probability of rolling two numbers whose sum is less than 10?

Answer Bank

E. $\frac{4}{9}$	S. 0	H. $\frac{1}{18}$	C. $\frac{11}{18}$	A. $\frac{1}{36}$
R. $\frac{3}{4}$	M. $\frac{1}{4}$	N. $\frac{7}{12}$	T. $\frac{1}{12}$	I. $\frac{1}{2}$

Compound events are two or more simple events happening _____.

$\overline{3}$ $\overline{7}$ $\overline{7}$ $\overline{1}$ $\overline{6}$ $\overline{2}$ $\overline{3}$ $\overline{4}$ $\overline{6}$ $\overline{7}$ $\overline{5}$ $\overline{4}$ $\overline{6}$

Name _____ Date _____ Period _____

6–15: FINDING PROBABILITIES OF COMPOUND EVENTS USING TABLES, LISTS, AND TREE DIAGRAMS

Organized lists and tree diagrams can be used to show data in a sample space. These lists and diagrams can be used to find probabilities of events.

Part One

Directions: Create an organized list or tree diagram to represent a sample space for the events below.

Event 1	Event 2	Event 3
A spinner with 4 equal-sized sectors is spun. Each sector is labeled with the letters A, B, C, or D.	A fair 6-sided die is rolled. Each side is labeled with the numbers 1, 2, 3, 4, 5, or 6.	A fair coin is tossed. One side is a head, and the other side is a tail.

Part Two

Directions: Use your organized list or tree diagram to find the following probabilities. Then match each answer with an answer in the Answer Bank. Some answers will be used more than once. Some answers will not be used. Write the letter of each answer in the space above its problem number to identify a term used in the study of probability (and in this assignment). You will need to reverse the order of the letters and divide the letters into words.

1. $P(A$ and 3 and $H)$

2. $P(D$ and 4 and $T)$

3. $P(H$ or $T)$

4. $P(A$ or B or $C)$

5. $P(5$ and $H)$

6. $P(\text{composite number})$

7. $P(C$ and $H)$

8. $P(B$ and a composite number)

9. $P(A)$

10. $P(D$ and $H)$

11. $P(C)$

Answer Bank

N. $\frac{1}{6}$	M. $\frac{1}{3}$	T. $\frac{2}{3}$	E. $\frac{1}{48}$	S. $\frac{1}{12}$	C. 1	V. $\frac{1}{2}$	P. $\frac{1}{4}$	A. $\frac{1}{8}$	L. $\frac{3}{4}$

$$\overline{}\quad \overline{}\quad \overline{}\quad \overline{}\quad \overline{}\quad \overline{}\quad \overline{}\quad \overline{}\quad \overline{}\quad \overline{}\quad \overline{}$$
$$\;1\qquad 3\qquad 7\qquad 9\qquad 5\qquad 2\qquad 4\qquad 11\qquad 6\qquad 10\qquad 8$$

Name_____ Date_____ Period_____

6–16: CONSTRUCTING AND INTERPRETING SCATTER PLOTS

A scatter plot is a graph in the coordinate plane that is used to find relationships between two quantities.

Twenty-four students in a college statistics class completed a survey about the number of hours they slept during an average night and their grade point average (GPA). The results of the survey are shown in the following table. Hours are rounded to the nearest half hour and GPAs are rounded to the nearest tenth.

Hours of Sleep	GPA	Hours of Sleep	GPA	Hours of Sleep	GPA	Hours of Sleep	GPA
7.0	3.6	4.0	2.2	6.0	3.2	7.0	3.4
8.5	3.8	7.0	4.0	7.0	3.5	6.5	3.1
6.0	3.0	8.5	3.5	5.0	2.9	6.0	3.2
6.5	2.9	5.0	2.7	10.5	3.0	5.5	2.8
8.0	3.4	6.5	3.4	6.5	3.1	8.0	3.5
5.5	3.0	5.0	2.6	4.5	2.5	7.5	3.4

Directions: Construct a scatter plot that represents the data. Then use your scatter plots to answer the questions.

1. Did you find any clusters? If yes, describe them.

2. Did you find any outliers? If yes, what were they?

3. What, if any, relationships did you find between the amount of sleep and GPA?

6-17: FITTING LINES TO DATA

The student council at Madison Middle School plans four dances a year for the eighth grade students. For each dance, there is a fee for admission, and raffle tickets are sold at the dance. Although each student must pay admission, students do not have to purchase a raffle ticket. The revenue and expenses for each dance for the last three years are in the table below. All amounts are rounded to the nearest dollar.

Dance	Number of Students	Admission Revenue	Revenue from Raffle Sales	Total Revenue	Expenses
1	116	$696	$380	$1,076	$1,276
2	94	$564	$351	$915	$998
3	108	$648	$364	$1,012	$1,105
4	106	$636	$361	$997	$1,100
5	120	$720	$375	$1,095	$1,300
6	125	$750	$358	$1,108	$1,405
7	96	$576	$345	$921	$968
8	94	$564	$320	$884	$940
9	120	$840	$332	$1,172	$1,307
10	110	$770	$318	$1,088	$1,120
11	100	$700	$328	$1,028	$1,065
12	128	$896	$370	$1,266	$1,380

Directions: Draw the four scatter plots described below. Then find the line of best fit for each scatter plot you drew.

1. Admission revenue as a function of the number of students who paid.

2. Revenue from raffle sales as a function of the number of students who paid.

3. Total revenue as a function of the number of students who paid.

4. Expenses as a function of the number of students who paid.

Following are possible lines of best fit. Not all will be used.

$y = -6x - 3$	$y = 13x - 287$	$y = 10x + 400$
$y = 20x - 300$	$y = 7.6x - 140$	$y = -10x + 400$
Relatively no linear correlation	$y = 20x + 300$	$y = 8.5x + 114$

Name_____ Date_____ Period_____

6-18: USING EQUATIONS OF LINEAR MODELS

Equations of linear models can be used to solve problems.

Directions: Use the equation to answer the questions for each problem.

Problem 1: Michaela hired an electrician to install some new lights in her home. The electrician charges $75 for the service call plus $50 per hour for any work he completes. The overall costs for this electrician can be modeled by the equation $y = 75 + 50x$, where x is the number of hours worked.

1. What does the slope represent?
2. What is the y-intercept?
3. What is the total charge if the electrician worked for 6 hours?
4. If the charge was $200, how many hours did the electrician work?

Problem 2: The score on one of Mrs. Rivera's 10-problem multiple-choice quizzes can be modeled by the equation $y = 100 - 10x$, where x is the number of incorrect answers.

1. What does the slope represent?
2. What does 100 represent?
3. Use the equation to find the score on a quiz if 3 answers were incorrect.
4. Use the equation to find how many answers were incorrect if the score was 80.

Problem 3: A small plain cheese pizza at Reggie's Pizzeria costs $9.99. Each additional topping is $0.75 extra. This can be modeled by the equation $y = \$0.75x + \$9.99$, where x is the number of toppings.

1. What is the slope?
2. What is the y-intercept?
3. Use the equation to find the cost if 3 toppings were ordered.
4. Use the equation to find how many toppings Bradley ordered if he paid $12.99 for one of Reggie's small plain cheese pizzas.

Problem 4: A nursery is having a spring sale in which the prices of all plants are reduced by 20%. The sale price of any plant can be modeled by the equation $y = 0.8x$, where x is the original price.

1. What is the slope, and what does it represent?
2. What is the y-intercept?
3. What is the sale price of a plant that originally cost $80?
4. If a plant is on sale for $80, what was its original price?

Name_____ Date_____ Period_____

6–19: CONSTRUCTING AND INTERPRETING TWO-WAY TABLES

Two-way tables are useful for organizing data and making data easy to interpret.

Ben Franklin Middle School has sixth, seventh, and eighth grades. There are 370 students in all of which 150 are eighth graders. For an upcoming school trip, 90 of the eighth graders said that they would attend. Overall 229 students (sixth, seventh, and eighth graders) said that they would not attend.

Directions: Use the above information to complete the following table. Then use the information in the table to answer the *true/false/cannot be determined* questions that follow. Finally, complete the statement at the end by writing the letter of each answer in the space above its problem number. You will need to divide the letters into words.

	Eighth Grade Student	Not an Eighth Grade Student	Totals
Will attend trip	(a)	(b)	(c)
Will not attend trip	(d)	(e)	(f)
Totals	(g)	(h)	(i)

1. 150 should be placed in space g. (T. True   U. False   M. Cannot be determined)

2. 90 should be placed in space d. (E. True   R. False   W. Cannot be determined)

3. 370 should be placed in space i. (E. True   A. False   L. Cannot be determined)

4. 141 should be placed in space h. (N. True   B. False   S. Cannot be determined)

5. 51 should be placed in space e. (G. True   D. False   O. Cannot be determined)

6. Most of the middle school students will attend the trip. (A. True   I. False   T. Cannot be determined)

7. Most of the seventh graders will attend the trip. (C. True   Y. False   V. Cannot be determined)

8. 60% of the eighth graders will attend the trip? (A. True   I. False   U. Cannot be determined)

_____ is used in this activity.

$$\overline{4}\ \ \overline{6}\ \ \overline{7}\ \ \overline{8}\ \ \overline{2}\ \ \overline{6}\ \ \overline{8}\ \ \overline{1}\ \ \overline{3}\ \ \overline{5}\ \ \overline{8}\ \ \overline{1}\ \ \overline{8}$$

Name_____ Date_____ Period_____

6-20: REPRESENTING DATA WITH PLOTS ON THE REAL NUMBER LINE

Data can often be represented on a number line.

Directions: Construct a dot plot and a box plot to represent the data below. Then answer the questions.

Test Scores of Mr. Rossi's First Period Math Class

85	60	75	100	95	90	85	85	90
75	85	90	100	95	75	85	90	80
90	80	90	85	95	75	85	85	80

1. Describe the test scores, based on your dot plot and box plot.

2. Which, if any, score or scores are outliers?

3. Which data display—the dot plot or box plot—did you find easier to construct? Explain.

4. Which data display do you feel shows the data more clearly? Explain.

5. What other kind of data display might you have used instead to show the test scores? Would this data display have shown the data more clearly than either the dot plot or box plot? Explain.

6-21: COMPARING TWO DATA SETS

Measures of center and spread are useful for comparing data sets.

Jon is thinking of purchasing a pre-owned car or a pre-owned SUV. He checked various ads and compiled the prices of cars or SUVs that he might be interested in purchasing. The data is shown below.

Costs of Pre-Owned Cars Less Than 10 Years Old

$5,995	$7,995	$12,975	$6,995	$6,500	$5,895	$4,995
$14,995	$4,995	$12,995	$16,995	$18,995	$7,595	$16,995

Costs of Pre-Owned SUVs Less Than 10 Years Old

$16,995	$18,895	$17,995	$23,995	$16,995	$22,995	$29,995

Directions: Determine how Jon might describe the data by filling in the blanks in the paragraph.

The data for the costs of the cars are not evenly distributed because the mean is
1. _____, the median is 2. _____ and the modes are
3. _____. The best way to describe the measure of center is with the
4. _____. I will use the 5. _____ to determine the measure of spread, which is 6. _____.

The data for the costs of the SUVs are also not evenly distributed because the mean is 7. _____, the median is 8. _____, and the mode is
9. _____. The best way to describe the measure of center is with the
10. _____.

I will use the 11. _____ to determine the measure of spread which is
12. _____.

Copyright © 2016 by Judith A. Muschla, Gary Robert Muschla, and Erin Muschla-Berry.

Name_____ Date_____ Period_____

6-22: INTERPRETING DIFFERENCES IN SHAPE, CENTER, AND SPREAD OF DATA DISTRIBUTIONS

Mrs. Hastings teaches four sections of statistics. The grades on her students' last test follow:

Section 1: 75, 80, 80, 90, 90, 95, 95, 95, 95, 100

Section 2: 60, 65, 70, 75, 75, 80, 80, 80, 90, 95, 95, 100

Section 3: 50, 70, 70, 70, 70, 75, 75, 80, 80, 80, 80, 100

Section 4: 40, 50, 50, 60, 70, 80, 90, 90, 90, 95

Directions: Find the shape, center, and spread of each section. Use this information to determine whether the statements are *correct* or *incorrect*. Correct any incorrect statements.

1. The test scores in section 4 have the largest IQR.

2. The test scores in section 3 have 1 outlier.

3. The test scores in sections 1 and 2 are the only data sets that have no outliers.

4. The test scores in section 4 are skewed right.

5. The test scores in section 1 are skewed left.

6. The mean and median of the test scores in section 3 are the same.

7. 40 is an outlier in the test scores for section 4.

8. The test scores in section 3 have the smallest IQR.

9. Every data set has one mode.

10. In general, removing an outlier has the largest effect on the mean of a data set.

6-23: RECOGNIZING CHARACTERISTICS OF NORMAL DISTRIBUTIONS

A normal distribution of data takes the form of a bell curve. Which figure below represents a normal distribution?

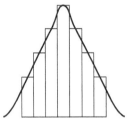 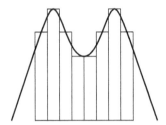

Directions: Decide whether each statement is *true* or *false*. Write the letter of each answer in the space above its statement number to complete the sentence at the end. You will need to divide the letters into words.

1. The curve of a normal distribution is symmetric about the vertical line through the mean of the distribution. (A. True U. False)

2. Normally distributed data may take the shape of a curve with a series of wavy lines. (E. True R. False)

3. For a normal distribution, about 60% of the data is within two standard deviations of the mean. (O. True I. False)

4. An example of a large data set that can be expected to be close to a normal distribution is the heights of 16-year-old boys. (U. True A. False)

5. The curve of a normal distribution nears the horizontal axis at both extremes. (E. True T. False)

6. In a normal distribution, the mean and median are located at a vertical line of symmetry for the curve, but the mode is located at an extreme near the horizontal axis. (N. True C. False)

7. By expressing the data points as percents, normal distributions can be described as frequency distributions. (P. True E. False)

8. Very large data sets are always normally distributed. (T. True L. False)

9. Histograms may be used to represent relative frequencies. (M. True H. False)

Given the mean and standard deviation, the _____ provides an estimate of the spread of data in a normal distribution.

$\overline{5}$ $\overline{9}$ $\overline{7}$ $\overline{3}$ $\overline{2}$ $\overline{3}$ $\overline{6}$ $\overline{1}$ $\overline{8}$ $\overline{2}$ $\overline{4}$ $\overline{8}$ $\overline{5}$

Name_____ Date_____ Period_____

6-24: SUMMARIZING CATEGORICAL DATA IN TWO-WAY FREQUENCY TABLES

Various related data can be displayed in two-way frequency tables.

In observance of Prevention of Cruelty to Animals Month, a representative of the local ASPCA visited Carter High School to speak to students about ways to rescue and adopt pets. 75 students attended the voluntary after-school presentation. To gauge the effectiveness of the presentation, student were asked if they would one day consider rescuing a pet. The results are tabulated in the following frequency table.

	Will Consider Rescuing a Pet	Will Not Consider Rescuing a Pet	Totals
Boys	25	10	35
Girls	32	8	40
Totals	57	18	75

Directions: Complete the relative frequency table. The first entry is done for you. Then answer the question at the end.

	Will Consider Rescuing a Pet	Will Not Consider Rescuing a Pet	Totals
Boys	$\frac{25}{75} = 0.\overline{3}$		
Girls			
Totals			

Based on the relative frequency table, do you feel that the presentation by the ASPCA representative was a success? Explain your answer.

Name _____ Date _____ Period _____

6-25: FINDING THE EQUATION OF THE LINE OF BEST FIT

Sometimes a line does not pass through all of the points of a set of data that have been plotted, even though the points may suggest a line. A line can be drawn that "fits" through most of the points. This line is called the line of best fit, and it is drawn as close as possible to the plotted points. To approximate the line of best fit, do the following:

- Plot the points.
- Use a ruler to sketch the line that fits the data.
- Locate two points on the line you have drawn.
- Use these two points to find the equation of the line of best fit.

Directions: For each set of data, plot the given points on graph paper, draw the line of best fit, and find the equation of the line of best fit.

1. Sandra is saving money for a trip. She read in a magazine that one way to save is to make purchases with paper money and not coins. Any change she would then receive would be saved in a cookie jar. Sandra followed this procedure and recorded the accumulated amount of change she had saved at the end of each week. After the first week, she had accumulated $2.00 in change, after the second she had accumulated $3.50, and so on as shown in the set of data below.

   (1, $2.00), (2, $3.50), (3, $7.00), (4, $8.00), (5, $9.75), (6, $10.99), (7, $15.00), (8, $17.25)

2. At the Happy Valley Community Swimming Pool, the pool manager wanted to track pool attendance, based on a day's high temperature. He recorded the number of people purchasing daily badges and the high temperature for each of the past 9 days. Following is his data. (Degrees are in Fahrenheit.)

   (200, 90°), (188, 87°), (160, 80°), (216, 94°), (140, 75°), (168, 82°), (120, 70°), (200, 90°), (108, 67°)

3. The students in Mrs. Valente's second period math class are measuring special pairs of angles. For example, the pair of numbers (5°, 86°) means that one angle of the pair measures 5° and the other measures 86°. Since measurements are not always exact, the results of the students vary. Following are the results of the measurements found by Mrs. Valente's students.

   (5°, 86°), (15°, 75°), (29°, 60°), (45°, 50°), (55°, 39°), (10°, 78°), (20°, 68°), (8°, 80°), (38°, 46°)

   What type of angles do you think the students are measuring? Use this fact to write the exact equation of the line.

Copyright © 2016 by Judith A. Muschla, Gary Robert Muschla, and Erin Muschla-Berry.

Name_____ Date_____ Period_____

6-26: USING LINEAR AND QUADRATIC MODELS

Scatter plots may suggest a straight line, a curved line, or no line, depending on the data.

   Directions: Each table shows how two quantities are related. There may be a linear relationship or a quadratic relationship. Find the relationship, and then identify how the quantities relate to the sides of the rectangular prism, the area of the rectangles, or the surface area of the prism as shown below.

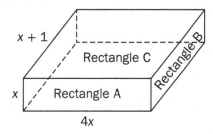

1.

x	0.1	0.25	0.75	1	1.5	2
y	0.11	0.3125	1.3125	2	3.75	6

2.

x	0.1	0.25	0.75	1	1.5	2
y	1.18	3.625	17.625	28	55.5	92

3.

x	0.1	0.25	0.75	1	1.5	2
y	0.4	1	3	4	6	8

4.

x	0.1	0.25	0.75	1	1.5	2
y	0.44	1.25	5.25	8	15	24

5.

x	0.1	0.25	0.75	1	1.5	2
y	1.1	1.25	1.75	2	2.5	3

6.

x	0.1	0.25	0.75	1	1.5	2
y	0.04	0.25	2.25	4	9	16

6–27: INTERPRETING THE SLOPE AND *Y*-INTERCEPT OF A LINEAR MODEL

Linear equations can be written as $y = mx + b$. m is the slope, and b is the *y*-intercept. *x* is the independent variable, and *y* is the dependent variable because the value of *y* depends on the value of *x*.

Directions: For each situation presented below, answer the questions, and then match each answer with an answer in the Answer Bank. Some answers will not be used. Complete the statement at the end by writing the letter of each answer in the space above its problem number. You will need to divide the letters into words.

A. Margie is studying for her final math exam. She began studying a little, and then she realized that for the next 5 days she needed to study 15 pages each day in order to review 100 pages of her math notes.

   1. What is the *y*-intercept of the line that models this situation?

   2. What is the slope of the line?

B. The price of movie tickets at two different theaters is modeled by the lines graphed below.

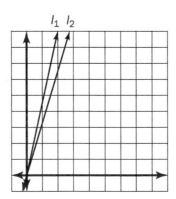

   3. Which line models the theater whose tickets cost more?

   4. What is the *y*-intercept of these lines?

C. A narrow 8-inch cylindrical vase is filled with water. The water evaporates at a rate of 1 inch per day. This can be modeled by $y = -x + 8$.

   5. What is the slope of the line that models this situation?

   6. What is the *y*-intercept of the line?

   7. What is the height of the water in the vase after two days?

   8. What is the independent variable?

   9. What is the dependent variable?

(Continued)

| D. x | N. −1 | T. 1 | A. 8 | I. 15 | Q. l_2 |
| E. y | L. 0 | S. 2 | O. 25 | R. l_1 | M. 6 |

_____ can be written as $y = mx + b$.

$\overline{6}$ $\quad$ $\overline{4}$ $\quad$ $\overline{2}$ $\quad$ $\overline{5}$ $\quad$ $\overline{9}$ $\quad$ $\overline{6}$ $\quad$ $\overline{3}$ $\quad$ $\overline{7}$ $\quad$ $\overline{1}$ $\quad$ $\overline{8}$ $\quad$ $\overline{9}$ $\quad$ $\overline{4}$

6-28: COMPUTING AND INTERPRETING THE CORRELATION COEFFICIENT

The correlation coefficient is a number r, such that $-1 \leq r \leq 1$. It is used to measure the strength of a linear relationship between x and y. When $r = 1$, the points on a scatter plot lie on a line that has a positive slope. When $r = -1$, the points on a scatter plot lie on a line that has a negative slope. The closer the value of r is to 1 or -1, the better the fit of the points on the scatter plot to the line.

Directions: Find the correlation coefficient for each set of data, and match each answer with a correlation coefficient (which has been rounded to the nearest thousandth) in the Answer Bank. Complete the statement at the end by writing the letter of each correlation coefficient in the space above its problem number. You will need to divide the letters into words. Also answer the final question.

1. x is time spent fishing (in hours). y is the number of fish caught.

x	3.5	2.75	5.0	1.25	7.5	6.25
y	3	6	5	5	7	3

2. x is the number of families in an extended family. y is the amount spent per family on the annual "family" vacation last year. (As more families attend, the cost per family goes down.)

x	1	2	3	4	5	6
y	$12,000	$6,000	$4,000	$3,000	$2,400	$2,000

3. x is the average number of hours players spent practicing shooting free throws each week. y is the percentage of free throws made during the season.

x	1	4.5	6	2	4	3.5
y	80%	52%	65%	93%	80%	75%

4. x is the number of people in a household. y is the number of pets in the house.

x	5	4	3	4	3	5
y	4	4	4	5	1	5

(Continued)

Copyright © 2016 by Judith A. Muschla, Gary Robert Muschla, and Erin Muschla-Berry.

5. *x* is the number of people in a household. *y* is the number of TVs in the house.

x	4	7	2	6	3	4
y	3	5	2	4	2	3

6. *x* is the average height (in inches) of teenage girls. *y* is the average weight (in pounds) of teenage girls.

	Age 13	Age 14	Age 15	Age 16	Age 17	Age 18	Age 19
x	61.7	62.5	62.9	64	64	64.2	64.3
y	101	105	115	118	120	125	126

7. *x* is the average height (in inches) of teenage boys. *y* is the average weight (in pounds) of teenage boys.

	Age 13	Age 14	Age 15	Age 16	Age 17	Age 18	Age 19
x	61.5	64.5	67	68.3	69	69.2	69.5
y	100	112	123.5	134	142	147.5	152

Answer Bank

R. 0.962   Y. 0.980   U. −0.878   S. 0.968   C. 0.141   E. −0.672   O. 0.608

Your knowledge in this activity positively correlates to _____.

$\overline{5}$ $\overline{4}$ $\overline{2}$ $\overline{6}$ $\overline{7}$ $\overline{1}$ $\overline{4}$ $\overline{6}$ $\overline{3}$

Which table shows the strongest correlation?

Name _____ Date _____ Period _____

6-29: DISTINGUISHING BETWEEN CORRELATION AND CAUSATION

When interpreting actions or events that seem to be linked, it is important to distinguish if the actions or events are correlated or if one action or event caused another.

- Correlation is when two or more actions or events occur at the same time and might be associated with each other.

- Causation is a specific action or event that causes another action or event to happen.

Directions: Decide whether each statement is an example of correlation or causation. Write the letter of each answer above its statement number to complete the statement at the end. You will need to divide the letters into words.

1. Under normal conditions, when the air temperature falls to 0° C, water begins to freeze. (R. Correlation   T. Causation)

2. Light from the sun warms the Earth. (O. Correlation   S. Causation)

3. Because many studies have linked diets high in saturated fat to heart disease, diets high in saturated fat cause heart disease. (E. Correlation   I. Causation)

4. Mandy always completes her math homework and maintains an "A" average in math. (N. Correlation   U. Causation)

5. Pressing on a brake pedal slows a car down. (R. Correlation   E. Causation)

6. When people stay up late at night, they are tired the next day. (U. Correlation   N. Causation)

7. When Jermaine became sick with the flu, his temperature rose from 98.6° F to 103.5° F. (I. Correlation   O. Causation)

8. Exercising burns calories. (E. Correlation   A. Causation)

9. Whenever Sami goes to bed early on the night before a test, she scores 80% or higher. (O. Correlation   S. Causation)

10. Yesterday the temperature was below freezing, and it snowed. (L. Correlation   N. Causation)

(Continued)

11. Students who eat a nutritious breakfast get good grades. (D. Correlation T. Causation)

12. Having overslept, Taylor missed his bus and was late for school. (N. Correlation Q. Causation)

Correlation _____ causation.

$\overline{11}$　$\overline{9}$　$\overline{5}$　$\overline{2}$　$\overline{4}$　$\overline{7}$　$\overline{1}$　$\overline{3}$　$\overline{12}$　$\overline{6}$　$\overline{8}$　$\overline{10}$

Name _____ Date _____ Period _____

6–30: UNDERSTANDING THE TERMINOLOGY OF STATISTICAL EXPERIMENTS

Understanding statistical terminology is necessary to understanding the processes that underlie statistical experiments.

Directions: Complete each statement with a word from the Answer Bank. Then complete the statement at the end by writing the designated letter of each answer in the space above its statement number. Some words will be used more than once; some words will not be used.

1. The purpose of a statistical study is to gather _____. (3rd letter)

2. A random poll of 1,250 registered voters in a state indicated that Candidate A would likely defeat Candidate B in an upcoming election. The _____ being studied is the registered voters of the state. (7th letter)

3. _____ can help to ensure an unbiased sample. (11th letter)

4. A population _____ is a defining, measurable characteristic of the population that is being studied. (2nd letter)

5. 50 students at Ramsey High School were surveyed about whether they favored starting the school day a half-hour earlier. The 50 students represent the _____ population. (1st letter)

6. Understanding and evaluating data is necessary to make _____ about the data. (10th letter)

7. Researchers must carefully control any variables they introduce in statistical _____. (6th letter)

8. A _____ is a subset of a population. (1st letter)

9. The _____ of a statistical study may be hundreds, thousands, millions, or more individuals. (7th letter)

10. A researcher can make _____ about a population based on a random sample of that population. (8th letter)

Answer Bank

researcher	data	evaluation	parameter	population
randomization	experiments	process	sample	inferences

_____ is an important branch of mathematics.

$\overline{8}$ $\overline{9}$ $\overline{4}$ $\overline{1}$ $\overline{3}$ $\overline{6}$ $\overline{2}$ $\overline{7}$ $\overline{10}$ $\overline{5}$

Name_____ Date_____ Period_____

6-31: EVALUATING PROBABILITY MODELS THROUGH SIMULATIONS

Although probability models may accurately predict the likelihood of events happening, randomness can affect results, especially in small samples.

Directions: Consider each problem, and then answer the questions.

1. A green marble and a red marble were in a jar. The marbles were exactly alike, except for their colors, and the jar was covered with dark paper so that students could not see the marbles inside. The probability model says that randomly picking either marble is 0.5. Raphael's teacher asked him to pick a marble from the jar. She recorded the color on the board. To ensure randomness, she put the marble back into the jar and shook it. Then she called another student to pick a marble. She followed this same procedure 8 more times until a total of 10 marbles were picked. The results were somewhat surprising: 7 students picked the red marble, and 3 students picked the green marble. This was not what the model predicted.

   Given these results, run simulations to evaluate the probability model. Are your results consistent with the model? What might be the reason for the results of the students in Raphael's class? Write a summary of your methods and findings.

2. A die has the numbers 1 to 6. A model says that tossing the die with the results being an odd number has a probability of 0.5. When Callie tossed the die 20 times, odd numbers came up only 7 times.

   Given these results, run simulations to evaluate the probability model. Are your results consistent with the model? What might be the reason for Callie's results? Write a summary of your methods and findings.

3. A spinner has 4 sectors, each of equal size and shape, numbered 1 to 4. A model says that spinning the arrow should result in the arrow landing on each number once every 4 spins. After 16 spins, Jamie got the following results: the arrow landed 4 times on 1, 3 times on 2, 1 time on 3, and 8 times on 4.

   Given these results, run simulations to evaluate the probability model. Are your results consistent with the model? What might be the reason for Jamie's results? Write a summary of your methods and findings.

6–32: RECOGNIZING SURVEYS, EXPERIMENTS, AND OBSERVATIONAL STUDIES

Researchers use various methods to gather data. Three common methods are surveys, experiments, and observational studies.

Directions: Read each statement and decide whether it describes a survey, an experiment, or an observational study. Answer the question at the end by writing the letter of each answer in the space above its statement number.

1. In collecting data on the hunting strategies of wolf packs, researchers made certain not to disturb the wolves in any way. (H. Survey   L. Experiment T. Observational Study)

2. Researchers asked randomly selected high school students the same questions about smartphone use. (M. Survey   R. Experiment   E. Observational Study)

3. In testing the effectiveness of the new drug, researchers gave some subjects the drug while others, called the control group, were not given any drug. (U. Survey A. Experiment   P. Observational Study)

4. Researchers gave a weight loss supplement to one group of test subjects and a placebo to another group, had both groups follow their usual eating habits, and then recorded any changes in weight. (M. Survey   D. Experiment   K. Observational Study)

5. Researchers conducted their investigation by randomly mailing questionnaires to a sample of the population. (I. Survey   E. Experiment   H. Observational Study)

6. Researchers took great precautions to make sure that the group of chimpanzees did not realize that they were being watched. (T. Survey   C. Experiment Z. Observational Study)

7. Researchers carefully wrote questions that members of the sample population would be asked to answer. (N. Survey   R. Experiment   E. Observational Study)

8. Researchers recorded the interaction of the kindergartners as they behave in actual classrooms. (M. Survey   P. Experiment   R. Observational Study)

9. Researchers controlled the conditions under which the relationship of exercise to weight control was investigated. (U. Survey   O. Experiment   I. Observational Study)

How can researchers ensure that a sample represents the members of a large population?

$\overline{8}$ $\overline{3}$ $\overline{7}$ $\overline{4}$ $\overline{9}$ $\overline{2}$ $\overline{5}$ $\overline{6}$ $\overline{3}$ $\overline{1}$ $\overline{5}$ $\overline{9}$ $\overline{7}$

Name_____ Date_____ Period_____

6-33: USING SIMULATIONS WITH RANDOM SAMPLING

Simulations can be useful for developing a margin of error for random sampling.
    Directions: Study the scenario below and then answer the questions.

In MacArthur High School, pizza was recently removed from the school lunch menu. Understandably, many students were upset. Deena, a student who counts pizza among her favorite foods, assumed that if at least 50% of the students wanted pizza on the menu, a strong case could be made to have pizza restored to the school's lunch offerings. She decided to take a random sample of 40 students and asked them the following question: "Should pizza be offered on the school lunch menu?" 18 students answered yes and 22 answered no. Based on these results, it would seem that more students do not want pizza on the menu than those that do. But this was a small sample, and Deena realized that another sample might result in different numbers. Before committing the time and effort to conduct more random samples of students, however, she decided to run simulations.

Your task is to help Deena by running at least 200 simulations of random samples of size 40 from a population of 50% ones (*yes*) and 50% zeroes (*no*). For each sample, calculate and plot the proportion of ones. Then answer the following questions:

1. Based on Deena's random sample of 40 students, what was the sample proportion of students who want pizza on the menu?

2. Describe the plot of the distribution of your sample proportions.

3. What was the mean of the plot of the distribution?

4. What was the standard deviation of the distribution of the sample proportions?

5. What was the margin of error for the sample proportions?

6. Using the data obtained from the simulations, the proportion of students who favor pizza being on the lunch menu is between what two numbers?

Name_____ Date_____ Period_____

6–34: COMPARING TWO TREATMENTS USING SIMULATIONS

A treatment is a procedure or substance that a researcher studies in an experiment. The researcher wants to find out the effect of the treatment, if any, on the subject.

Directions: Consider the data below, obtained from a sample trial using a new weight-loss supplement. Then answer the questions that follow.

Researchers developed a new weight-loss supplement that is based entirely on natural ingredients. A small, initial trial of the supplement showed promising results. The trial consisted of 20 adults, chosen randomly from a large group of volunteers. Each of the volunteers weighed between 200 and 250 pounds, which was significantly above their ideal weight. The researchers felt that using volunteers who fit this profile would provide data that would be statistically significant.

Of the 20 volunteers, 10 were randomly chosen to receive the supplement while the other 10 would not receive the supplement. Both groups were to maintain their typical eating habits and diets for three months, at which time any change in weight in the test subjects would be recorded. After the three-month period, it was found that the group receiving the supplement lost weight compared to the group that did not take the supplement.

The next step for the researchers is to conduct a much larger trial. But before they move forward, they want to be as sure as possible that the weight loss they recorded is a result of the supplement and not a result of randomization in a very small sample. Following are the results of the initial trial.

Results of the Initial Trial of a New Weight-Loss Supplement

Weight Change (in pounds) of Ten Volunteers with Supplement after Three Months	Weight Change (in pounds) of Ten Volunteers without Supplement after Three Months
−7.4	1.5
−9.5	0.8
−0.6	−0.5
−8.0	5.3
−10.7	−2.5
−12.3	1.6
−9.8	0
2.0	2.7
−8.6	3.4
−11.2	4.7

(Continued)

1. What was the mean of the weight change for the group taking the supplement? What was the mean of the weight change for the group not taking the supplement? What was the absolute value of the difference of these two sample means?

2. How could you re-randomize the data and use simulations to help you decide if the results of the initial trial are likely to be valid?

3. How many simulations did you run? After running the simulations, what can you conclude about the data? How certain are you that your conclusions are correct? Explain.

6–35: EVALUATING DATA IN REPORTS

Evaluating reports based on data is critical to drawing inferences, conclusions, and making decisions. Effective evaluation is dependent on analysis and interpretation of the data.

Directions: Assume that you have been tasked with evaluating a report on a Special Traffic Safety Program for McKinley Township. Evaluate the data, and answer the questions. Following is information you are to consider in your evaluation.

McKinley Township has two major highways and several roads that have a high incidence of speeding. In an effort to discourage speeding and reduce accidents, injuries, and fatalities, the police department implemented a Special Traffic Safety Program. Additional police officers were assigned to patrol the township's highways and roads on which most speeding occurred. The additional officers were paid overtime, which some people in the township's government feel is a cost that strains the police budget. These individuals have come to question the value of the Special Traffic Safety Program. To determine if the program is in fact worthwhile, the police chief has ordered a report containing data on speeding, costs, revenues, and other information related to the program. The data included in the report is shown below.

Data for the McKinley Township Special Traffic Safety Program, 2015–2016

Highways/Roads	Posted Speed (mph)	Average Speed (mph) with Program, 2016	Average Speed (mph) without Program, 2015
Highway 30	55	62.5	66.0
Highway 51	50	50.0	58.5
Connors Road	45	53.5	52.0
Valley Road	45	50.5	53.5
Winter Road	45	54.5	55.0
River Road	40	51.0	50.5
Sherman Road	35	42.0	43.5
Freeman Road	35	36.5	36.0

Note: Speeds were rounded to the nearest half mile per hour (mph).

(Continued)

ADDITIONAL INFORMATION

The following information pertains only to the highways and roads that were a part of the Special Traffic Safety Program.

- Overtime costs for additional police officers (2016): $320,622

- Overtime costs for additional police officers (2015): $0

- Revenue for speeding tickets and other traffic violations (2016): $288,545

- Revenue for speeding tickets and other traffic violations (2015): $204,130

- Traffic accidents on highways and roads with the program (2016): 251

- Traffic accidents on highways and roads without the program (2015): 279

- Fatalities on highways and roads with the program (2016): 5

- Fatalities on highways and roads without the program (2015): 8

1. Based on the overall data (the table and additional information), do you feel that the Special Traffic Safety Program is successful? Explain.

2. Do you feel that given the results of the program, its costs are justified? Explain.

3. What, if any, additional data might have been helpful to your evaluation? How would this data have helped you in drawing inferences or conclusions about the program?

4. Would you recommend that the Special Traffic Safety Program be continued? Would you recommend that a modified version of the program be implemented? Explain.

Name _____ Date _____ Period _____

6-36: DESCRIBING EVENTS AS SUBSETS OF A SAMPLE SPACE

A sample space is the set of all possible outcomes of an experiment. An event is a set of possible outcomes. It is a subset of the sample space.

The two spinners shown below can be used to generate proper fractions.

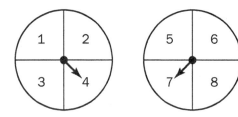

The number spun on the first spinner generates the numerator of the fraction. The number spun on the second spinner generates the denominator. The sample space of all of the possible outcomes is listed below:

(1, 5)	(1, 6)	(1, 7)	(1, 8)	(2, 5)	(2, 6)	(2, 7)	(2, 8)
(3, 5)	(3, 6)	(3, 7)	(3, 8)	(4, 5)	(4, 6)	(4, 7)	(4, 8)

Directions. Find the outcomes of the sample spaces described below and match your answers with the answers in the Answer Bank. Some answers will not be used. Write the letter of each answer in the space above its problem number to complete the statement at the end. You will need to divide the letters into words

1. The fraction generated has the smallest value.

2. The fraction generated is equivalent to $0.\overline{6}$.

3. The fraction generated is equivalent to 0.5, and the numerator is not 3.

4. The fraction generated is equivalent to a repeating decimal, both numerator and denominator are prime, and neither is 2.

5. The fraction generated is a repeating decimal, and the numerator is 1.

6. The fraction generated is larger than 0.6.

7. The fraction generated is equivalent to 0.25.

8. The fraction generated is a repeating decimal, the denominator is not 7, and the numerator is neither prime nor composite.

9. The fraction generated is a repeating decimal, and the numerator is composite.

(Continued)

Answer Bank

F. (4, 6) and (4, 7)	R. (2, 8)	B. (1, 7)	U. (4, 7)
A. (1, 6) and (1, 7)	T. (2, 6)	I. (1, 6)	C. (1, 8)
E. (4, 5) and (4, 6)	S. (3, 7)	N. (4, 6)	O. (4, 8)

The mathematical theory of probability _____ in the seventeenth century.

$\overline{5}$ $\overline{7}$ $\overline{3}$ $\overline{4}$ $\overline{6}$ $\overline{8}$ $\overline{2}$ $\overline{9}$ $\overline{7}$ $\overline{5}$ $\overline{2}$ $\overline{1}$ $\overline{6}$

6–37: IDENTIFYING INDEPENDENT EVENTS

Two events are independent if the occurrence of Event A has no effect on the occurrence of Event B. If A and B are independent events, the probability of A and B occurring together is $P(A \text{ and } B) = P(A) \cdot P(B)$.

Directions: Decide whether each set of events is independent. Circle the letter of your answer, *yes* or *no*, and write the letter of each answer in the space above its problem number to complete the statement at the end.

1. A 3 of hearts is pulled from a deck of 52 cards. A 3 is rolled on a standard 6-sided die. Are these events independent? (W. Yes   B. No)

2. Michael took the bus to school, but he arrived at school 5 minutes late. Are these events independent? (I. Yes   E. No)

3. Laveran took an umbrella to work, and it rained. Are these events independent? (L. Yes   H. No)

4. A jar contained 10 red marbles and 10 green marbles. Hannah picked a green marble, put it back into the jar, and picked a red marble. Are these events independent? (O. Yes   E. No)

5. Marcus had a set of 10 cards, numbered 1 to 10. He picked the 4, put this card aside, and then he picked the 6. Are these events independent? (S. Yes   E. No)

6. Sara parked in a no parking zone for only a few minutes, and, unfortunately, she got a ticket for parking illegally. Are these events independent? (H. Yes   D. No)

7. At an amusement park, Tomas played a game that involved spinning a wheel. The wheel had 24 equal-sized spaces—12 spaces for winning a token (tokens could be accumulated and cashed in for prizes) and 12 spaces for losing. He paid for two spins. He lost on the first spin but won a token on the second spin. Are these events independent? (K. Yes   T. No)

8. A spinner has 9 equal-sized sectors, numbered 1 to 9. A 3 was spun, a 5 was spun, and a 3 was spun again. Are these events independent? (G. Yes   E. No)

9. A box of candy contained an equal number of chocolate-covered candies (of the same size and shape) with either caramel, coconut, or fudge filling. Elisha picked a candy with coconut filling and then picked a candy with fudge filling. Are these events independent? (R. Yes   N. No)

Your score on this assignment depends on your _____ of events.

$\overline{7}$ $\quad$ $\overline{9}$ $\quad$ $\overline{4}$ $\quad$ $\overline{1}$ $\quad$ $\overline{3}$ $\quad$ $\overline{2}$ $\quad$ $\overline{6}$ $\quad$ $\overline{8}$ $\quad$ $\overline{5}$

Name _____ Date _____ Period _____

6-38: INTERPRETING CONDITIONAL PROBABILITY

$P(A|B)$ is the probability of Event A occurring given that Event B has occurred. When Event B occurs, the size of the sample space changes.

- When two events are independent, $P(A|B) = P(A)$ and $P(B|A) = P(B)$.

- When two events are not independent, they are dependent, and $P(A|B) \neq P(A)$ and $P(B|A) \neq P(B)$.

Directions: Three scenarios are described below. Find the probabilities for each problem and match each answer with an answer in the Answer Bank. Some answers will be used more than once. Write the letter of the answer in the space above its problem number to complete the statement at the end, and then answer the question.

A. 9 women and 12 men are standing in line at a fast-food restaurant. A pollster is conducting a survey. Event W is randomly selecting a woman. Event M is randomly selecting a man. Find the probability of the following.

    1. $P(W)$ 2. $P(M)$ 3. $P(W|M)$ 4. $P(M|W)$

B. A spinner with 3 congruent sectors labeled 1 to 3 and a fair coin are tossed. Event 3 is spinning a 3. Event H is tossing a head. Find the probabilities of the following.

    5. $P(3)$ 6. $P(H)$ 7. $P(3|H)$ 8. $P(H|3)$

C. 8 students got a B or higher on the algebra midterm. 14 students got a C or less. Event B is randomly selecting a student who got a B or higher. Event C is randomly selecting a student who got a C or lower. Find the probabilities of the following.

    9. $P(B)$ 10. $P(C)$ 11. $P(B|C)$ 12. $P(C|B)$

Answer Bank

| B. $\frac{1}{2}$ | U. $\frac{9}{20}$ | L. $\frac{8}{21}$ | R. $\frac{7}{11}$ | O. $\frac{3}{5}$ | A. $\frac{4}{7}$ | E. $\frac{1}{3}$ | Q. $\frac{2}{3}$ | P. $\frac{3}{7}$ | I. $\frac{4}{11}$ |

A probability space where each simple event has an equal probability is called an

_____ space.

$\overline{5}$ $\overline{12}$ $\overline{3}$ $\overline{9}$ $\overline{1}$ $\overline{10}$ $\overline{4}$ $\overline{8}$ $\overline{2}$ $\overline{6}$ $\overline{11}$ $\overline{7}$

Which pairs of events are independent? Explain your reasoning.

6–39: UNDERSTANDING TWO-WAY FREQUENCY TABLES

Two-way frequency tables are useful for organizing data. They can also be used to determine probabilities.

Michael is writing an article for the school newspaper. He asked the 130 students in Mrs. Perez's math classes the following question: For which one of the following five tasks do you use a personal computer (PC) or laptop the most? The tasks are social media, e-mail, playing video games, research and writing reports, and watching videos.

Following are the results: Of the boys, 8 picked social media, 11 picked e-mail, 15 picked playing video games, 20 picked research and writing reports, and 6 picked watching videos. Of the girls, 12 picked social media, 14 picked e-mail, 9 picked playing video games, 25 picked research and writing reports, and 10 picked watching videos.

Directions: Construct a two-way frequency table to represent Michael's data. Find the probabilities for the events and match your answers with the answers in the Answer Bank. Then complete the statement at the end by writing the letter of each answer in the space above its problem number. You will need to divide the letters into words.

M is randomly selecting a boy.

F is randomly selecting a girl.

S is randomly selecting a student who picked social media.

E is randomly selecting a student who picked e-mail.

G is randomly selecting a student who picked playing video games.

R is randomly selecting a student who picked research and writing reports.

W is randomly selecting a student who picked watching videos.

1. $P(E|M)$ 2. $P(M|R)$ 3. $P(M)$ 4. $P(S)$ 5. $P(F|G)$

6. $P(M|E)$ 7. $P(F)$ 8. $P(R)$ 9. $P(W|F)$

Answer Bank

| I. $\frac{1}{7}$ | V. $\frac{2}{13}$ | A. $\frac{11}{60}$ | N. $\frac{6}{13}$ | P. $\frac{3}{8}$ | R. $\frac{9}{26}$ | T. $\frac{11}{25}$ | D. $\frac{4}{9}$ | E. $\frac{7}{13}$ |

Dependent events _____.

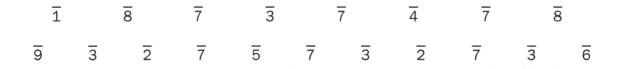

$\overline{1}$ $\overline{8}$ $\overline{7}$ $\overline{3}$ $\overline{7}$ $\overline{4}$ $\overline{7}$ $\overline{8}$

$\overline{9}$ $\overline{3}$ $\overline{2}$ $\overline{7}$ $\overline{5}$ $\overline{7}$ $\overline{3}$ $\overline{2}$ $\overline{7}$ $\overline{3}$ $\overline{6}$

Name_____ Date_____ Period_____

6–40: EXPLORING CONCEPTS OF CONDITIONAL PROBABILITY

Conditional probability is the probability of an event based on the occurrence of a previous event. It can be applied to everyday situations.

- Two events are independent if $P(A|B) = P(A)$ and $P(B|A) = P(B)$.

- Two events are dependent if $P(A|B) \neq P(A)$ and $P(B|A) \neq P(B)$.

Directions: Consider the two scenarios below. Determine whether the events in each scenario are dependent or independent.

SCENARIO 1

Marianna kept a record of her study time and grades on her 12 math tests last year. She studied more than 2 hours for 11 of the tests. She earned an "A" on 10 of these math tests. Are studying more than 2 hours for a test and getting an "A" independent events? Support your answer using conditional probability equations.

SCENARIO 2

Kelvin is an avid football fan who also believes he is very lucky. His high school team played 12 games last year and won 6. (No games ended in a tie.) Kelvin attended 3 of the 6 games they won. He also attended 3 of the 6 games they lost. Are Kelvin's attendance and the football team winning the games independent events? Support your answer using conditional probability equations.

Name_____ Date_____ Period_____

6-41: FINDING CONDITIONAL PROBABILITIES AS A FRACTION OF OUTCOMES

It is possible to find conditional probabilities without using a formula. The table below shows 3 types of bagels and 4 types of toppings.

	Sesame Seeds	Crumbs	Nuts	Onions	Totals
Bran	5	4	10	6	25
Whole Wheat	1	3	2	8	14
Egg	7	9	11	12	39
Totals	13	16	23	26	78

Following are events:

S, Randomly selecting a bagel topped with sesame seeds

C, Randomly selecting a bagel topped with crumbs

N, Randomly selecting a bagel topped with nuts

O, Randomly selecting a bagel topped with onions

B, Randomly selecting a bran bagel

W, Randomly selecting a whole wheat bagel

E, Randomly selecting an egg bagel

Directions: Find each probability below and match each answer with an answer in the Answer Bank. Not all of the answers will be used. Complete the statement at the end by writing the letter of each answer in the space above its problem number. You will need to divide the letters into words and include an apostrophe.

1. $P(E|N)$ 2. $P(E|O)$ 3. $P(E|C)$ 4. $P(S|C)$ 5. $P(B|S)$

6. $P(O|E)$ 7. $P(B|O)$ 8. $P(C|W)$ 9. $P(S|E)$ 10. $P(N|B)$

Answer Bank

A. $\frac{4}{13}$	U. $\frac{7}{9}$	D. $\frac{2}{5}$	E. $\frac{9}{16}$	S. $\frac{3}{13}$	R. $\frac{7}{39}$
Z. $\frac{11}{23}$	O. $\frac{5}{13}$	M. $\frac{1}{3}$	N. $\frac{3}{14}$	B. $\frac{1}{4}$	K. $\frac{6}{13}$

_____ equals 13.

$\overline{6}$ $\overline{4}$ $\overline{6}$ $\overline{2}$ $\overline{3}$ $\overline{9}$ $\overline{7}$ $\overline{10}$ $\overline{5}$ $\overline{1}$ $\overline{3}$ $\overline{8}$

Name _____ Date _____ Period _____

6–42: APPLYING THE ADDITION RULE

The Addition Rule $P(A \text{ or } B) = P(A) + P(B) - P(A \text{ and } B)$ can be used to find the probability of events A or B.

Directions: Ten numbers, 1 to 10, are placed in a hat. Use the Addition Rule to find each probability below, and then match your answers with the answers in the Answer Bank. Some answers will be used more than once. Some answers will not be used. Write the letter of each answer in the space above its problem number to answer the question at the end. You will need to divide the letters into words.

1. P(a prime or a composite number)

2. P(a multiple of 2 or a two-digit number)

3. P(an odd or a two-digit number)

4. P(an odd number or a number greater than 5)

5. P(an even number or a number divisible by 3)

6. P(a number less than 5 or an even number)

7. P(a number more than 8 or a multiple of 3)

8. P(a multiple of 5 or a multiple of 2)

9. P(1 or an even number)

10. P(an odd number or a number less than 6)

11. P(a number greater than 8 or less than 7)

Answer Bank

B. $\frac{9}{10}$ L. $\frac{2}{5}$ A. $\frac{1}{5}$ I. $\frac{1}{10}$ S. $\frac{3}{10}$ E. $\frac{3}{5}$ R. $\frac{1}{2}$ O. $\frac{7}{10}$ G. $\frac{4}{5}$

This mathematician wrote $A + B$ for $A \cup B$. Who was he?

$\overline{11}$ $\overline{3}$ $\overline{10}$ $\overline{2}$ $\overline{4}$ $\overline{9}$ $\overline{1}$ $\overline{6}$ $\overline{5}$ $\overline{7}$ $\overline{8}$

INDEX

E

Empirical rule, 238

Equations: defining, 62; deriving $y = mx$, 72–73, 98; finding, of line of best fit, 239–240, 280; identifying, that have one, no, or infinitely many solutions, 73, 99; identifying solutions to, 64, 82; justifying solutions to, 113–114, 139–140; relating graphs to solutions of, 119, 150; solving, and inequalities, 68–69, 92; solving, with variables on both sides, 73–74, 100; solving rational and radical, 114; using, of linear models, 234; writing and graphing, in two variables, 111–112, 135–136; writing and solving, 65, 84–85; writing and solving exponential, 170–171, 213; writing and solving, in one variable, 111, 134

Equations, linear: adding, subtracting, factoring, and expanding, 89; finding, of line of best fit, 280; solving multi-step, in one variable, 115, 142; solving rational and radical, 114; solving systems of, 118, 148; solving systems of, algebraically, 74, 101; solving systems of, and quadratic equations, 118–119, 149

Equations, systems of: solving, 117, 146–147; solving, by graphing, 74, 102; and solving system of linear and quadratic equation, 118–119, 149; using graphs and tables to find solutions to, 120, 151–152

Equivalent expressions, 63, 64, 80, 81

Equivalent ratios, and coordinate plane, 3, 10

Eratosthenes, 215

Euler, Leonhard, 210

Events: describing, as subsets of sample space, 246, 296–297; identifying independent, 247, 298; understanding probability of, 264–265; using probability models to find probabilities of, 267–268

Experiments, recognizing, 244, 290

Exponential decay, 209

Exponential equations, writing and solving, 170–171, 213

Exponential growth, 209

Exponential functions: constructing linear and, 169–170, 209–210; interpreting parameters in linear or, 171–172, 214; and observing behavior of quantities that increase exponentially, 170, 211–212; proving growth of, by equal factors over equal intervals, 168–169, 208; writing and solving, 170–171, 213

Exponents: applying properties of integer, 69, 93; rewriting expressions involving radicals and rational, 29–30, 52; using properties of, 29, 51; writing and evaluating numerical expressions with whole-number, 61, 76

Expressions: adding, subtracting, factoring, and expanding linear, 67, 89; interpreting, 104, 122; rewriting, in different forms, 67–68, 90; rewriting, involving radicals and rational exponents, 29–30, 52; using structure of, to identify ways to rewrite them, 104–105, 123; writing, in which variables represent numbers, 64–65, 83; writing and evaluating numerical expressions with whole-number, 61, 76

Expressions, equivalent: applying properties of operations to generate, 63, 80; identifying, 63–64, 81

Expressions, quadratic, factoring, to reveal zeros, 105

Expressions, rational, rewriting, 110, 133

Extraneous solutions, 114, 141

F

Formulas, highlighting qualities of interest in, 113, 138

Fractions, expressing, as repeating decimals, 27–28, 48–49

Function (s): analyzing and graphing, 158–159, 184; comparing, 157, 177–179; comparing properties of, 165, 199–200; constructing linear and exponential, 169–170; domain of, 161; finding inverses of, 167, 206; finding values of, 159–160, 186; finding values of sine, cosine, and tangent, 174–175, 220; graphing linear and quadratic, 162–163, 195; graphing polynomial functions, 163–164; identifying, 156, 176; proving linear, grow by equal differences over equal intervals, 168, 207; relating domain of, to its graph or description, 161, 190–191; transforming, 166–167, 204–205; understanding, 159, 185; writing, 165, 201–202

Functions, exponential: constructing linear and, 169–170, 209–210; interpreting parameters in linear or, 171–172, 214; and observing behavior of quantities that increase exponentially, 170, 211–212; proving, grow by equal factors over equal intervals, 168–169, 208; writing and solving, 170–171, 213

G

Galois, Evariste, 198
Garfield, James, 220
Geometric sequences, writing, 166, 203
Geometric series, finite, finding sums of, 106–107, 128
Graphing: functions, 158–159, 184; linear and quadratic functions, 162–163, 195; points in coordinate plane, 21, 38; polynomial functions, 163–164, 196–197; proportional relationships, 4–5, 14, 71–72, 97; rational numbers on number line, 20–21, 37; solving systems of equations by, 75, 102; solving systems of inequalities by, 120–121, 153–154
Graphs: identifying key features of, 160, 188–189; relating, to solutions of equations, 119, 150; relating domain of function to its, 161, 190–191; using, and tables to find solutions to systems of equations, 120, 151–152; using zeros to construct rough, of polynomial function, 131

H

Hume, James, 51

I

Identity Property, 24, 25
Imaginary numbers, 33, 34, 57, 58
Independent events, identifying, 247, 298
Inequalities: defining, 65; identifying solutions of, 64, 82; solving equations and, 68–69, 92; solving multi-step linear, in one variable, 115–116, 143; using, 65–66, 86–87; writing and solving, in one variable, 111, 134
Inequalities, systems of, solving, by graphing, 120–121, 153–154
Inferences: drawing, about population using random samples, 227–228, 261; drawing,

about populations, 229, 263; drawing, from samples, 227–228, 259–260
Integer exponents, 69, 93
Intercepts, 162, 165, 188
Interquartile range (IQR), 226, 237
Interpreting, units, 31, 54
Inverse Property of Multiplication, 25
IQR. *See* Interquartile range (IQR)
Irrational numbers, 26, 50; sums and products of, 30–31, 53; using rational approximations of, 28, 50

L

Line: determining whether data lies on, 157, 180; finding slope and y-intercept of, 157–158, 181–183; fitting, to data, 272; of best fit, 239–240, 280; representing data with plots on real number, 236, 275
Linear equations: adding, subtracting, factoring, and expanding, 89; finding, of line of best fit, 280; solving multi-step, in one variable, 115, 142; solving rational and radical, 114; solving systems of, 118, 148; solving systems of, algebraically, 74, 101; solving systems of, and quadratic equations, 118–119, 149
Linear expressions, adding, subtracting, factoring, and expanding, 67, 89
Linear functions: constructing, and exponential functions, 169–170, 209–210; graphing, 162–163, 195; proving, grow by equal differences over equal intervals, 162, 163, 168, 169, 177, 194, 207
Linear models: equations of, 234, 273; interpreting slope and y-intercept of, 241, 282–283; using, 240, 281

M

Margin of error, 244
Mean, finding, 223–225, 229, 253–254
Measurement: appropriate levels of accuracy for, 32–33, 56; and using radian and degree measures, 172, 215
Median, finding, 223–225, 229, 253–254
Mode, finding, 223–226, 229, 253–254
Monomial, 104
Multi-step problems, solving, 68, 91
Multiplication Property of Equality, 117, 126

Q

Quadratic equations: rewriting, 164, 198; solving, by completing square, 116, 144; solving, in variety of ways, 116–117, 145; solving, that have complex solutions, 34–35, 59; solving system of linear and, 118–119, 149

Quadratic expressions, factoring, to reveal zeros, 105, 124–125

Quadratic functions, 162, 163, 195

Quadratic models, using, 240, 281

Quantities: defining appropriate, 31–32, 55; observing behavior of, that increase exponentially, 211–212; of interest, 113, 138; using variables to represent two, 88

R

Radian, 172, 215

Radical equations, solving, 114, 141

Radicals, rewriting expressions involving, and rational exponents, 29–30, 52

Random samples, 227–228, 244, 261, 291

Range, finding, 223–224, 229, 253–254

Rate of change, finding average, over specified intervals, 162, 192–194

Rational approximations, 28–29

Rational equations, solving, 114, 141

Rational Exponent Property, 29, 30, 51, 52

Rational numbers: absolute value and order of, 22, 39–40; converting, to decimals, 26, 45; graphing, on numbered line, 37; multiplying and dividing, 25–26, 44; solving word problems involving, 27, 46; sums and products of, 30–31, 53; using number line to add and subtract, 23–24, 42; using properties to add and subtract, 24–25, 43

Ratios: equivalent, and coordinate plane, 3, 10; understanding, 2, 7–8; unit rates and, 2–3, 9

Real numbers, 58, 73, 165, 236, 275

Remainder Theorem, applying, 107–108, 130

Reports, evaluating data in, 246, 294–295

Rudolff, Christoff, 30, 52

S

Sample mean, 244

Sample proportion, 244

Sample space, describing events as subsets of, 246, 296–297

Samples: drawing inferences about a population using random, 227–228, 261; drawing inferences from, 227, 259–260; using simulation with random, 244–245

Scatter plots, constructing and interpreting, 233, 271

Scientific notation: operations with, 70, 96; using numbers expressed in, 70, 95

Sequences, defining, recursively, 160, 187

Series, defining, 106

Simulations: comparing two treatments using, 245, 292–293; evaluating probability models through, 243, 289; using, with random sampling, 244–245, 291

Sine, finding value of, 174–175, 220

Slope: finding, 157–158, 181–183; interpreting, and Y-intercept of linear model, 241

Slope-intercept form, 157, 181

Solutions: complex, 34–35, 59; identifying equations that have one, no, or infinitely many, 73, 99; justifying, to equations, 113–114, 139–140; relating graphs to, of equations, 119, 150; representing constraints and interpreting, 112–113, 137; using graphs and tables to find, to systems of equations, 120

Square, 104; completing, to reveal maximum or minimum values, 106, 126–127; solving quadratic equation by completing, 116, 144

Square roots, using, 69–70, 94

Standard deviation, 244

Statistical experiments, understanding terminology of, 242–243, 288

Statistical questions, identifying, 222, 251

Subsets, 246, 296–297, 332

Subtraction, 23

Surveys, recognizing, 244, 290

T

Tables: constructing and interpreting two-way, 235, 274; summarizing categorical data in two-way frequency tables, 238–239, 279; understanding two-way frequency, 248–249, 300; using graphs and, to find solutions to systems of equations, 120, 151–152